GONE A LONG JOURNEY

Leonard Charles Williams

ISBN 0-9542487-0-8

Published by Hillmead Publications
3 Hillmead Gardens
Bedhampton
Havant
Hampshire
PO9 3NL
United Kingdom

Design & production co-ordinated by:
The Better Book Company Ltd
Havant
Hampshire PO9 2XH

Printed in England.

Leonard Charles Willliams

1911-1990

For my darling wife Kay, with all my love.

Every married sailor worth his salt has divided loves. His wife and his ship. The latter must always be the rival of the former. In this book you will read about some of your rivals and understand that they too, were something more than steel and wood. They possessed a soul and were always referred to as *SHE* which was probably why we sailors loved them and why our wives had to share them. That you appreciated and respected this tradition has made you, too, something very special in my life and was why my Navy days were so happy!

Len
15th April, 1967

INTRODUCTION

I have written this so that my family will know what I got up to in my youth. This is my story. A story with the Navy as its scenery, the ships as its props, and their crews as my friends.

It is not a great story because I am not a great person, merely mediocre, but it is the mediocre people without whose help the great men cannot attain their greatness. The little cogs which keep the big machine turning over. It has been my privilege for 26 odd years to be one of those little cogs in the Navy machine.

A thirst for seeing the world; the companionship of fine messmates; and working for the good of one's ship and not for one's self, has been the oil to keep my particular cog working smoothly. This, combined with the ability to keep out of trouble, has made my passage through the service a particularly happy one.

The fact that I met a war half way through was unfortunate, but nevertheless an adventure, which, after all, was what I was trained for. We mediocre people did our best during this period, and some of us, including most of my friends, left their bleaching bones, trapped in the rusting hulls of their ships, at the bottom of practically every sea and ocean in the world. I hope this part of my story will be remembered, for they were, as I have said, fine messmates. They ceased to be mediocre, for in giving their all, they became the greatest of the great.

As time went on, we emerged from the darkness of war into the sunshine of a new age; an atomic age, with all its advantages and fearful possibilities. Then, a few more happy years afloat, and my membership of the Royal Navy came to an end, as all good things do.

As I sat in my office in the Electrical Training School in H.M.S. *Collingwood* on the last day of my service, I contemplated the morrow and my release to "Civvy Street" with all its doubts and fears and I suddenly knew what Horace meant, when he wrote centuries ago:-

> Happy the man, and happy he alone,
>
> He who can call today his own:
> He who, secure within, can say,
> Tomorrow do thy worst, for I have lived today.

"GONE A LONG JOURNEY"

An exciting experience

To Snowy, in whose gay and carefree company I have spent so many happy hours; and to the people of Malta G.C. in whose enchanted island we spent them.

"For the goodman is not at home, he is gone a long journey"

Proverbs 7 Verse 19

Leonard Charles Williams

Chapter One

The Royal Hospital School, Greenwich.

<u>1924 – 1927</u>

In the first place, I think I inherited my love of the sea from my father, and with it, the yen to go abroad and see places. A Chief Stoker in the Royal Navy, Dad was a quiet unassuming person, with hidden depths. For instance, at one stage in his career, he volunteered to go with Captain Scott to the South Pole in 1911, only the fact that he was a married man with a family kept him out of the ill-fated expedition. A single man, Chief Stoker Lashley, was chosen instead, but for a number of years, Dad kept up a correspondence with Lieutenant E.R.G.R.Evans, one of the expedition, who was to become famous as "Evans of the Broke", and later in life as Admiral Lord Mountevans.

In all, my father served 27 years in the Royal Navy, leaving it in 1920 when he got a job as a Watcher in H.M. Customs and Excise. His initial posting was to Hull, where we all moved from Portsmouth. It was at Hull, during my school holidays and half days that I first began to show interest in ships and the sea. Most of my spare time was spent haunting the docks and watching the ships unloading their various cargoes. The spicy smells from the holds and the ports of registration printed on the sterns of the ships, conjured up far distant lands and produced an urge in me to go and see them.

Then there was the *Fighting Temeraire,* that famous picture of Turner's. As a youngster I was fascinated by it, and this too, helped to turn my footsteps seawards. Even now I have a reproduction of it hanging in my lounge. Long after my retirement from the Royal Navy I still feel that pull of the sea and begin to wonder afresh as to what lies beyond the horizon.

Lying at the foot of Observatory Hill in Greenwich Park and immediately opposite the Royal Naval College, is what is now known as the National Maritime Museum. This ancient pile of buildings was, in my boyhood days, The Royal Hospital School for the sons of seamen. It was here, at the tender age of 13, that I began a career which was to take me across the world in some of the most famous vessels in the Royal Navy.

A few days after my thirteenth birthday I left the family home in Hull and took a train for London, to join the Royal Hospital School at Greenwich, as my brother had done before me. This was entirely my own decision for my parents had been paying fees for me to train for a shorthand typist and book-keeper, but I had other ideas, there was going to be no office job for me, not if I could help it! My mother came with me to make sure that I would arrive safe and sound and, after a tiring day's journey, we eventually reached the school and were directed to the annexe which was an old building situated in Park Row at the side of the R.N.College. The building was known as Trafalgar, and it was here that all new entries to the school spent their first three weeks.

I well remember the day, it was murky and damp and by the time we arrived inside the gloomy looking building, tea was being served to the boys already there, under the yellow glare of several gas lamps. The dining room was some thirty feet long and contained several long deal tables and stools. Adjoining this room was the kitchen or galley as it was called, and behind this, in a separate building, was the dormitory, a large barn of a place containing about seventy beds.

After a cup of tea and a cake or two, mother and I said our good-byes and she left to catch the night train back to Hull, leaving me, for the first time in my life, to stand on my own two feet. I did not feel at all happy , but then I was in good company, for there were about thirty of us boys in like situation and it did not take us long to settle in and to get to know each other.

After tea, we sat around the dining room swapping life stories and discussing our prospects at the school. Some of the boys had relations already in the main school and of course, they had heard all about the routine, schooling, work and discipline and lost no time in relating all the worst points for the benefit of we newcomers.

At 7 p.m. we had an issue of dry bread and cheese and a basin of hot cocoa, the latter being the same as is issued to the Navy. It is supplied in large thick slabs and has to be broken up and boiled.

When made properly it is a hot and nourishing beverage, but made as ours was, it was like dishwater and tasted like it too! After this meagre supper we were ushered to the bathrooms in the basement for a wash before going to bed. By 8.30p.m. we were all in bed and listening to a talk on the school routine, given by the duty instructor.

It was a scene reminiscent of the Charles Dickens period. The dismal looking dormitory, the spluttering yellow gas lamps and the cold murkiness of the night outside. My spirits were extremely low and as the instructor's voice droned on, I began to wonder why on earth I ever left home. It was the ultimate aim of going to sea which kept me going and I accepted this meagre existence only as a means to an end.

After explanations and telling us that we would be called at 6 a.m., the instructor bade us goodnight and left the dormitory. As soon as his footsteps died away a buzz of conversation commenced, and the live-wires among us began a pillow fight which only stopped when one of the pillows burst and scattered its contents over the room. We were excited, because the next day we were to go to the main school to be fitted out with our navy uniforms.

At 6 a.m. sharp we were awakened by the duty instructor. It was still dark and the current of cold air sweeping into the room did little to cheer us on this, our first morning at Greenwich. The chains controlling the gas lamps were pulled and the room was flooded with the limey yellow glare from the grouped mantles. We were all chivvied out of our warm beds and chased along to the washplace to sluice ourselves with cold water. After washing, we were shown how to make up our beds, with the blankets neatly folded at the head of the mattress and the pillows placed on top. After this, we went into the dining room for our first breakfast in the school.

The meal consisted of a basin of cocoa, a half of a pound loaf and a cube of margarine. With this we had a lump of steamed sausage-meat with gravy or a piece of smoked haddock. Sometimes we got a kipper and on Sundays it was usually egg and bacon. It was not an appetising meal by any means, but we were hungry and amid a babble of conversation, we soon disposed of it, and like Oliver Twist, we left the table feeling as if we could eat another. After the meal was over, we all went back to the dormitory and began to sweep and polish it under the supervision of a Petty Officer boy, who had been placed in charge of us. About a dozen of us were sent back to the dining room to scrub it out and soon, hot water, soap and scrubbing brushes were busy, until the messroom was looking like a new pin.

At 9 a.m. sharp we were fallen in and marched across to the main school, where we were to receive our uniforms. The school was situated in Romney Road, and my first impression was of its size. In a huge parade ground stretching some 300 yards in length, was the school building in the form of a letter "H". The outer legs being the dormitory blocks and the cross bar consisting of the Queen's House which was connected to the outer blocks by a collonade on either side. Immediately in front of the Queen's House, and cemented into the parade ground, was the famous old frigate *Fame*, complete with figurehead and bowsprit. Her topmasts had long since been removed in the interests of safety, but her lower masts and fighting tops remained.

In addition to the buildings I have already mentioned, there was a huge gymnasium, workshops, school rooms and swimming baths etc. Behind the Queen's House and on top of a hill in the park, was the Royal Observatory. As a point of interest, the zero line of Longitude, from which the world takes its time, runs from the Observatory and through the school gates.

All the school buildings were constructed of stone blocks and were erected, I believe, circa 1635. The Queen's House, a Palladian villa, was built by Inigo Jones for Anne of Denmark, the wife of Charles the First. There is an inscription over the north front which reads:- HENRICA MARIA REGINA 1635. Looking in from the road, the whole architectural appearance was most pleasing to the eye.

We marched across the large parade ground and into the clothing store, which smelled of damp serge and mothballs. The gentleman in charge of this emporium was a naval pensioner, about 50 years of age. He was tall, upright and possessed a neatly trimmed black beard, shaded with grey. He sized us up and called out a string of unintelligible jargon to his assistant, one of the older boys, who began to toss the uniform to us as our turn came in the queue. I received two blue serge uniforms, two white duck suits, three flannel shirts, two pairs of boots, three pairs of socks, a cap and cap ribbon which bore the words GREENWICH R.H. SCHOOL in gold lettering.

Our next problem was the marking of all our kit. We were not troubled by having to write our names on every item because when one joined Greenwich School, two things happened. First, you forgot you had a name, and instead you used a number which identified you during the whole of the time you were in the school. Secondly, one had to have the regulation school haircut which removed most of one's hair close to the scalp until one looked a fair imitation of a Buddhist monk. We all hated both of these rather barbaric practices and considered them both humiliating and totally unnecessary. I, for one, never forgave the short sighted idiots who insisted on perpetuating these customs.

The issue of identity numbers to each of us proceeded and I was given the number 6/16, which meant that I had been allocated to number six company and that my number in that company was sixteen. From that moment onwards and for the rest of the time I was in the school, we always referred to each other by number, and were addressed as such by members of the staff. It was a soul destroying system and I hated it, because it seemed to put us on the level with convicts.

After marking all the clothes with our numbers, we packed them into a bundle and were marched back to our Trafalgar quarters where we changed into our naval uniforms for the first time. For a working dress during the week, we wore white duck suits with the check shirt, flannel and jersey; the latter during the winter months only. The new duck was as stiff as cardboard and swished and crackled as we moved about. We then had to pack up our civilian clothes, so that they could be posted home to our parents. From now on we would only be wearing naval uniform.

Saturday dawned and, as is the custom in the navy, so it was at Greenwich. The whole building was spring cleaned, scrubbed and polished from top to bottom, and was inspected to see that it had been done properly. This spit and polishing went on until noon and the rest of the Saturday we had off, although we were never allowed to leave the grounds. We were at a loose end and apart from reading, writing letters or conversing with each other, our activities were severely restricted. This state of affairs would change when we were transferred to the main school, where the facilities and opportunities for recreation were greater.

Our ages ranged from 11 to 14 and we mainly came from naval families. We were a mixed lot and like all boys were full of high spirits, and of course, this monastic life was strange to us. However, until these first three weeks of our introduction to school life were completed, we had to put up with it. This was fair treatment towards us, because it would have been very hard on us had we started our new life in the main school without this more gentle breaking in period, to equip us for the more tough life ahead.

Saturday and Wednesday nights were bath nights and I shall always remember my first experience of having to bath with other boys. All of us had come from fairly good homes, where privacy in such matters as personal hygiene was an accepted fact. My first bath in Greenwich School was a mixture of shyness, hilarity and downright fear. To begin with, the bath was situated in a stone-walled room under the building, and a series of stone corridors or tunnels ran off the room in all directions. These corridors were hideouts and escape routes such as were found under many of these 16th and 17th century buildings. They were dimly lit by single gas jets, which used to flare and splutter in the draught and we boys had to use these tunnels as our dressing rooms.

As for the actual bathing, we took our towels, soap and clean underwear and undressed in one or other of the tunnels, then proceeded to the bath, which was a large concrete square pit about three feet deep by fifteen feet square and mounted over the top were several rows of showers. We boys piled in under the hot downpour and bathed the best way we could, washing each other's backs and generally larking about. Personal shyness and any other peculiarities went by the board. This experience soon reduced us to a common level, for we found that we were all made alike!

Getting out of the bath, we were then inspected by the Company officer and, if passed as clean, we ran off down the draughty corridors, all wet and naked, until we found our towels and clothes. Laughter and squeals echoed around those gloomy tunnels as we chased each other about. In fact, looking back to those days, I wonder how we ever escaped getting pneumonia.

During my stay at Trafalgar, I had to visit the school dentist, whose surgery was situated in the sick quarters in the main school. This was the result of our medical inspection on joining. Apparently I had one or two of my milk teeth which had to be removed, also a broken root. The notoriety of the school dentist was widespread, even among we newcomers. I was to have a practical demonstration, which, after the experience, kept me away from dentists for a very long time. To cut a long story short, I had three teeth and the broken root extracted without any pain killer being used at all! For a youngster only just thirteen, the experience was burned into my memory.

Our three weeks' stay at Trafalgar soon came to an end and in due course, we were transferred to the main school. The arrival of new boys was always a source of interest to those already established, and as we arrived outside the administration block, a crowd soon gathered around us, in the hope of seeing a familiar face. One felt like a fly under a microscope, but in a moment or so we had been split up into our various companies and our company officers took us over.

There were about twenty of us allocated to number six, and our C. O. was a stocky Scot named James McBratney, who, we discovered later, was the best of all the company officers. A naval pensioner, about 55 years of age, Mac was a fatherly type and we all liked him. He took us under his wing and so began our real life at Greenwich School.

First of all Mac took us over to the large gymnasium where the various company kit lockers were sited, and we were each given a locker bearing our number, and we began to stow our spare clothing. The gymnasium was a huge building, with large arched metal girders supporting its roof. At the far end was a large stage, and at the entrance, over the main doors, was the clock under which was a heraldic scroll bearing the words "FEAR GOD HONOUR THE KING" in letters of gold on a blue ground. On either side of the hall and running its full length, were the gymnastic wall bars. The whole place gave one the impression of being in a mainline railway station without the rails and platforms. Just below and to the right of the gym clock was the canteen, or tuck shop, where one could buy sweets, delicious cream buns and lemonade, if one's parents provided the wherewithal!

After putting away our clothes, we were taken across the parade ground to our dormitory, which was on the top floor in the front wing. Our beds were in numerical order. On the left as one entered, the beds commenced at two, four, six and so on. The two left hand columns of beds containing all the even numbers and the two right, the odd numbers. Altogether there were 123 and our company had exactly that number of boys in it. Of these beds, two were raised up on individual platforms, one at each end of the dormitory. These belonged to the two Chief Petty Officer Boys, the beds being so raised so that they could keep an eye on the rest of us. The whole dormitory was spotlessly clean, and an odour of floor polish was in the air. We sorted out our own beds and hung our towels over the foot-rail, then Mac took us on a tour of the school.

We discovered that there were nine companies of boys in the school, and a special company known as the Boreman Foundation. These were day boys only, and although they wore uniforms, they lived at home in the normal way. Of our companies, number nine was known as the Advanced Class, and their uniforms differed from ours inasmuch that they wore a brass buttoned bum freezer jacket instead of the normal jumper type. To get into this elite company one had to have a standard of education equivalent to that of a Grammar School and the general standard was very high.

The school staff consisted of the Admiral Superintendent, who was a retired Rear Admiral, a Chief Officer, a Surgeon Captain,

Paymaster, Captain, Chaplain, R.N. and a nursing staff. Then we had Company Officers, Cooks, Bakers, Laundry Staff and a Dining Hall Master. These were the main staff, although there were one or two others such as the Bandmaster, to make up the complement.

We were conducted around all the buildings, which included two swimming baths, school rooms, science laboratory, seamanship room and a host of places such as the kitchens, laundry, bakehouse etc. After our tour was over, the day was practically finished and I had time to take stock of all I had seen. The most impressive part of the school as far as I was concerned was the school classrooms. These rooms breathed history. High up on their walls were huge murals of old frigates and clipper ships and a faint odour of tarred hemp and tallow pervaded these rooms. The desks were covered with carved initials and judging from the dates, went back over a hundred years or more. One could sense maritime history in these old rooms and I loved every minute I spent in them. Also, there were large photographs of our modern cruisers and battleships and coloured posters depicting scenes from the West Indies, Ceylon, India and other far flung places, all of which conjured up romantic dreams of things to come.

Our routine at the school commenced when we were called at 6 a.m. and after making our beds, we went below to the washrooms to perform our toilet, after which we were marched across the parade to the gymnasium for the breakfast assembly. Here all the boys assembled in their respective companies, and when all were present and correct, each company was doubled into the Dining Hall under the eagle eye of the Dining Hall Master. We all stood by our own particular Mess table and waited for the last company to arrive, then, when every boy was present, grace was sung, after which we all sat down to breakfast, which after the delay was usually stone cold.

Food was the big disappointment as far as most of us were concerned. For one thing there was never enough of it for a healthy boy, or at least this was our opinion. Secondly, it was slap happily prepared and indifferently cooked. Our breakfast usually consisted of half of a one pound loaf, a dollop of margarine, with perhaps a kipper, a piece of haddock or a lump of sausagemeat, with the inevitable basin of cocoa. Dinner was very similar to the normal mid-day meal one is accustomed to, apart from the fact that it was usually ruined in both the preparation and the cooking. Tea, of course, was the last real meal of the day and was made up of a basin of tea, a third of a one pound loaf, margarine and either jam or treacle. Before we went to bed we either had a couple of hard navy biscuits or a slice of dry bread with a small cube of cheese to go with it. This was served in the gymnasium at 7 p.m. without any drink.

Once a month a competition was held among the messes to see which was the cleanest mess. The prize was cake for tea on the Sunday following the competition. For days before the actual judging we would stay behind in our spare time and polish all the metal mess kettles, knives, forks and spoons and scrub the tables and stools until they were almost white, in the hope that they would produce the cake for us. We even went to the trouble of inventing special cleaning polishes in the hope that it would produce a shine just that much better than the next mess. This was the only occasion when cake was issued. A runners-up-prize of jam tarts was also awarded and these were made and presented by the Dining Hall Master's wife.

As a result of the badly cooked food, and the small amount of it, I spent all of my pocket money on buying bread and dripping from one or other of the boys who worked in the bakehouse, and who ran a profitable little racket of selling loaves and dripping to those of us who were prepared to buy from them. It was a bad system, but as far as I was concerned, I was glad such racketeers existed.

We placed certain values on these black market deals. For instance, the lower half of a pound loaf which always had the tasty crust, cost fourpence, when cut along its length and was heavily lathered with rich beef dripping. The upper half with the soft crust, only fetched tuppence, such was the market value! We had our names for various foodstuffs, the origins of which I have never been able to trace. Names such as Wang for meat, Toke for bread, Torch for dripping and a torch stungee was the name given to the half loaf sandwich stuffed with dripping. A feast worthy of the gods!

Discipline at the school was very strict, and extra work was doled out for minor offences. Serious misbehaviour such as stealing and smoking, was punished by six of the best where it did the most good. The rare and more serious cases such as repeated theft or indecency cases, resulted in expulsion from the school, with disgrace.

I soon settled down to this strange disciplined life, and apart from the food, gradually began to like it. Our education was continued, but it was split into various sections, as follows:- One had half a day at school and the other half at a trade such as Laundry Hand, Baker, Tailor, etc. or, if one was musically minded, one could join the school's brass band, in which case this was classed as a trade. I, of course, joined the band; not because in any way I was a budding Beethoven, but rather because it entailed less work!

Lots of the older boys were wearing red stripes on their uniforms and I discovered that in order to qualify for the first of these, one had to be in the school at least nine months, be of good character, and must have passed the swimming test. Now at this particular stage I could not swim, so I made up my mind to learn. When I approached Mac about this, he made it quite clear that we should all have a chance to do this, since two periods a week of our training were given over to the swimming instructor, as I soon discovered.

On two mornings a week we finished our school lessons an hour early and we were marched across the parade ground to the small swimming bath, which was situated adjacent to my dormitory. The denizen in charge of the bath was a corpulent company officer, who turned out to be the C.O. of number three company. He was a jolly, fat person, again a naval pensioner. His name was Searle, and since he was bald, was popularly known as Curly.

The actual bath was small, being about sixty feet long by about twenty wide. On one side was a large space with long stools for laying our clothes on and also a small office. On the other, a wire was stretched along on which to hang the wet bathing slips. Curly did not waste any time. He soon sorted us out into two groups. Those who thought they could swim and those who knew that they couldn't. He then told us to get undressed and said that if we did not like putting on wet slips we could go in without any at all. Most of us preferred to go naked, since it is a chilly experience to put wet slips on a warm body.

The first in were the professed swimmers, and Curly soon decided who could and who could not swim. Then he got around to us. He made no bones about it. He took us one at a time and gave us the option of either jumping in or being thrown in. I decided that it might be more pleasant if I got in under my own steam and with a couldn't care less attitude (or so I thought) I made a belly landing which must have been heard for miles around. And so I learned to swim!

After about a dozen or so lessons, I put on a duck suit, and after managing to swim the length of the bath and remain afloat for three minutes, I successfully passed the prescribed test. It was only a question of time now, before I got my first stripe.

Our only contact with the outside world, apart from our seasonal leaves, was the once a week march through Greenwich Park with the school band up front. Every Wednesday, weather permitting, we finished school early and forming up on the Parade Ground, we marched out of the gates, along the Romney Road and into the park. It was a pleasant march, swinging along to the music of our band, but later on, when I became a member of the band, it was not so funny, because the instrument I learned to play was the largest and the heaviest to carry, the "E" flat Bass. And since we always had to clean our instruments before this weekly ramble, I had quite a lot of brass to polish!

Sunday was our main parade, when we wore our full uniform and were inspected by the Rear Admiral. As a bandsman, I had to parade with the band and play for the Admiral as he walked around the companies. After the inspection we marched across the road to church in the Royal Naval College. The President of the College, usually a Vice Admiral, also attended, in fact the scene was a colourful one, the blue and gold of the uniforms, blending with the banners and ensigns of ships long since gone, and the polished brasses around the walls commemorating past victories and Admirals. The very place breathed centuries of sea history. It was thrilling to know that one was worshipping at the same place as had Nelson, Anson and a host of other historically great seamen.

Next door to the chapel was the famous Painted Hall. A large marble hall containing priceless relics and paintings depicting Britain's maritime history. Its huge ceiling is one great masterpiece in oils and is said to have taken the artist years to paint. At the far end on a raised floor, is a glass case containing the actual uniform Lord Nelson wore when he was fatally wounded at Trafalgar, the faded bloodstains being still visible. His sword and cocked hat are here too, including the glorious diamond cockade he wore in it, with its spray of scintillating diamonds. The doors of the Hall, with those of the chapel next door, are of beautiful polished wood and bevelled glass and are reputed to be worth a small fortune. I began to realise that, hard life though it may be, we were very privileged boys at the Royal Hospital School and I did not wish to be anywhere else, except perhaps at sea.

After I had been at the school a year, I was recommended for promotion to Petty Officer boy 2nd class. This was the junior rank in the school's chain of command. Each Company had two Chief Petty Officer Boys, two 1st class Petty Officers and four 2nd class Petty Officers. These were responsible for the day to day discipline and organisation of the company. It was a similar system to the Public School prefects and it worked extremely well.

The recommendations were usually made by the schoolmasters, whom it was considered, were in the best position to judge a boy's character and capabilities. I was therefore honoured to be selected for such promotion after only barely a year in the school. In due course I had to appear before the Rear Admiral, who, after a few words of very good advice, promoted me to Petty Officer 2nd class, for which I would receive pay at the princely figure of four shillings a month, an unexpected windfall! It also gave me a stripe with a crown above it, to wear on my right arm, thereby balancing up the one already on my left.

As a Petty Officer Boy, life was a lot easier for me, although I now had to assume responsibilities which sometimes became irksome, particularly when in charge of high spirited boys. This early training in command stood me in good stead throughout my whole service life and also in civilian life. It made me an extremely good judge of character, and a fairly good psychologist to boot. I have much to thank my old school for. It taught me responsibility at an early age.

We had our annual sports in the summer months and I was fortunate in winning one or two events such as the 100 yards race and the long jump, mainly, I think, because of my long legs. Other highlights of the year were the annual trip to the Lyceum in January to see the pantomime, the Royal Tournament at Olympia, and Foundation Day, when we had a day's holiday and a special pudding for dinner known as Foundation Pong; why it was called "Pong" I do not know, because it tasted delicious, like Christmas pudding.

We had two weeks holiday at Christmas and Easter. And six weeks at mid-summer when we would all gather in our best uniforms, carrying a blue check bundle handkerchief containing our spare underclothes etc. and be marched to the station. These were great occasions and we had high jinks once we got aboard the train. Most of us bought cigarettes and became real devils smoking them. Leave, coming as it did, only three times a year, was a real luxury and respite from the rigid discipline of the school, but I was always glad to be back in school, pleasant as the break had been. At school, one was among one's peers and one's friends.

We of the school band, had occasional excursions, since we were often booked by local organisations such as charity fetes and church bazaars, and on one occasion, a torchlight procession on the Isle of Dogs, although I never did know what the procession was all about. These outings were very much appreciated by us since they always terminated in a big feed or tea for the band members. Whilst on this subject I must mention our Bandmaster, Mr. Brown, affectionately known to us as "Tatcho". A short, very dapper man with a Van Dyke beard, always meticulously trimmed. I can see him now, in front, conducting us and listening for the spare and illegal notes (of which there were many) or marching in front of the band with his short mincing steps, baton tucked under his arm. He was a gentle, but firm man, who always got the best out of us and we worshipped the ground he walked on.

Whilst at Greenwich, we saw the return of Alan Cobham from his sensational flight to Australia and back. We saw his seaplane dipping down behind the domes of the Royal Naval College. We also had the experience of the General Strike and saw our food being brought in to the school in Naval lorries with an armed escort onboard.

During this period I was again promoted, this time to Petty Officer Boy 1st Class, but by now my time in the school was running out and in the March of 1927, at the age of 15 and six months, I passed into the Royal Navy, being sent to H.M.S. *Ganges* at Shotley. It had been a memorable two years in which I had grown immeasurably in experience and responsibility. They were days I shall never forget. Days in which "I" became "We" and "Mine" became "Ours", for they laid the foundations of my life, foundations which were set in rock!

Greenwich School

First leave, age 13 years.

Chapter Two

H.M.S. *GANGES*

<u>1927 – 1928</u>

One Tuesday mid-day in early March, found me waiting on the quay at Harwich in the company of about 14 other Greenwich Schoolboys and a handful of other youngsters from all parts of the country. We were a nondescript lot – the long and the short and the tall, but we had one thing in common, we were all eager to get into the Navy. We gazed across the windswept water at the high bank of land, crowned with trees, which concealed the barracks beyond. Although wanting to belong, we were apprehensive at the unknown before us, for yonder lay H.M.S. *Ganges*, our "Baptism of Fire".

We saw a smart steam launch, fussing its way across the intervening stretch of water and soon it curved alongside the quayside steps in a flurry of disturbed water. A smart Petty Officer bounded up the steps and, in no time at all, produced a list and began checking our names, after which we were ushered down the steps and into the boat.

The launch itself gave us a good idea of the standard the Navy expected, for its deck was scrubbed white and the brasswork and paint positively gleamed. With a clang of engine room telegraphs, the boat moved away from the quay and headed for Shotley Pier.

It was a low tide as we steamed across the river and the wind was strong enough to whip the spray high over our bows. I caught the sharp, fresh smell of seaweed and heard the cry of the wheeling gulls over our heads. At last I was a name again, and not a number, and this short trip across to Shotley was a taste of the wide salt-laden future ahead. For the first time in a long while, I was glad.

H.M.S. *Ganges*, or Shotley R.N. Barracks, is situated on a promontory, on the north side of which runs the river Orwell, and on the south, the river Stour, and is directly opposite Parkeston Quay, Harwich on the Stour side. As our launch slid alongside Shotley Pier I had a good view of the Hook of Holland steamers lying alongside Parkeston Quay and, over in the distance, one could see the R.A.F.

Flying boat base at Felixstowe. We disembarked and were marched along the wooden pier leading to the steps cut into the hillside, which took us up to the barracks. It was a long climb, and by the time we had reached the top we were all out of breath. Of course, we were out of condition, a state soon to be corrected!

Arriving at the top, we were again fallen in and marched along the road to the Regulating Office, where we were mustered in and victualled up. I was very interested in all my surroundings and discovered that the road where we were standing was known as the Quarterdeck. At the end of it was the main parade ground at the head of which was mounted a large sailing ship's mast, complete with all its rigging and in front of this stood the *Ganges* figurehead facing the road.

Everything and everybody in this place looked clean, neat and tidy and I particularly noticed the smartness of the boys being marched about on the huge parade ground. *Ganges* was run to a meticulous pattern, that much was evident.

After the preliminary inspection by the doctor and dentist, we were marched off the quarterdeck and turning left by the figurehead, we proceeded out of the gates and along a country road. About half a mile up this road we came to a small encampment of wooden huts known as the Annexe. Here we were to stay for our first three weeks in the Navy.

Annexe was simply a staging post to enable us to be kitted up with our uniforms and to gently break us in to the stringent routine of the larger barracks up the road. No training was given other than showing us how to sew our names into our kit and to keep the camp clean. However, we were kept at it, with only a couple of hours a day left to ourselves to enable us to write our letters home.

Food was tolerably good and we had plenty of it, although most of us spent the little pocket money as we had in the small canteen, buying sweets and chocolates. These first few weeks were perfect bliss and we made the most of them. Once we left here we would begin to go through the mill.

We Greenwich Schoolboys had two advantages over our civilian colleagues. Firstly, we already wore naval uniform and knew how to

wear it correctly, secondly, we had received a strict disciplinary training at the school and knew something of service routine. However,
there the difference ended, for taking stock of our situation here in
this vast training barracks, I realised that we were all strangers in what
was anything but paradise!

The sight of the huge parade ground and the several squads of
boys being relentlessly drilled upon its asphalt surface, to the accom-
paniment of the harsh grating voices of their instructors, scared the
life out of we new entrants. However, we had three weeks at the
Annexe before we too, experienced our first taste of parade work, so
it was a question of living today and to the devil with tomorrow.

At the end of our last week at the Annexe, we were classed up
and I, and about 40 others, formed 65 class, and we were informed
that we would be victualled in 17 Mess.

On Friday afternoon, we were given a kit inspection, after which
we loaded a lorry with all our belongings and were then transferred
up the road to the main barracks – and here we came down to earth
with a bang!

Our new mess was situated at the bottom of a long covered way,
which sloped from the quarterdeck down to the lower playing fields
and foreshore. The hut itself was the usual service bungalow style,
holding about fifty beds. At either end was a coal burning stove and
at the entrance was the bedding store, toilets and bathrooms. The
latter were only equipped with wash basins and mirrors, the actual
showers being at the top of the covered way.

We were marched to the entrance by a Petty Officer Instructor
Boy, a smart, fresh looking lad of 16, who turned us over to the two
Petty Officers who were to be our instructors in Gunnery and Seamanship for the next nine months, besides being responsible for our
general welfare and the upkeep of our mess, and of course, discipline.

I do not intend to name these two for obvious reasons, but for
identification purposes the gunnery instructor shall be known as
'Bungy' and the seamanship instructor as 'Ben'. Both of them were
extremely good instructors, but there the similarity ended. Bungy
was a short, thin, hatchet-faced individual, who turned out to be a

sadistic bully, although in fairness to him, he produced first class results as an instructor. Ben, on the other hand, was gentle but firm, and he too got the best out of us, but we all liked him for the way he obtained it. These two provided me with a first class lesson in psychology and its application to training methods.

Of these two characters, it was inevitable that Bungy took charge of us and in no uncertain terms, he made it quite clear what he expected of us, to which he added a few dire threats of punishment if we failed to reach his standards.

I took an immediate dislike to Bungy, as did most of the class. He had an extremely jaundiced outlook on life in general and us in particular. For myself, I managed to get along with him tolerably well, mainly because I was interested in gunnery and managed to do fairly well at it, and his instructional technique, although backed by his boot and his vitriolic tongue, was such that to this day I remember most of what he taught us.

After lecturing on the routine, meals, and various other items, he told us we were free for the rest of the afternoon and evening, finishing up with the warning that he was on duty at 6 a.m. the next day and that we had better be sharp out of bed. With this parting shot, both instructors departed and we were left to our own devices to unpack, make our beds and get tea ready. It was quite a relief to sit on one's bed and relax awhile and most of us devoted the rest of the day to unpacking and stowing our kit, reading or writing letters.

So far, I had not made any particular friends. We had only been together for three weeks and our time was so occupied that sorting out possible friends was out of the question, besides which, I did not make friends easily, due probably to shyness plus the fact that I had to know a person a long time before I got on really intimate terms with him. At the moment we were all pals in adversity, so to speak, and I was content to leave it like that, at any rate for the time being.

Saturday dawned with Bungy's raucous voice bidding us to "Rise and shine, the sun is burning yer bloody eyes out!" Such a refined one, our Bungy. It was 6 a.m. and blowing a hooligan outside. In the distance we could hear the bugle notes of "Reveille" drifting down on the wind, and with great reluctance we staggered out of our warm beds and made our way to the bathroom and toilets. Outside the rain drove against the windows, which were rattling against the pressure of the wind. It was one of those days, and we were the poor orphans of the storm.

Between 6 a.m. and 6.30 a.m., biscuits and cocoa could be drawn from the galley and two of us had to be detailed by the class leader to collect this issue each morning from the duty cook. On six days of the week, the biscuits were the standard issue, – hard, square and tasting of castor oil, in fact we all swore they were made with it purposely to keep our bowels regular – but on Tuesdays we got an issue of round biscuits which were much sweeter and better tasting and these were greatly sought after. It is not surprising therefore, to find that on Tuesdays it was the custom for messes to waylay the boys sent to draw this special issue and to burgle them, with the inevitable result that we soon learned to send an escort to the galley on Tuesday mornings to safeguard our ration.

Today being Saturday, it was the day the Captain inspected all messes, which meant that everything had to be clean, spick and span, and woe betide anybody who left any of his personal clothing or property lying about.

Immediately we had finished our breakfast, Ben and Bungy appeared and had us turning to with hot soapy water, scrubbers and cloths and whilst some of us shifted the beds across to one side of the room, others began to scrub the cleared side. Some scrubbed the mess tables and stools until they were white, and two or three were engaged on cleaning windows, polishing brasswork, cleaning cutlery and white-washing the bases of the two coal stoves. This went on until 11 a.m. then, with the mess looking fresh and clean, all the boys were sent down to the playing fields, except the class leaders and our two instructors, who would have to receive the Captain and his retinue and await for either the praise or the trouble. It usually amounted to a bit of each.

After the great man had made his inspection, we were all allowed back in the mess again, by which time our dinner was ready and we laid the table and were soon enjoying the hard earned meal amidst the babble of young, hearty voices, going over the events of the morning.

The rest of Saturday we had free, but whilst enjoying this freedom, one always had to keep Sunday in mind, because on that day we had the weekly parade and inspection of all divisions by the Captain, followed by church in the gymnasium. This meant that our best uniforms had to be pressed and spotlessly clean, shoes highly polished and lanyards white, and of course, our collars washed and properly ironed. When properly turned out, there is no fresher looking or smarter uniform that that of the British sailor and *Ganges* made certain that we kept it that way. With this in view, a great part of our Saturday was devoted to ensuring a smart turn-out on the following morning.

Saturday night was also one of our bath nights, the other being Wednesday. After tea we would muster outside the mess with our clean clothes, towels and soap and the class leader would march us up to the shower room at the top end of the covered way. As it was at Greenwich School, this bath night was quite an experience, and there was certainly no room for shyness in our make up. There was of course, the inevitable ribald horseplay and remarks as we washed each other's backs and commented heartlessly on each other's physical peculiarities. A duty Petty Officer was always in charge to maintain order and discipline, also to inspect us to see that we had bathed properly. He usually provided himself with a pliable ruler or whippy little cane, and if one had not rinsed the soap off properly or had left any tide marks, then a whack across the bare bottom was one's reward. Since most of the duty P.O's were good for a lark, one usually collected a whack regardless!

Sunday mornings were, of course, the "Bull" period of the week. They began with all of us being called at 6.45 a.m. instead of 6, so we all enjoyed an extra three quarters of an hour in bed and this privilege was greatly valued. After breakfast, we cleaned up the hut and at 9 a.m. we changed, or as they say in the service, "cleaned" into our best uniforms. Everyone was fussing in front of the many mirrors, getting their lanyards and silks straight and putting various brands of hair oil on their hair. The whole hut reminded one of the chorus back stage, getting ready for a gala performance! We were only allowed 30 minutes to change and to get up on the parade ground. Some of us did it easily; others did not and were still fussing about a few minutes before the bugle sounded "Divisions."

The parade ground itself was a huge sweep of tarmac bordered on two sides by low buildings and on the other two by playing fields. It was overshadowed at the quarterdeck end by the huge mast, in front of which was the Rostrum, from whose platform the Captain took the salute at the march past.

Sharp at 9.30 a.m. the Royal Marine Buglers sounded "Divisions" and in one mad rush, over fifteen hundred boys ran to fall in on their divisional markers, shepherded by instructors, class leaders and divisional officers. The next twenty minutes or so was taken up in sizing and dressing the divisions into straight lines and inspections by divisional officers, who, when they were satisfied with their divisions, then reported to the Commander that his men had been preliminary inspected and were now ready for the Captain's own inspection. After all reports had been received, the Commander called the entire parade to attention and reported to the Captain that all was ready for his inspection. The skipper usually began by taking a look at the Boy's Guard first.

Followed by the Surgeon, Paymaster, Guard Commander and a host of minor pop-in-jays, the skipper would inspect each boy carefully, indicating minor faults here and there, dirty boots this one, haircut for that one, "When did you shave last?" etc. , the Divisional Officer noting it all down in his little book. All throughout the entire inspection, the Royal Marine Band, resplendent in their white helmets, and the big drummer arrayed in his gorgeous leopard-skin, played selections of music in slow time.

Divisions usually lasted about an hour, during which time everyone was thoroughly fed up with standing about. The Grande Finale was the whole parade marching past the rostrum with the Captain taking the salute and picking up this division, or that, for faulty marching, after which the whole parade – except for the Roman Catholics and other special denominations – would then march to the gymnasium for the Church of England Service.

The gym was the ideal place in which to accommodate so large a congregation, either for Church, Cinema shows or theatricals and on Sunday mornings it was rigged up as a church. It was a huge lofty building, with a stage at the far end. Wall bars were fitted along the walls on two sides and box horses, parallel bars and other items of physical training equipment lay scattered about the vast floor area.

The duty watch of boys had already placed the seating, which in true naval style, consisted of capstan bars, buckets and planks and we boys filed in and took our seats. In the front half dozen rows chairs had been placed for the Officers and their wives.

Two things always stand out in my memory when I recall these Sunday services. The perfume from the hair oils used by the boys, which pervaded the gymnasium, and the words of Rudyard Kipling's wonderful poem "IF", which adorned either side of the stage on two gigantic wall panels.

The whole scene was one of colour. The rows of fresh young seamen in the making, with their navy blue uniforms, lighter blue collars and white shirt fronts. The blue and gold of the officers uniforms, the variety of colours of the ladies' dresses, the huge white ensign hanging down behind the pulpit and the Royal Marine Orchestra (no common organ for us) which accompanied our lusty voices as we sang those good old -fashioned hymns.

I always enjoyed those services, with their very much alive congregations. Here we were all young and healthy, and very grateful for it. With the pronouncing of the blessing and the singing of the National Anthem, the service came to an end, and the Captain and Officers and their wives, filed out, followed by we small fry, whilst the duty watch remained behind to un-rig the seating and to restore the room to its original use, a gymnasium.

After church, the rest of Sunday was ours. The non-duty watch could proceed ashore until 6 p.m. but only a few took advantage of this, since one could only walk along the country lanes. Quite a few took part in organised games, such as football or cricket, according to the season, but I was not keen on these. My own sports were athletics and rowing.

If the weather was fine, some of us would spend the afternoon up the mast, climbing among the rigging, or relaxing on the lower platform with a book and a bar of chocolate. Or one could lie in the long grass bordering the playing fields, lazily watching the clouds roll by. We made the most of these Sunday afternoons, because next morning another strenuous week of training would begin.

On Monday morning, through the warm fog of sleep, we heard the now familiar voice of Bungy calling us back to reality. It was 6 a.m. and it was our first day of what was to be eight months of concentrated training. As we tumbled out of bed, Bungy was reminding us of the dress we had to wear and the routine to be followed when we arrived on the parade ground at 8.30 a.m. This was enough to put the wind up the class before we started, but in spite of all his do's and don'ts, we all managed to eat a hearty breakfast.

At 8.30 a.m. sharp we were on parade with the rest of the barracks, wearing clean white duck uniform. Half of the class wearing cleaned webb belts and gaiters. This was due to the training programme which worked as follows:- For one week, half of the class did gunnery instruction in the forenoons and school after lunch, then the following week it would be seamanship in the mornings and school after lunch, so that the whole class had gunnery and seamanship on alternate weeks, with school every week. The gunnery section therefore, had to wear khaki belts and gaiters which was the "uniform" of the gunnery world. It has been said that even the seagulls flying around Whale Island (the Navy's premier gunnery school) wear gaiters!

After "Divisions" and prayers were over, the whole of the class was addressed by the Training Commander, a tall, stern looking officer, with an air of "no nonsense" about him. He commenced by warning us that the Navy was a very old institution, that it had met blokes like us before and had survived hundreds of years regardless, so we must not imagine that any feeble efforts of ours to try and alter things were likely to shake its foundations. "If," he went on, "we cared to dig out, and put our best into it," he saw no reason why, one day, we should not fly our flags from the masthead of one of His Majesty's ships, etc., etc. And so we budding Admirals began our training.

My half of the class started our first week with gunnery instruction a.m. and school p.m., and Bungy, with a gleam in his eye, marched us off to the dreaded parade ground. First he gave us a short talk on why it was necessary to have drill at all, pointing out that this sort of training made a person react automatically to orders given, and because of it, might one day be the means of saving life. He then changed his voice, which up till now, had been soft and purring, like a cat with a saucer of cream before it. In a menacing voice, he warned us that whilst he might be prepared to overlook one mistake, a second would bring disaster on our heads, and with this little pleasantry, we began our day.

We marched – oh how we marched! – all the forenoon. "Right Turn; Left Turn"; "Right Incline"; "Left Incline", "Keep yer ruddy heads up." This way, that way, until we were giddy and thoroughly footsore. As is usually found in every class, we had a fool in our midst who could not distinguish his left from his right. We also had a rarity, one who had great difficulty in swinging his arms alternately. He would insist on swinging them both together in the same direction, to the great hilarity of the class and the chagrin of Bungy, who of course, took it out of all of us. Altogether we were glad when the forenoon came to an end.

After our morning on the Parade ground we had appetites like horses, and I was glad to find a dinner I liked waiting for us. Pea soup, sausages, mashed potatoes with fried onions, followed by suet pudding and treacle. A meal fit for the gods and we all thoroughly enjoyed it.

Lunch over, we paraded on the Main parade ground and under the charge of our class leader, we were marched off to the school classrooms. In contrast to our morning, the peaceful atmosphere of the schoolroom was sheer heaven, even if it did mean racking our brains over missing decimal points and wondering who Pythagoras was!

Naval schoolmasters of my day held the rank of Warrant or Commissioned Warrant Officers. These worthy gentlemen spent years in this low rank and to my mind were worth far more than they got in the way of pay and promotion. I am glad to say that nowadays they start as Sub-Lieutenants and can go right to the top.

This first week was one of sweat and tears in the mornings and peace and quiet in the afternoons. It was a real down to earth introduction to the ways of the Navy and, although at the time we thought it tough and ourselves hard done by, looking back over the years I realise that it did all of us a power of good, and I thank those hard case instructors for making something of me.

After tea, we would sit around on our beds discussing the day's happenings. The seamanship half of the class relating their experiences to the gunnery half and vice versa, and of course, the gunnery section lost no opportunity of putting the fear of old nick into the other half.

We had the usual blithe spirits one finds in a community of boys, and they did much to brighten our lives, particularly after a heavy day on the parade ground, when one or the other would give a fair imitation of Bungy instructing us in rifle drill. This sort of episode made our early days in *Ganges* tolerable and we were grateful for it.

Altogether, they were exciting days. We slowly divorced ourselves from civilian life and learned to work together and to share our lives and experiences. We even began to speak a different language. One spiced and laced with nautical expressions foreign to the ordinary man in the street. We were sailors in the making and we were very proud of that.

To say that we were all angels would be stretching things a little. We had our secret smokers and our minor delinquents and the odd one or two who tried to kick over the traces. However, the Navy is an old firm and knew the answers to this problem, and gradually these few were won over and began to toe the line with the rest of us.

Those first few weeks passed quickly. We pounded the Parade Ground to dust. We learned how to turn, march, salute and stand to attention without moving an inch. We practised all the movements of drill under arms until we were like automatons. First mistakes were tolerated, but heaven help those who repeated them, because quite apart from the individual attention of Bungy, the culprit invariably got the rest of us a period of doubling around the parade ground, with the result that we would take it out of him as well.

In addition to the parade work, we had our periods of Physical Training, when we were put through our paces in the gymnasium. I have always hated this form of physical torture and could never understand the mentality of those muscle-bound worshippers of physical culture, whose attitude seemed to be that everyone else should be as enthusiastic as themselves in leaping over box horses and swinging about on bars and trapezes like a lot of Barbary apes. With few exceptions, we were always glad when these sessions in the gymnasium were over.

We also had an introduction to the swimming bath, where we had to take the naval swimming test, which consisted of swimming two lengths of the bath, then keeping afloat for three minutes, dressed in a duck suit. I was fortunate in getting through this and was therefore excused further instruction, but quite a few failed to make the grade. Presumably they had never had to swim in clothes before! These had further instruction until such times as they finally passed the test. No boy was ever sent to sea from *Ganges* unless he could swim.

During the evening, on his duty day, Ben would sometimes come down to our hut and talk to us. I well remember one such occasion. That morning we had been put through the mill on the parade ground. Bungy had really gone to town on us and we were near breaking point. Ben sensed this, and like the wise bird he was, began to ferret out our grievances.

We told him of our trials and tribulations and of the way Bungy was hazing us on the parade. Ben was sympathetic, but he was also very loyal to his kind. He pointed out that the real Navy was not at all like *Ganges*. Here they had the job of breaking in undisciplined civilians and turning out smart seamen, who would re-act to emergency automatically. This was not a job for amateurs. It required many qualities. One had to be patient – very patient – we did not all learn at the same speed, in fact some did not learn at all! Drill was not a popular subject, either to teach or be taught and tempers were therefore easily frayed.

Ben, with his quiet way of reasoning, gradually brought us round to looking at Bungy in a more sympathetic light and we began to realise that perhaps, after all, he was doing as fair a job as possible, even if it was at our expense.

This was Ben's greatest quality. We could speak outright to him and he had the priceless knack of putting us right with the world. If my own Naval career was considered successful – and I think the powers that be were well satisfied with their servant – then a large part of that success was due to his wisdom and teaching. I shall always remember him with gratitude.

We always looked forward to our seamanship weeks and Ben taught us the rudiments of the art. He showed us how to heave the lead, steer a ship, knot, splice and do fancy rope work. We were taken out on the river Stour and taught how to row a 32 foot cutter and how to manage her under sail in all sorts of weather. We learned navigation and pilotage, and had the Rule of the Road at Sea off by heart. He told us that seamanship was largely the practice of common sense and proved it to us on more than one occasion. I have found all this knowledge of great assistance to me during my lifetime, both in and out of the service.

About the middle of summer, we completed our first twelve weeks training and, after passing a brief examination, we were then advanced to Boy 1st class. The special privilege allowed us was the casting off of our soft serge caps and the adoption of the normal service cap, which indicated to all and sundry our new status. We also received an extra sixpence a week pocket money, making 1/6d. a week, which we thought was magnificent bounty!

We now commenced our final five months training. At this stage, those of us who wished to become signal and wireless ratings had the chance of changing over to this branch. About twelve of our class did so, amid the ribald comments of the rest of us, since it was considered that a boy who so transferred, did so because he couldn't take the more tough life of the seaman. This, of course, was simply not true, but youth is always unsympathetic towards its own generation and we were no exception.

As I remember, it was a beautiful summer and we were all hard at it. We crammed drill, explosives, fire control, heavy gun drill and allied gunnery subjects, followed by boatwork, and all the seamanship subjects. We did this until early August when we got our first spell of leave. Fourteen days of sheer heaven after all we had gone through, and of course, everyone made the most of this temporary reprieve.

Shortly after returning from leave, I developed a septic callous on the sole of my right foot which necessitated my having to spend a week in the Sick Bay. My chief worry was that of being put back a class, since it was the custom to do this should a boy be too long away from his instructions. However, this did not happen to me, although one was always faced with this possibility and I dreaded having to start in a new class with fresh faces and unknown instructors.

It was my first experience of a naval sick bay and I was most impressed by the clean orderly efficiency everywhere. After the daily hub-bub of our normal life, this was calm and peaceful. With kippers and jam for tea, and eggs which we secretly boiled in the ward sterilizer, I really enjoyed myself.

In those days I was a great reader and the Chaplain used to bring me books and papers, and for me, the time passed all too soon. However, by the end of the week my foot had healed and I was pronounced fit for duty, and I rejoined my old class in time to continue training on the following Monday.

Although I had been absent for a week, I was able to catch up such instruction as was missing by borrowing my classmates' books and swotting during the evenings. The theory of gunnery, explosives, shells etc. and the intricate systems of fire control interested me greatly, consequently this knowledge came to me easily and at this stage, I had almost decided that this would be the branch of the service in which I'd most like to qualify. However, this was not to be as later on I fell in love with the more interesting and complicated Torpedo Branch and I finally made this my choice.

During the last quarter of the year, the Boxing Tournament commenced. To find likely candidates, it was the custom to hold eliminating contests between the various messes. There was no question of volunteers or whether one liked boxing or not. Each mess in turn, mustered in the gymnasium and the boys were sorted out into pairs of roughly the same height and weight. These pairs were then put into the ring in rotation and for one minute, knocked the living daylights out of each other. Any boy showing signs of becoming a likely boxer, was noted and found himself entered for further coaching. The whole affair was known to we boys as "Inter-mess slaughter". It certainly recalled to mind the ancient stories of the Gladiators of Rome. Very few of us liked the idea, but since it was part of the training system, we had to accept it. Needless to say, we non boxers were glad to be eliminated at the earliest possible moment! This was the training policy; like it or not, one had to have a go. Looking back on those days, I must admit how right that policy was.

Another facet of our life at *Ganges* was our weekly wash day. Every Wednesday afternoon our class collected together all our dirty clothes, and complete with bar of soap, we were marched to the laundry. This was housed in a large room with a tiled floor. Along one side was a row of deep Butlers sinks, each with its hot and cold water tap. In the centre of the room was a large bank of drying frames which one pulled out like a drawer, then, having hung up one's washing, the frame was pushed back into its housing. Hot air circulated between the frames, thoroughly drying the clothes overnight.

Also in the centre of the room were two giant sized high speed hydro extractors, or spin dryers, which we used to spin dry our clothes before placing them in the hot frames, and woe betide any boy who tried to put his washing in the frame before he had spun it.

Our washing methods were all "handraulic", every piece having to be hand-washed, except perhaps for our white duck suits. These suits were stiff and to attempt to wash them by rubbing through the hands, resulted in one skinning one's knuckles. The easy way, therefore, was to use a scrubbing brush, with the suit stretched out on the floor. Our only weapons were the scrubber and the pound bar of yellow navy soap. We had no soap powders or "whiter than white" aids, it was simply a question of hot water, soap and plain elbow grease. The washing session took us all afternoon to complete and I, for one, was glad when it was over.

As the autumn shades began to appear on the trees around the camp, our intensive training course came to an end and we began our final week of swotting for the passing out examinations at the end of October.

For the past eight months we had slogged on the parade ground, on the water and at our books, until our brains were fit to burst. From the nondescript, undisciplined rabble at the pierhead eight months ago, we had been transformed into smart, alert and fairly intelligent youngsters. Not yet sailors perhaps, but sound material for the sea to start on.

For my part, I had enjoyed every stage of the training, except perhaps the parade work, but then this was not popular with anyone in their right minds, so I was not alone in this respect. And so we came to the end of the last week of our course.

Sunday afternoon and evening we spent asking each other questions and going through the examination syllabus. First we tested each other's knowledge in gunnery subjects, then we swapped to seamanship. Some of us practised arms drill, with broom handles used as rifles and we all went to bed that night, mentally and physically exhausted, hoping to wake in the morning refreshed, and trusting that we would be asked the questions we knew, rather than those we did not.

My section began with the gunnery examinations and our first ordeal was a written paper on explosives, ammunition and magazine regulations. It was held in a classroom and conducted by a Warrant Officer of the Gunnery Branch. Of Bungy we saw no sign, we were now on our own, and after first reading the paper through we commenced the exam at 9.30 a.m. the official finishing time being 11.30 a.m.

As far as I was concerned, it was a good paper, since the subject had always interested me, and taking up my pen I began to scribble away, answering such questions as "What are the ingredients of cordite?" and "How would you recognise a target practice smoke shell?" etc. I was soon deep in the realms of explosives, fireworks, shells and magazine safety regulations and before I knew it, the paper was finished and our time was up. When we left the building to go to dinner, I felt that I had turned in a reasonable paper.

Over dinner we discussed our morning's work, comparing answers given and generally trying to analyse each other's efforts, so that by the time the meal was over, we had a general idea of how we might have fared in the Ammunition examination.

At the time we had been racking our brains over ammunition, the other section of the class had been examined in seamanship subjects. They had turned in a paper on "Rules of the Road at Sea", Lights, Pilotage and Chart Work and of course, we in the gunnery section were very much interested, since it would be our turn next.

It was an exciting week, we were all very much alive and eager to have done with this barrack life and to get to sea, but we realised that these examinations had to be faced first. After tea some of us went down to the lower foreshore and in the late sunshine, with the fresh sharp smell of the seaweed in our nostrils and wheeling gulls overhead, we would discuss the exams, our hopes and our desires. Classmates such as Lofty Lazenby, Swifty, Kimber, Brum Pengelly whom we always referred to as "Flannel Belly". I have often wondered since, how many of those fresh young classmates of mine are still alive today. We had our dreams, but we also had a war.

And so we came to the end of the week and the completion of our course. All that remained now were the much awaited exam results. The weekend passed all too slowly, leaving us to stew in doubt. We woke up on Monday morning in a state of mind bordering between success and failure. Some of us were confident, others apprehensive and some just dead sure that they had failed to make the grade.

There was an air of expectancy at breakfast. We were eager to get the interview with the Training Officer over and behind us. We had stewed ourselves all the weekend and now we were ready to hear our fate. After clearing up the mess, we all got into our clean duck suits and at 9 a.m. we were marched off to the Instructional Office.

We paraded in two lines outside the office, with both our Instructors out in front and, at 9.30 a.m. the Training Commander came out, accompanied by his Chief Petty Officer assistant. Bungy called us to attention and reported that we were all present and correct, then he stood us at ease.

With a preliminary cough, the Commander began with a speech outlining our progress during the past eight months, pointing out that from irresponsible civilian dogsbodies, we had been converted into tolerable human beings with a purpose in the world and, although we had finished our course here in *Ganges*, we must not suppose that we were now fully fledged sailors. "No sailor," he added, "was ever produced on dry land," and therefore, when we were drafted to a sea-going ship, we would only then begin our real training. He pointed out that of our class of forty, only three had failed to make the grade and that they would be transferred to another class which was three months behind us.

Like a theatre impressario, the Commander kept his best turn until last and, after praising our two Instructors for the high standard obtained, he then read out the long awaited results. Dame fortune was with me, and my name appeared among the top bracket. I had an idea that I hadn't done too badly, but this result pleased me immensely, for it was better than I had expected. After all the results were known, the Commander wished us well and his assistant then took over and since we had now finished with instructions, we were detailed into camp working parties.

I was chosen to be the Gunnery Officer's messenger, my job being to keep his office clean and to run any errands for him. At the same time, since he discovered that I could use a typewriter, I also did most of his correspondence as well.

These camp duties usually lasted for a week at a time, then one would change to another duty; however, owing to my typing ability,

I was kept on at the Gunnery Office as a permanent feature until drafted to sea.

The rest of the year slid peacefully by and before long our Christmas leave loomed over the horizon. However, a week before it was due to start, our class list appeared in the drafting orders. We were all being sent to ships of the Third Battle Squadron, which was the Training Squadron of the Atlantic Fleet and we were to be drafted on our return from Christmas leave.

We were all highly delighted at the news, particularly me. With a fortnight's leave due and a ship awaiting my return, life was exceedingly good. A study of the drafting list showed that, with ten others, I was being drafted to H.M.S. *Marlborough*, a coal-fired battleship, whilst the rest of the class were spread among the other three ships of the squadron; *Iron Duke, Benbow* and *Emperor of India*.

Next day, after packing a few things in a blue check bundle handkerchief (no attaché cases for us), we were ferried across to Harwich to catch the train to London and home for Christmas leave.

All through my leave I could not think of anything else but *Marlborough*, and managed to learn quite a bit about her pedigree before returning to *Ganges*. Like all leave, it passed too quickly and before long, I found myself in the Harwich train at Liverpool Street station, with some of my class mates as travelling companions. This time we were excited at returning from leave. We were on the threshold of a new experience and the rain, beating against the carriage windows could not dampen our spirits.

We were due to join our ships a week after our return from leave and this last week in *Ganges* was busy for us, inasmuch that we had to draw our hammocks from the store, and fit them up with the clews and lashings. We had to muster all our kit, see that it was properly marked, clean, and all the deficiencies made good. We had to pass the doctor and dentist and do a hundred and one things necessary before going on draft. All was hustle and bustle, but I loved it, for this was the beginning of an adventure and that was sufficient for me.

In the second week of January 1928 we bade farewell to *Ganges*, the furnace that had tempered us, and as we crossed the water to Harwich, with all our baggage, I looked back and saw the white ensign of the barracks, proudly stiffening in the salt laden breeze, and I realised that this was but the end of the beginning!

Chapter Three

H.M.S. *MARLBOROUGH*

<u>1928 – 1929</u>

It was late afternoon when our train arrived at North Road Station, Plymouth and, as is usual at Plymouth, it was pouring with rain. Looking through the rain-streaked carriage windows, we could see the R.N. lorry drawn up outside the station, waiting to take us and our kit down to Devonport Dockyard.

We were met by a Petty Officer from *Marlborough*, who soon had us unloading our kit from the train and stowing it aboard the lorry. This only took a few minutes and, climbing onboard, we soon got under way and headed towards Devonport.

Dockyards are normally a dismal picture, but add this to the steady rain and the failing light of a late January afternoon and you have some idea of my first impression. Our lorry bumped over old fashioned cobblestones, and lurched across railway lines running in all directions. All the buildings were constructed of drab grey stone which, in the half light, added gloom to the already murky conditions.

We passed dry docks and basins containing all types of warships, from submarines to aircraft carriers, some in various states of repair. I could see the intermittent violet flash of an arc welding tool being used on a cruiser's superstructure. Elsewhere the distant clatter of a pneumatic rivetting hammer echoed around the yard.

We crossed a caisson and there, before us, sitting on her fat bottom in a large dry dock, was H.M.S. *Marlborough*. My heart sank into my boots. I had pictured her in all her glittering glory of fresh paint and sparkling brasswork, but what did we see? A dirty looking battleship, dressed in dark grey with splotches of red lead paint daubed here and there; her decks covered with dirt and patches of grease and oil and littered with pneumatic air lines spreading in all directions.

Here and there, one could see dockyardmen's tool boxes, empty paint drums and wood shavings. Overall hung the pungent, acrid smell of the anti-fouling paint used to coat the ship's bottom. In the dim light and the rain, *Marlborough* looked a pretty dismal sight and we, the newest members of her company, felt equally dejected!

As our lorry came to a halt near the forward brow, I had time to take in her outline. About twenty nine thousand tons, she mounted ten thirteen point five inch guns, disposed in five twin turrets, two forward, two aft and one amidships. There were twelve six inch guns arranged in a battery of six each side of the ship, each gun mounted in its own casemate. A tripod mast immediately behind the bridge, surmounted by a spotting top and gun director, followed by two slender "woodbine" funnels and a short stumpy mainmast, completed the picture.

My dreams were shattered by the need to unload our kit and to get onboard out of the rain and, within ten minutes or so, I was standing on the deck of one of His Majesty's battleships for the first time. It might have been King George's but at the moment it was mine, dirt and all!

We were shepherded into the starboard six inch gun battery and were shown our new mess, which was a gun casemate containing a six inch gun, a table and two long stools. The inboard side of the casemate contained a steel breakwater about three feet high, which marked the boundary of our mess. The Leading Seaman in charge of our particular mess (who shall be known as 'Tubby') was introduced to us, and from then on he took over.

Tubby, as his nickname suggests, was a plump and short individual, but unlike most fat people, not very amiable. Perhaps it was because of his long association with the training of boys, but we soon discovered that he had a very short temper and consequently, we treated him delicately. We also discovered that *Marlborough* had about six hundred boys on board (some were still on Christmas leave) and a skeleton crew of seamen ratings, which meant that the boys practically ran the ship themselves.

There is a definite atmosphere about a ship when going between decks for the first time. There is the "shippy" smell of new paint combined with tinned air from the ventilating system. Then there is the odour of damp serge and mothballs, mingling with the smell of cooking and perhaps, paraffin. Also the perpetual hum of the ventilating fan motors, although one gets used to this until the noise is not noticed.

The deckhead above is coated with cork chippings to absorb moisture, and is usually covered with a maze of pipes and cables of varying sizes and with all sorts of coloured bands and markings around them to indicate the contents passing through them.

It is a strange fact that, on coming aboard one's own ship, it can be identified by its noises. For instance, after serving a short while in a ship, one gets accustomed to the particular sound of the ventilating fans. On visiting a friend in another ship, the pitch of the fan motors in that ship would be different and I could always detect this. In hundreds of other acoustic ways, one sensed the difference between one's own and other vessels. This was but one of the many facets of shipboard life which made one think of one's own particular ship as home, and so it was with me on joining *Marlborough*.

Marlborough herself had quite a history, having descended from a long line of other *Marlboroughs*. Built around about 1913-14 she had taken part in the battle of Jutland, when she flew the flag of Vice Admiral Sir Cecil Burney. During the action she was struck by a torpedo and assumed a slight list, but was able to maintain the fleet speed of 17 knots by the prodigious efforts of her stokers.

Now, however, she was commanded by Captain Alfred Carpenter, V.C., the hero of the famous Zeebrugge raid in 1918. He was in command of H.M.S. *Vindictive* on that brilliant St. George's Day. Our executive officer was a rather irritable gentleman, one, Commander F. Johnson. No doubt with 600 boys to look after, this would account for his not infrequent bouts of irritability.

We ten from *Ganges* had the mess to ourselves, and we were all placed in the Maintop Division under a very fine officer, Lieut. Commander M. Fogg-Elliott, and our Petty Officer Captain of the Top was one, Spike Marlin, a real pirate.

Our first hot meal was at 7 p.m. which was the ship's normal supper time, after which Tubby helped us to settle in. He showed us how to sling a hammock, gave us our kit locker numbers and, after warning us that, as boys, we had to be turned in by 9 p.m., he left us to ourselves. For the short time left before turning in, we toured the ship between decks, exploring this space and that, and locating the canteen and bathrooms. It was all new and exciting to us, we were on the threshold of a new experience and the thought of the coming months kept me awake long after the others were asleep.

The training we had received in *Ganges* stood us in good stead, since we found that the ship's routine, with very little exception, was much the same. One of the major differences of course, was our having to get up at 5.30 a.m. and commence scrubbing down the decks at 6 a.m. regardless of the weather. However, since we were at the moment, in dry dock and the decks littered with all sorts of junk, we could only sweep down.

At 6.30 on most mornings, whilst the ship was in dock, we were called away from our sweeping and taken for a run around the dockyard by the Physical Training Instructor, known as 'Beefy Evans'. It was ship's routine and each morning he would collect a bunch of boys and put them through various P.T. exercises, or as in our case, and if we were berthed alongside a jetty, he would take us for a sort of cross country run around the dockyard. "Beefy" was a rough diamond, at one time a Navy Heavy Weight Boxing Champion. We all grew extremely fond of "Beefy" despite the fact that few of us took kindly to his brand of P.T.

Another surprise we had was the coming aboard of the famous "Shotley Terror", a certain gunnery instructor by the name of "Nutty Gardiner."This character had the reputation at *Ganges* of being the most dreaded instructor on the parade ground. With a voice like a nutmeg grater, he used to hound his classes to distraction, but his boys always obtained record marks in their examinations. We poor fools, thought we had seen the last of him, but here he was, large as life, joining our ship! Worse was to follow, because we found that he had been allocated to our division, the Maintop.

We soon discovered that the "Terror" of *Ganges* fame was a totally different kind of man onboard ship. Here, shipboard life was a lot less strenuous for an instructor than was the parade ground of a rigid training depot. Onboard the "Shotley Terror" became human again, and we all grew to like him immensely. He was direct and straight to the point. Off duty, one couldn't find a better shipmate or friend; but he will always be remembered by generations of sailors as the "Shotley Terror". A first class seaman and instructor.

Towards the end of January, with the rest of the crew back from leave and the refit practically complete, *Marlborough* was moved from the dry dock to one of the big basins, where the completion of the dockyard work was carried out.

By this time, we had more or less settled down to our strange new life and had fitted in with the rest of the crew very well. I had been introduced to the art of painting by Spike Marlin, who, when I had told him that I had never done any painting or decorating before, simply laughed in his black beard and roared, "Well sonnie, now's yer bloody chance to learn – get up that so and so mast!" And so I became an expert painter overnight. We learned the hard way, but the method was very effective.

Life in a dockyard basin is extremely primitive for any ship's company. To begin with, since we could not pump refuse into the basin, we had a two day camel ride to the dockside toilets. This also applied to bathing and washing and since the weather was wet and freezing cold, one can imagine the inconvenience to our crew. To make matters worse, our galley was under repair and all our meals were cooked onshore and had to be carried inboard each meal time, consequently, by the time we got them on the table they were invariably cold and tasteless. It was with some measure of relief that we were finally moved out of the basin and towed out into tidal waters to be ultimately berthed alongside the coaling jetty to receive our quota of coal.

Marlborough and her three sisters, *Iron Duke, Benbow* and *Emperor of India* were the last of our coal fired capital ships. When drafted to *Marlborough* this fact was, as far as I was concerned, a very interesting one, because whilst most of my classmates were deploring it, I was looking forward to the experience of coaling ship. This does not mean that I liked hard work any more than the next man, but at least

I would be able to say that I had served in one, and also be able to spin my crop of yarns about them.

The atmosphere on coal ship days was a mixture of jollity and hard work. Every man in the ship, with the exception of the Captain, Medical staff and the Paymaster, was engaged in getting the coal onboard and stowed in the bunkers. During the whole of the day, the Royal Marine Band, perched precariously on top of the centre gun turret, played selections of popular music, with clouds of coal dust ascending around them and their instruments, until they resembled coloured minstrels. Discipline was relaxed, boys allowed to smoke and a competitive spirit prevailed everywhere.

It was one of those evolutions which was in complete contrast to any other drill or job. The dress worn on these occasions was entirely optional and many and varied were the rigs worn. I have seen elderly A.B's dressed in striped trousers and battered toppers, heaven only knows where they got them, and one old timer was seen shovelling coal dressed as a parson.

As soon as the collier had secured alongside, the various parties detailed for their particular hold, descended on the ship. Four gangs of men and boys were allocated to each hold, one gang to each corner. The bags we used each held two hundredweights and it was the job of each gang to fill ten of these bags to make up a one ton hoist. Once the coaling commenced and the first gang had got its ton load ready and away, the race began to fill ten more bags before the coaling whip got around to them again. To miss a hoist due to not having the ten bags ready was considered a poor show, and the rest of the gangs soon let their feelings on the subject be known.

To keep up this pressure, hour after hour with only a thirty minute break for lunch, was hard work, in fact, back breaking work. Throughout the day, limejuice was sent around to all hands and one usually drank it straight out of the fanny, after first blowing the coal dust scum away from the drinking edge of the receptacle.

Every hour, signal flags were hoisted at the yard arms, indicating how many tons of coal had been stowed during the previous hour and, when the whole squadron were coaling together, there was great competition to see which ship had taken onboard the most coal.

All during the coaling, vast clouds of dust ascended from the holds and from the ship's bunkers, settling everywhere throughout the ship. In addition to this it clogged one's eyelashes and the rim of one's eyes. We smeared our eyelids and lashes with margarine or vaseline so that the dust could be easily washed off, but even after this treatment, for days afterwards, most of the crew looked as if they had been using mascara on their eyelashes.

I think, of all men, the stokers whose duty it was to trim the bunkers, probably had the worst job of all. At least we seamen were in the fresh air, even if it was loaded with suffocating dust; but down below in the bunkers, conditions must have been well nigh intolerable.

At the end of the day, with bunkers full, all hands were engaged in washing down the ship from truck to keel, whilst a tug steamed slowly around the ship, washing down our upperworks with high pressure hoses. Our last act of the day would be to bath ourselves with limited quantities of fresh water, and washing our coaling clothes all ready for the next time.

Although welcoming the unique experience of coaling ship, I sometimes envied those serving in oil-fired vessels, where the refuelling simply consisted of connecting up a flexible hose and that was the end of the matter. However, I was glad that I was able to take some small part in these operations because of the historical fact that I was serving in one of the last four coal-fired battleships in the Royal Navy, and to me, that was something worth boasting about.

Next day we were moved out to a buoy in the middle of the stream, ready for the ammunition lighters to secure alongside. For the day following, we were going to ammunition ship and there were certain safety regulations to be observed.

For the job of ammunitioning, the ship's company dressed in their blue overall suits, and the various derricks were rigged ready to swing out over the lighters. We boys were split up and attached to various parties, some to deal with 6" cordite, 13.5" cordite and small arms ammunition; others to strike down below the huge 13.5" shells and the smaller 6" variety.

It was a job where one had to be nimble and keep one's eyes open, or fingers soon became jammed or broken when handling the heavy cordite cases, or the three quarter ton 13.5" shells. Ammunitioning usually took two full days and none of us were really sorry when the lighters, now empty, finally closed their hatches down and cast off for home.

There remained one more job before we finally sailed. That of provisioning and storing ship, and we commenced that the next morning. We were lucky with the weather for a change, it was sunny, though cold and by 5 p.m. we had embarked all our needs and then went to tea. We were now ready for sea, and were due to sail for Gibraltar to join the rest of our squadron and the Atlantic Fleet, of which we were a part.

This was Friday, and our last weekend in Devonport, since we were sailing on Monday on the afternoon tide and, everyone who was eligible for weekend leave, (not the boys of course) was busy changing and getting ready for shore leave. As boys we were allowed leave on Saturday and Sunday afternoons from 1 p.m. to 7 p.m. Most of us took this leave and went for a walk around Devonport and Plymouth, finishing up at Agnes Weston's Royal Sailors Rest for tea, before returning onboard.

On Monday afternoon (I believe it was the first week in February), we slipped our buoy and steamed slowly out of Plymouth Sound into the teeth of a heavy South Westerly gale. Although some twenty nine thousand tons, *Marlborough* began to dip her bows before she had gone through the breakwater, and when clear of the Sound the ship was rolling and pitching heavily, with that slow corkscrew motion which left one's stomach in the air whilst one's feet were still on the deck!

By the time we had altered course to the south west and began heading towards Ushant, I, and most of our new crew members were cursing the day we ever decided to become sailors. We were literally green. Although feeling half dead and fervently wishing that we were, we were chased up on deck and made to work, securing gear which might be washed overboard.

Every time the bows dipped, a heavy green comber would break over the forecastle and sweep aft, to throw itself skywards in a huge fountain as it struck the breakwater. To add to our trials, there were the smells peculiar to every ship, such as paraffin, cooking, paint and damp serge clothing, all of which helped to turn us a more vivid shade of green and make us wish we had never been born. And, of course, there were always the old hands with pieces of fat bacon on the end of a piece of string, doing their utmost to worsen our condition and bring about our downfall.

Since our cruising speed was only ten knots, we did not reach the Bay of Biscay until next day, then for thirty six miserable hours, we buffeted and rolled our way southward, each hour an agony, with me wishing each one was my last. The ship did everything but turn over. It was as if the old lady was putting on a special show for our benefit; then turning out one morning, 36 hours later, we found the ship on an even keel, with smooth seas, blue skies and brilliant sunshine. It was as if a miracle had happened and we were grateful for it, for we came to life again and all hands turned to and cleaned up the ship.

After tea, with nothing to do, we would get right forward in the bows and, lying on our bellies, watch the porpoises playing around our forefoot. Now and again, flying fishes would rise out of the startling blue sea and, skimming low across the surface, plop back some fifty or sixty yards further on. Up to this moment, I had only read about such things and we were all fascinated as we watched the porpoises racing the ship and leaping lazily across her bows. Over to port we saw the faint outline of the Portugese coast and occasionally, a distant lighthouse could be seen standing out white against the blue blur of the coast.

Since we were in the main shipping lane, we were passed by several homeward bound vessels, ranging from huge P & O liners to small tramp steamers. Each vessel as it passed us, lowered its ensign in salute, to which we replied in kind. This is an old sea tradition which still survives and is one of the little courtesies which help to make life worth while. In all my sea experience I cannot recall a single instance where this custom has not been observed.

On the fourth morning out, the ship entered the straits of Gibraltar and there, a distant smudge on the port bow, could be seen the famous Rock. As we steamed through the straits, or the Pillars of Hercules as it is sometimes called, we were busily preparing for entering harbour.

After breakfast, the crew took up stations for entering harbour, and we boys were fallen in on the upper deck in our respective divisions. The Royal Marine Guard and Band were paraded on the quarter deck and two buglers stood on top of "B" turret ready to do the honours of saluting senior officers as we passed their respective ships.

Shortly after 9 a.m. *Marlborough* slowly turned to port to make the run into Gibraltar Bay, and as we steadied on our new course, there before us lay the Atlantic Fleet, peacefully at anchor in the lines of their respective squadrons.

Over to Starboard loomed the huge edifice of the Rock. A mass of green and limestone with the township huddled around its base and the dockyard with its harbour breakwaters completed the picture. Immediately ahead of us, as we slowly steamed to our anchorage, and mounted on the top of a hill, was the stone structure known as "The Queen of Spain's Chair", whilst over to port lay the town of Algiciras.

In the fresh clean air of the morning one could smell the odour of spice, scent and oranges, wafting off the shore, and these were our first impressions of Gibraltar. We were intoxicated by the freshness of the morning and the romance of sighting our first foreign land beyond the Rock. There was a picturesque atmosphere about the place. One often reads about the spicy off-shore scents of sub-tropical places, now for the first time we were experiencing it, and like Cortez gazing at his Pacific Ocean, we drank in the scene greedily and felt glad to be alive.

Most of the fleet were anchored in the Bay, but as was the custom of the Navy, senior officer's ships had preference of berths, therefore one could see the flagships of the various squadrons berthed inside the breakwaters of the harbour. I picked out *Nelson*, the C-in-C's ship; *Hood*, the flagship of the battlecruiser squadron, and *Iron Duke* our own squadron's flagship, with Rear Admiral John

Casement onboard. Beyond these and secured to buoys lay *Curacoa* flagship of the 2nd cruiser squadron and against the inner jetty, the light cruiser *Centaur*, the flagship of the Atlantic Fleet Destroyer Flotillas. Berthed in the pens nearby were the destroyers themselves, eighteen in all. In the brilliant sunshine it was a magnificent sight, this vast panoply of sea power anchored under the shadow of the Rock of Gibraltar.

With a rattle of cable and the sounding of the "G" on the bugle, *Marlborough* simultaneously dropped anchor, spread awnings, got out lower and quarter booms, and began to lower the boats required for duty during the day. This was a smart evolution, which earned us a "Well Done" signal from the flagship. A good start for the day.

Although the morning was bright and sunny, a wind sprang up, which raised a considerable chop on the water and made boatwork wet and hazardous. We were surrounded in no time by bum boats plying their wares, although how their owners expected to sell anything with their boats plunging violently about was beyond me, but at least they tried, and more than one box of cigars or bottle of perfume found its way up the ship's side.

We boys could not go ashore until the following day, which was Saturday, and for the rest of the day we were employed painting or holystoning the decks. There was one consolation however, we had been paid, which meant we would have a few shillings in our pockets. It was with a thrill, next day, that my messmates and I stepped ashore in Gibraltar for the first time. We quickly walked through the old dockyard and soon found ourselves in the Main Street. Most goods are duty free in Gibraltar and of course, perfumes and cigars were the main attractions, although one could get exceptionally good crystal beads here.

After poking around the various shops and haggling with their owners, we began to find our way up the path that led to the summit of the Rock. On the way up we saw some of the famous apes who eyed us curiously as we passed them.

Eventually we reached the top and gazed spellbound at the magnificent views. Looking down on the harbour and bay, the fleet looked like miniature models resting on a sheet of hammered glass, whilst southwards, across the Straits, one could see the low white buildings of Tangier on the North African coast. To the north we saw the interior of Spain, with its south eastern coastline curving away in stretches of golden sand, washed by the blue of the Mediterranean sea; a vivid contrast to the green and brown of the terrain behind.

It had taken us the best part of an hour to reach the top, but the marvellous views we obtained of the surrounding country, and the sea, dancing and sparkling in the brilliant sunshine, was well worth the physical effort involved.

We spent most of the afternoon at the top of the Rock, then we began our descent, finishing up in a café in the Main Street for tea, before returning onboard.

Even the harbour scene was full of interest to me, for the landing stage consisted of floating pontoons, alongside which was berthed the old depot ship, H.M.S. *Cormorant*. With the whole fleet berthed inside and outside the harbour breakwaters, there was quite a lot of boat traffic, and, whilst awaiting our own launch, we were interested in the various ship's boats as they came alongside. I can picture the scene now, in the hot sun, with a light breeze sweeping in from the bay. The phut-phut of the motor launches, and the smell of the blue smoke from their exhausts. The sounds of the boats' engine-room bells, as their coxswains rang down for more or less speed; while the wheeling seagulls, their white wings flashing against the blue of the sky and the shoals of fish one could plainly see in the clear water, contributed in providing a vivid sparkling scene not easily forgotten.

Our spell at Gibraltar was further enlivened by the arrival of the Mediterranean Fleet, led by their flagship *Queen Elizabeth*. The new-comers looked positively brilliant in their very light grey paint and freshly polished brasswork, which sparkled in the morning sunlight.

This famous fleet was noted throughout the navy for its excellent gunnery and general all-round efficiency, and was the prime post for any Admiral, since invariably it was the jumping off stage for the highest naval command, i.e. First Sea Lord. As I watched them entering harbour, I made up my mind that this was the fleet in which most of my time would be served. This resolve was kept, because later on I was to serve over seven years with the Mediterranean Fleet, and I enjoyed every minute of it.

Whilst at Gibraltar, the combined fleets took part in mock battles in the Atlantic, the Red Fleet being the Mediterranean Fleet and the Blue Fleet, the Atlantic Fleet; and for about a week to ten days, both sides would be at action stations under war conditions. Then, on completion of the exercises, we would part company, the Mediterranean Fleet proceeding on their Spring cruise around the French and Italian Riviera, whilst we of the Atlantic Fleet would visit a few spots around the Spanish coast before returning to England to give Easter Leave.

On the way home, we of the Third Battle Squadron, carried out a full calibre 13.5" firing practice, using a Battle Practice target towed some 600 yards behind an ocean going tug. We boys had to stand in two ranks on the upper deck to watch this and were almost lifted off of our feet by the gun blast. This was done to season us to heavy gunfire. It may have been considered good training, but none of us liked being almost on top of the guns when they fired, since the blast was most unpleasant, quite apart from the possible injury to one's eardrums.

We arrived back at Sheerness, which was *Marlborough's* home port, just before Easter and we were given 14 days leave. I can still picture the old paddle steamer *Harlequin* coming alongside to take us down stream to Gillingham Pier. We were a boisterous, happy lot that boarded the steamer. We were sailors, home from the sea!

On return from Easter leave we painted the ship overall. This involved the boys and we were all allocated to our respective parts of the ship. My own division was responsible for the starboard side of the ship from the after end of the forecastle to the beginning of the quarterdeck, also the two funnels and the starboard side of the bridge. I, and another boy were soon over the side on a stage, with a pot of dark grey paint (known to all sailors as "crab fat") and two large brushes.

Painting ship overall is quite an evolution in the Navy. First of all the weekly orders would read something like this: Monday...

"Prepare to Paint Ship", parts of ship to provide stages etc, side party to rig bowsing wire. Tuesday…"Hands to paint ship", Officer of the Watch to ensure that safety regulations re men working aloft are carried out.

To explain further – the side party referred to is a party of seamen, about eight, with a Leading Seaman or Petty Officer (known as the Captain of the side) in charge. They are responsible that the ship's side, at all times, is kept clean and smart, and that no rust patches or other marks appear. On paint ship occasions it is their responsibility to rig the bowsing in wire, and to cut in the black painted waterline. For the "landlubber", the bowsing in wire is a thin wire rope which runs from the bow of the ship to a position about a third of the ship's length along both sides. It is rigged so that the men painting the part of the forecastle which flares inwards, are able to lash their stages in close to the side to paint it.

As regards the safety regulations for men working aloft when the radio staff are transmitting, fairly high voltages are likely to be passing through the W/T aerial system, and since when working aloft, men are liable to come in contact with these aerials, some sort of safety arrangement had to be introduced. This consists of a small board fitted with through contacts, which, when inserted in the transmitting circuit, allows the operator to transmit, but, when removed from its normal position, it breaks the circuit thereby cutting off current to the aerials aloft. Before sending a man aloft to work, this board must be removed from the W/T office and handed to the Officer of the Watch, who will retain it until such times as the man or men aloft have returned to deck level, when the board may be returned to the W/T office. During this period, the radio transmitter cannot be used.

I learned a lot from my first experience of painting ship. For instance, I soon discovered it was safer to lower one's own stage, than let others do it for you, although lowerers were specially detailed for the job. These jocular types had the nasty habit of lowering one's stage in jerks; or letting it down with a run, spilling the paint and sometimes putting one in the "drink". After my first experience, I soon learned to run the free end of the stage lanyard around a convenient awning stanchion or deck cleat, and secure the end around the cross jack of my stage. This way, one could control one's own speed of descent and also one's own nerves!

Painting over the side could be very entertaining. We had our humorous types and we sang as we painted, – songs so ribald and salty as to forbid repetition here. I always enjoyed it, and swinging about on a stage below forecastle level, on a fine sunny morning was really something!

It was on such a fine morning in Gibraltar harbour, when serving in *Hood* that I had an amusing experience. A rather corpulent messmate, by name, Tug Wilson, and myself were over the port side of the ship painting the outboard doors of the torpedo tubes. As we swung lazily to and fro on the stage the "Defaulters" bugle call rang out. Now at the Commander's defaulters session, the various Divisional Officers who "owned" the defaulters, had to be in attendance to speak for or against their protégées. We, on the lower deck, always referred to this gathering of officers as the "Jury". A few moments later, the bugle again sounded, this time the "Officer's Call". As the bugle notes echoed around the ship, the Commander, "Big Hearted Dave" happened to look over the side where we were painting. Tug, on hearing the bugle and not aware of the presence of the great man above him, remarked in a voice which was loaded with scorn, "There goes the bloody jury, some poor sod is going to get it in the neck!" Tug nearly fell off the stage when he heard an Oxford accent above him reply, "Quite right Wilson, and if you don't get cracking on that painting, it will be your neck under the chopper!" Tug and I often laughed about this particular episode. It made our day – but back to *Marlborough*.

We spent all day over the side, and because of the swift current at Sheerness, we had to work with a lifeline around our waists. Two days were required to complete the whole ship and, after topping up with stores and provisions, we sailed for exercises with the fleet and the beginning of the summer cruise.

During this cruise I was put into a torpedo training class, and from the beginning, these contrary weapons completely won me over. Add to this the fact that the maintenance of a ship's electrical installation was also the responsibility of the torpedo branch, and you have another reason why I was captivated by this branch of the service. However, this was only a minor course designed to qualify one for Able Seaman's rate, and it was some years later before I was able to get into the torpedo branch as a specialist rating.

The summer cruise took us on courtesy visits to Folkestone and Oban, and we finished up by having a Regatta at Lamlash, in which quite a few of us got sore bottoms due to the intensive regatta training programme. It is hard work pulling a two and a quarter ton cutter for two miles, twice a day for practice, and finishing up with the actual regatta some four weeks later. However, this energetic sport became my first love during my service career, and I took part in most regattas in whichever ship I happened to be serving.

After the regatta, we sailed for Sheerness and our Summer leave. Leave was always a welcome break from the everyday ship's routine, but in my case I always seemed to become bored after the first few days leave. This was probably because I had no friends at home, due mainly to my family moving about, and the early age at which I had left home for sea training.

Girl friends at this period of my life were not for me; (a) because of the brief intervals spent at home and (b) because of the poor pay we received. I did not wish to become involved too early with the opposite sex, for I wanted to see the world first. Apart from the cinema, and long cycle rides into the Hampshire and Sussex countryside, I was not altogether sorry when my leaves came to an end.

Arriving back from leave, we had to coal ship from a collier; a dirty looking vessel named *Agnes Duncan*. We hated this particular ship because of the number of accidents we had when coaling from her. Her sister ship the *Francis Duncan*, we got on well with, but whenever *Agnes* came to us, we usually had a few broken arms or legs among our company. On this particular occasion, *Agnes Duncan* excelled herself. We lost one of our boys, killed when a hoist of coal swung across the hold and jammed him up against the ship's side, breaking his back. Another of us broke a leg. We were heartily glad when this "Hoodoo" ship cast off and left us in peace.

After coaling, we sailed for Portland and joined up with the rest of the fleet and, a day later, the whole assembly sailed for Scottish waters, carrying out exercises in the North Sea on the way.

Four days later we arrived at Invergordon. On the way in, we passed the capsized wreck of H.M.S. *Natal*, a cruiser which, during the first world war had blown up at anchor whilst giving a cinema show onboard. Each vessel of the fleet saluted the wreck as she passed it; a poignant reminder of the tragic disaster.

Our stay at Invergordon largely consisted of football, rugby and cross country running for the ship's company, and golf and shooting for the Officers. We boys continued our training programme and, having finished the torpedo course during our previous cruise, I now found myself in a seamanship class. This was also interesting, but of course, was not up to the standard of torpedo work

During our stay here, we had the annual Admiral's Inspection, which meant that for almost a fortnight before the event, everyone went mad in a burst of cleaning, painting, polishing and drills; also bringing one's kit and bedding up to standard, in case one was select-ed to lay it out for the Admiral's inspection. It was a hectic fortnight, and we were all very glad when it was over and we could once more get back to our normal way of life.

In due course we left Invergordon and visited Scapa Flow, where a fleet sailing regatta was held. This immense, bleak stretch of water, surrounded by the low and barren hills of the Orkney Islands was an ideal spot for sailing, and the fifty odd boats of all sizes, bowling along in a spanking breeze, some with their crews sitting on the weather gunwhales to prevent them capsizing, was a sight to behold.

From Scapa we went to sea for our quarterly full calibre gun practice, both with 13.5" and 6" guns; we also carried out various fleet evolutions, such as taking another ship in tow, or exercising the lifeboat's crew at sea, and numerous other drills to exercise the ship's company in their professional capacity. Our days were fully occupied and, before we knew where we were, the fleet dispersed to its home ports to give Christmas leave.

I had now served twelve months in *Marlborough*, during which time I had learned a lot about a seaman's life. We had worked and played hard. We had formed duty boat's crews, to run inshore under oars and sail, in all sorts of weather to pick up mails and stores; not because we did not have power boats to do this sort of thing, but simply to give us training in operating under oars and sail, and extremely good training it was.

We learned to use a paint brush to good effect; splice ropes and wires; sew canvas and the thousand and one jobs required of a good seaman. Some of us had been members of gun's crews. Others, like myself, had manned the submerged torpedo tubes, and had helped to prepare, fire, and recover the torpedoes. We had rowed our hearts out in the Fleet Regatta, and had got wet bottoms and no fish in the sailing races at Scapa. It had been a good year and we had all profited by it. It was no surprise, therefore, when just before going on Christmas leave, I was sent for by the Regulating Office staff and informed that, on my return from leave, I was being drafted to H.M.S. *Centaur*, the flagship of the Atlantic Fleet destroyer flotillas.

This draft, to my mind, was a plum appointment, since light cruisers were considered to be good ships to serve in. Not too big, and not too small, the best of both worlds so to speak. Apart from this, *Centaur* was a Portsmouth manned ship, whereas *Marlborough* belonged to the Chatham port division, and since my home was in Portsmouth I was more than delighted at the prospects ahead of me. Now, when the ship came in for leave or repairs, I would be able to get home each night.

Once again we packed our bundle handkerchiefs, and boarding *Harlequin*, began our journey homeward for Christmas leave. *Harlequin* was fitted with a bar below decks, and, on the journey to Gillingham, this was well patronized by the elder members of our ship's company, and it was not long before we had a few ribald songs and sea shanties. It was a happy, if slightly tipsy cargo of sailors who finally disembarked at Gillingham Pier.

I returned onboard after spending a quiet Christmas, and began to gather my things together for draft. A week later I was once more onboard *Harlequin*, this time with all my kit. As the paddle steamer moved away from *Marlborough's* side, I felt a pang of regret as the old lady slipped away from us in the morning mist, and I hoped that during the past year she had enjoyed my company as much as I had hers. So passed another milestone in my life.

H.M.S. *Marlborough*

Chapter Four

H.M.S. *CENTAUR* and H.M.S. *NELSON*

<u>1929 – 1931</u>

It was a bright day in January 1929, one of those rare occasions when the winter sun excelled itself. The lorry bearing me and my baggage, bumped across the railway lines as it headed towards the tidal basin where *Centaur* was berthed. A few more minutes and the lorry drew to a halt, and there she was, 4,000 tons of trim cruiser, with a difference; for unlike *Marlborough*, this ship was a flagship, flying the broad pennant of Commodore Robin Dalgleish. She was also painted in enamel paint, and positively gleamed in the morning sunshine. With her snowy decks and scintillating brasswork, *Centaur* was a delight to any seaman's eye.

Since I was still only 17 years old, I was put in the boys' mess, and attached to the Foretop division as my part of ship. The Petty Officer in charge of we boys was a Physical Training Instructor by the name of Sims, who was an extremely able and likeable man, and we boys all got on well with him.

Our executive officer was Commander Charles Peploe, D.S.C., a very smart officer with a great sense of humour. Among other things, I believe he was a member of the Royal Yacht Squadron, and was fairly well-to-do, a fact which showed itself in the ship's immaculate appearance.

Since *Centaur* was the Atlantic Fleet destroyer flagship, most of her officers had, at some time or other, been destroyer men, and an exceptionally good lot they were. I was to serve with some of them in other ships later on. Commander Peploe himself had won a Distinguished Service Cross at the Battle of the Heligoland Bight in 1914, when, as a young Lieutenant, he had taken over command of the destroyer *Laurel* when her captain had been severely wounded and had continued to fight the ship, bringing her safely home after the action.

We also had a bluejacket band on board. As a light cruiser with a junior flag officer, we were not entitled to a Royal Marine Band, but there was nothing in the regulations to prevent us forming a blue-jacket band and, I think we were the only vessel, apart from the Naval Barracks, who possessed one. Our band was swollen in numbers when the destroyers were with us, since their crews often sported amateur bandsmen.

Centaur was a happy ship, I saw this from the moment I stepped onboard. Everyone seemed to take a pride in everything they did. Charles Peploe, the Commander, was a strict disciplinarian, but for all that, he was a loveable character, with chubby cheeks and twinkling eyes. There was nothing we would not do for him. He kept us on our toes and the ship was absolutely spotless.

I well remember the day when Charlie came up on deck and spotted the oily impression of somebody's bottom on his otherwise white deck. Since it was immediately outside the engineroom door, it was reasonable to suppose that a stoker was the guilty party. Sure enough, after a piece of brilliant detective work, Charlie got his man and for the rest of that week, in his spare time, the culprit was to be seen holystoning the deck. We never saw any further oil stains on the deck after that.

Another type of menace we had to contend with was the thoughtless person who threw his cigarette ends and matchsticks, either on the deck or over the side. The seamen, seldom, if ever, did this, since they had to clear up the mess. The guilty ones usually belonged to one or other of the other branches, such as stokers, cooks, stewards, etc. Charlie was determined to stamp out this habit because, apart from the litter on the deck, there was the ever present danger of fire caused by a cigarette end thrown carelessly over the side, to be blown into an open scuttle by the wind, thereby starting a fire in a possibly unoccupied compartment

One day the Commander caught a Stores Assistant dropping his cigarette end on the deck. He ordered the culprit to pick up the spitoon or spitkid as they are called, and to take it to the Engineer's workshop to have two holes drilled in its rim. When this was done, a piece of codline was threaded through the holes and a loop made. Then the unfortunate man had to patrol the deck with the spitkid around his neck, collecting his shipmate's leavings until he too, caught someone else dropping rubbish on the deck. Needless to say, a miraculous improvement in the ship's company's smoking habits came about.

During the second week in January, we sailed for Gibraltar with the rest of the fleet. After passing the Nab Tower at the entrance to the Solent, we altered course to the south west and headed for Ushant. At about 3 p.m. we were joined by the rest of our destroyer flotillas. These were the ships based at Chatham and Devonport and with the Portsmouth ships made up a total of sixteen vessels, i.e. the 5th and 6th destroyer flotillas. If my memory serves me right, the 5th was led by *Wallace* and the 6th by *Campbell* the flotillas consisting of the famous "V" and "W" class ships, such as *Vimy, Vortigern, Windsor* etc., built around about 1917 – 1918

They provided a magnificent sight as they manoeuvred at high speed, then, with a wide sweep and leaving a curve of creaming foam behind them, they took station astern of us in two columns, each led by its own Captain "D".

By nightfall we had reached Ushant, and turning to port we entered the notorious Bay of Biscay, and for once the Bay was behaving itself, although there was a ground swell which caused *Centaur* to roll like a barrel. During the passage we exercised with the destroyers, carrying out dummy night attacks on the rest of the fleet.

Unlike *Marlborough*, our cruising speed was 15 knots, with the result that we were out of the Bay within 24 hours and steaming down the coast of Portugal. It was a beautiful trip and a thrilling sight to see the bulk of the fleet ploughing along in their respective squadrons. There was *Nelson, Rodney, Hood, Repulse, Renown* and the famous Jutland veteran *Tiger*. Then came the 2nd Cruiser Squadron, consisting of *Curacoa, Comus, Canterbury* and *Cambrian*. The cruiser-minelayer *Adventure* and, way behind, the slower 3rd Battle Squadron, *Iron Duke, Benbow, Marlborough* and *Emperor of India*.

Arriving at Gibraltar, we found the Mediterranean Fleet already there, and this time, since I was now in a flagship, we secured alongside the main dockyard wall, which was a much better arrangement than the previous year in *Marlborough*, where we had all the boat work between ship and shore.

There is not a great deal to say about our visit to Gibraltar. We followed the same programme as before, with sports events between the two fleets and the customary cocktail parties for the officers. However, this year we did have a ceremonial "March Past" consisting of landing parties from all the ships present. The parade was held in the Alameida Gardens, the salute being taken by the Commander-in-Chief of the Mediterranean Fleet, Admiral Sir Ernle Chatfield, who had been Beatty's Flag Captain in H.M.S. *Lion* at the Battle of Jutland. It was a brilliant day and both civilian and army personnel gathered to watch what turned out to be a highly successful display.

After leaving Gibraltar, *Centaur* and destroyers paid a courtesy visit to Barcelona. We moored in the inner harbour, stern to the wall and our destroyers did likewise. It was a colourful scene, with orange vendors in their brightly coloured dresses and everywhere the odour of cigars and perfume. In brilliant sunshine I went ashore with some of the boys. We had been given an invitation to attend a bull fight, and took this opportunity to look around the city.

We had a little trouble with the policeman controlling traffic. It is an offence to cross the road until the officer gives the pedestrians the right of way. We, of course, strangers in a foreign country, were not aware of this, but the policeman was very nice about it all, and we passed on, wiser men!

We eventually arrived at the Barcelona Bull Ring, a huge arena like structure, with terraced seats like an ancient Roman coliseum. It was a picturesque scene which met our eyes as we took our seats. There was colour everywhere, with large Spanish flags draped around the back, their red and yellow standing out against the vivid blue backdrop of the sky. Everywhere gaiety prevailed and the multi-coloured dresses of the senoritas, the perfume and the cigar smoke, created an exciting and colourful scene which I would not have missed for the world.

I like to keep an open mind on controversial subjects until in a position to judge for myself and, having seen this particular afternoon's bullfighting, I was thoroughly disgusted, so much so, that with a few more who thought the same way as myself, I got up and left the bullring. It was a great pity that the wonderful scene of the multi-coloured audience and its exciting atmosphere, should have been spoiled for us by the actual bullfighting.

Leaving Barcelona, we carried out exercises with our destroyers, particularly night attacks, and eventually we arrived at Gibraltar where, topping up with oil, fuel and water, and our ship's company loaded with cigars, perfume and other knick-knacks, we sailed for home and Easter leave.

Leave came and went and the beginning of May found us on our way up the North Sea en-route to Invergordon, where, with the rest of the fleet, we carried out drills, inspections, exercises and firing practices. My own action station being a 3" A.A.Gun which almost split one's eardrums when it was fired.

During this cruise, we in *Centaur*, visited Aarhus, in the Jutland Bight, where the ship's company had a wonderful time among the Danish population. In fact, when we left Aarhus, to the strains of "Auld Lang Syne", played by the ship's band, I saw tears in more than one pair of eyes. A most successful visit!

Another port of call was Oslo, which we reached after a picturesque trip up the Oslo Fjord. The scenery was really magnificent, in weather warm and sunny, the like of which we had not experienced for many a year. During our stay, we had a visit from Queen Maud and King Haakon. On Sunday we landed a church party, who, on taking their seats in the local church were surprised to see the Norwegian Royal Family sitting in the front pews. No fuss or formality, just another family attending church.

We next visited Gothenburg, a busy Swedish city, where we spent a very pleasant week. It was very noticeable how clean everything was and how fair their people. It was with real regret that we left their shores for home and after a short visit to Brighton, we headed once more for Portsmouth and Summer leave. It had been a memorable and very enjoyable cruise.

Early September found us heading northwards to Rosyth, Invergordon and Scapa Flow, with the usual exercises on the way. However, my stay in *Centaur* was cut short whilst in Rosyth, for a few days after my 18th birthday (on which I was rated Ordinary Seaman), I developed Paratyphoid fever and was taken the few miles to the West of Fife Infectious Diseases Hospital at Dunfermline.

Whilst in this wonderful hospital, I received every care and attention during the five months of my stay. It was also discovered that I had an abscess over my left kidney which necessitated an operation and caused me to be detained longer than would otherwise have been the case.

In March 1930 a rather tottery Ordinary Seaman left the hospital, after saying farewell and thanking the doctors and wonderful staff for their many kindnesses, and with a naval Sick Berth Petty Officer as an escort, I was taken to the Royal Naval Hospital at Haslar, who, after giving me a thorough medical check up, sent me on a month's convalescent leave. After my return, I was drafted to the R.N. Barracks for disposal. Before leaving the hospital, I was given the chance to leave the Navy if I so desired, but this was my life and I enjoyed it, so I tactfully declined their kind offer (and I think they were surprised at my so doing) and was called all sorts of fools by my naval friends when they heard of it.

After a month of light duties in the Naval Barracks, I received a draft to H.M.S. *Nelson*, the flagship of the now re-named Home Fleet. A monster of 33,000 tons and armed with 16" guns, she had been built under the Washington Treaty and, with her sister ship *Rodney* were the most powerful battleships afloat. One did not join a ship like *Nelson*, it was more like entering a skyscraper.

Coming aboard *Nelson* was like climbing the side of a mountain. After the relatively small trim *Centaur*, *Nelson* was a veritable colossus. She towered above the South Railway Jetty like a giant, and looking up at her vast bulk, I felt very small indeed!

Arriving on deck, I looked towards her bows and wondered when they were going to terminate. In fact, it would not have surprised me to see a bus drive around from behind her huge gun turrets. She gave one the impression of being in a big city, so great were her areas and spaces. However, I once more had that feeling, as with *Centaur*, that this was a happy ship. After being victualled in, and given a mess number, I began to unpack and stow my kit, by which time the mess was preparing for tea.

Since I was not of the duty watch, I was free to go ashore, but before doing so, Ronnie Burgess, one of my new messmates, took me on a tour of the ship in order that I could find my way about. Burge, as we all called him, was a curly headed Ordinary Seaman of nearly 19. He too, lived in Portsmouth, but it was his duty night onboard. He was an infectious character and was liked by everyone, and we became fast friends for the whole of the time I was in *Nelson*.

We went up to the compass platform at the top of the bridge superstructure and, from this height, looking down on the ship was like looking down from a tall building onto a street below, except that we had three giant gun turrets in the way. Even after Burge's conducted tour, it took me almost six weeks to really find my way around this giant.

At the beginning of June, *Nelson*, flying the flag of Admiral Sir Michael Hodges, sailed with the rest of the fleet for the summer cruise. We had the customary exercises, firing programmes and drills, and during the cruise I finished my training for Able Seaman by taking the Gunnery Course.

After all the drills etc. were over, the fleet split up for the courtesy visiting programme and *Nelson's* first port of call was a small Norwegian township called Odda, which nestled at the foot of a mountain at the end of the Hardanger Fjord. To reach it necessitated a day long trip up this fjord, with mountains and waterfalls on either side of us. The water was like a mirror, disturbed only by our wash as we steamed slowly along. It was a magnificent trip with gorgeous scenery all the way. The brilliant sunshine and the cool mountain air made it a visit which has always stood out in my memory. At about 5 p.m. we arrived at Odda and dropped our anchor in very deep water; so deep that we ran most of our cable out of the locker.

Apart from a match factory, there did not appear to be any industry here, which left us wondering what the rest of the inhabitants did for a living. We woke up each morning with heads as clear as bells, for the cold mountain air, flavoured with the smell of pine, was most invigorating.

Whilst here, we had our annual Admiral's inspection and finished the week by giving a dance onboard for the local population, which went down very well indeed. All good things come to an end and soon we were steaming slowly back down the fjord and heading across the North Sea to Scarborough, our next port of call.

It was the height of the British holiday season when we arrived at Scarborough and, due to the tidefall, *Nelson* had to anchor a fair way off shore, but this did not prevent us being surrounded by speedboats and other pleasure craft almost as soon as we had anchored. The weather was fine and the sea calm and with dinner over, we opened the ship to visitors.

Burge and I did not intend to go ashore until after tea, so we passed the first afternoon away showing visitors around the ship. This was something I liked doing, particularly if the person was really interested and like the real Yorkshire people they were, they usually wanted to know everything.

About this period, H.M.Ships had been fitted with S.R.E. equipment, which, in common parlance meant, a radio and local broadcasting apparatus with extension loudspeakers fitted in all parts of the ship. In off duty hours we could enjoy radio programmes or records and, whilst at Scarborough, some of our female visitors enjoyed impromptu dancing onboard, the music being provided by records on our S.R.E. outfit.

Burge, Mo (another of our friends) and I, had one or two trips ashore and among the northern holidaymakers, we bluejackets seemed to be very popular, with everyone "touching our collars for luck." We were particularly embarrassed in one restaurant where, when we three entered with a view to having tea, we were greeted by the orchestra playing "All the nice girls love a Sailor." It was a nice friendly gesture which secretly we appreciated, but were our faces red!

We stayed at Scarborough a week, during which time the warm hearted Yorkshire folk and their holiday guests, took us to their hearts and it was with real regret that we sailed away into the early morning mist and headed south for St. Peter Port in the Channel Island of Guernsey.

On a brilliant morning in early July, we anchored off the harbour breakwater of St. Peter Port on what was to be the last visit of our cruise. We three went ashore for a look around and had not gone far when a parson, passing in his open car, stopped and offered to show us around the island. We accept his kind offer and piled into his car and, for the rest of the afternoon toured the island.

The Vicar turned out to be most interesting to talk to and we asked him to come onboard, when we in our turn would be pleased to show him over the ship. He never did, but then, no doubt he was a busy man, parsons usually are.

We had a very pleasant stay at St. Peter Port and were entertained ashore by various committees etc. then once more we weighed anchor and shaped course for Portsmouth and Summer leave.

For the first three months of my service in *Nelson* I was attached to the Double Bottom Party. This consisted of a party of about a dozen seamen under the charge of a Chief Stoker, whose job it was to clean out and re-paint the double bottoms and oil fuel tanks of the ship.

It was a very dirty job, and could, unless safety precautions were thoroughly observed, be a very dangerous one. Before any man was allowed to enter a double bottom compartment, a portable electric fan was brought up to the manhole and a large leather flexible hose lowered into the space, then for 24 hours the fan would thoroughly ventilate the compartment, extracting the poisonous carbon-monoxide fumes which had accumulated. After this, a miner's lamp was lowered into the compartment to test for gas. Only after these precautions had been taken was the cleaning party allowed inside and even then, a ventilating fan ran continuously to keep a flow of fresh air passing through the compartment. We had to chip off all the old paint and, after wire scrubbing the metal, re-paint it with thick red oxide paint. We had to work in cramped conditions, using wandering lead electric lights to see what we were doing. Sometimes the spaces were so low we had to lie on our stomachs to work. The filthiest and most dangerous part was the cleaning out of the oil fuel tanks, when we had to breathe the fumes of the oil in a confined space. Before we could do anything else we had to wipe the treacly black oil off the metal with rags. We were covered from head to foot with the stuff, and the fumes got right down into one's belly. The job was certainly not for those who suffer from claustrophobia! For this dirty and dangerous work we received one shilling and sixpence a day extra, known as "Danger Pay". For all that, we were a happy lot and nearly always sang as we worked, not that anybody could hear us down there in the bilges of the ship.

By this time I had fully recovered from my illness earlier in the year, although I had to miss taking part in the fleet regatta since it was too soon after my operation to exert my back muscles. *Nelson* was proving herself to be a good ship to serve in and I was extremely happy. Burge and Mo, my two friends were first class and we three were inseparable. We did not see much of each other whilst the ship was at Portsmouth, due mainly to all of us being natives of the port and living ashore each night, but once on a cruise we were the "three Musketeers!"

Early in September *Nelson* sailed for Portland where we met up with the rest of the Home Fleet, and after a fortnight of drills and heavy gun practice we sailed for Invergordon. Here the routine was much the same as in previous years so I will not repeat it here, but we did visit Rosyth and one or two other places ere we returned to give Christmas leave at Portsmouth.

We were more interested than usual in the coming Spring cruise because due to the prevailing economic depression in the West Indies, it was decided to send the entire Home Fleet on a cruise around the islands. The idea being to let the fleet personnel circulate their money in the hard hit islands.

It was announced that, during this cruise *Nelson* would pay a courtesy visit to the United States Pacific Fleet at Panama. We were all warned to see that we had two white drill uniforms in our kit ready for this visit. With this pleasant prospect in mind we went on

Christmas leave and whilst on leave I ordered two white uniforms from my tailor ready for the cruise to come.

About the middle of January we sailed with the fleet for the Caribbean. During the passage we carried out the usual tactical exercises one came to expect on these occasions. The Atlantic behaved itself, considering that it was January, and after fourteen days we arrived in Caribbean waters. Our first port of call being Bridgetown, Barbados.

We anchored off the harbour with the usual ceremonial spreading of awnings, blowing of bugles and lowering of duty boats and we were soon surrounded by bumboats and coloured boys, completely naked, diving for pennies thrown by our seamen.

It was a glorious morning and my first impression of Barbados was the almost white, sandy beaches, fringed by the white creaming surf of an otherwise deep blue sea, beyond which were palm trees and vivid green foliage; the whole backed by a brilliant blue sky on which was mounted an occasional white fleecy cloud. Inside the harbour one could see the forest of masts belonging to the innumerable small schooners used for inter-island trading. It was a lovely setting after our fourteen days of nothing but heaving ocean.

During our "Stand Easy" break we watched the native boys dive for our pennies, the drops of sea water sparkling on their brown bodies as they climbed back into their rickety boats, clutching their pennies. We admired their courage, for these waters were infested with sharks. It was amusing to see these boys, some of them barely 10 years old, flashing down in the clear depths, chasing their pennies. One could follow them easily because the soles of their feet and the palms of their hands were much lighter in colour than the rest of their bodies. I was fascinated by them and spent a lot of time watching their antics.

During our visit to the Caribbean, the ship's company ceased normal work at noon each day and, apart from the duty watch, we were allowed ashore until 7 a.m. each morning. This was to give us the maximum amount of time in which to spend our money and help boost trade. Needless to say "we three" changed into our white uniforms and went ashore to see the town.

It soon became evident to us that the islanders were having a lean time and before we had gone very far, we had given away practically all of our cigarettes which we had brought for our own use. We visited one or two bars and had cold beer, and after an interesting afternoon and evening, we found a Missions to Seamen hostel and fixed ourselves a bed for the night, when we were a sumptuous feast for the local mosquitoes!

Our ship's company spent a terrific amount of their pay whilst at Bridgetown, so it was hoped that we did the islanders a bit of good.

Whilst at Bridgetown we caught a monster hammerhead shark, by baiting a meat hook with a joint of meat and attaching it to a heaving line, rove through a block on one of our lower booms. When the hands turned to, to scrub decks at 6 a.m. we found the boom shaking violently, and hauling in the line we discovered a fifteen foot shark on the end. We finally managed to get it inboard, but only after the gunnery officer had emptied his revolver into its head. We hoisted it at one of the davits and placing a sailor's hat on its head we photographed it. The ship's butcher then skinned it, giving us a large supply of shark's skin, which is widely used in the navy for cleaning woodwork, whilst the butcher had the jaws as a souvenir.

During the whole of February we visited most of the Windward and Leeward group of islands, so that between the Home Fleet, each island was well visited and we discovered afterwards that our visits had been much appreciated both from a financial, as well as a social point of view.

Now came the climax of our Spring cruise, when our Commander-in-Chief was to visit the U.S. Pacific Fleet. This meant a passage through the Panama Canal and since *Nelson* had a beam of 106 feet and the width of the canal locks were only approximately 108 feet in width, a considerable problem was presented to the canal authorities. It meant that *Nelson* had to be dead in line with the centre of each lock and kept there. There was some doubt at first as to whether we should get through without damage, but the risk was accepted and we left Jamaica and headed for Colon, the Atlantic entrance to the canal.

We arrived early, about 7 a.m. and the canal pilot came onboard to take us through. There was a light breeze blowing across our beam and due to the ship's high freeboard and large superstructure, we entered the first of the locks slightly on an angle, with the result that we brushed the starboard side against the side of the lock, shearing off a number of scuttle rigols and waterline eyebolts.

I happened to be in the bathroom at the time and smoke caused by the friction as we touched the side, plus the squeal of the tortured metal, caused me to beat a hasty retreat from the bathroom in a state of nudity!

This damage to our ship's side, although slight and of little consequence, annoyed the Commander quite a lot, since it had taken a large amount of best quality enamel paint off the side. We had spent almost three weeks rubbing down and enamelling the side in preparation for our meeting with the American fleet and now this had happened. Small wonder our normally touchy executive officer was almost unapproachable for the rest of that day.

The trip through the canal was most interesting and we saw several alligators basking in the sun along the canal banks as we steamed slowly along. It was quite an experience and we were told by the pilot that *Nelson* was the largest ship to have passed through the canal to date.

At about 3.30 p.m. after an interesting and sometimes hair-raising passage, we arrived at Panama and berthed alongside the jetty immediately astern of U.S.S. *California*, an American battleship. We exchanged 21 gun salutes and the rest of the day, until sunset, was taken up with paying and returning official calls. By sunset, all the "Official Bull" was completed and all those who could, made their way ashore.

A good week was had by all and our ship's company got on well with their Pacific fleet counterparts. We exchanged visits with various U.S. ships and some of their men were invited onboard to sample our navy rum, and since their service was "dry", this was a popular visit.

Our diesel Picket boats were a source of admiration among the U.S. Navy men. These were 17 ton boats with a single funnel, brass trimmed and enamelled in dark blue, with white enamel upperworks. Their polished brass, snow white decks and smart white uniformed crews presented a picture of cleanliness and efficiency which was greatly admired by the Americans, who as we discovered, were sticklers for these virtues themselves.

We finally left Panama with a host of "Bon Voyage" and "Come again" signals flying from the yard arms of our hosts ships and, once more we negotiated the tricky canal to arrive at the Atlantic end, where we re-joined the rest of the Home Fleet and heading out into the Atlantic, we shaped course for Gibraltar. A week out from Colon we began tactical exercises with the Mediterranean fleet who had emerged from their domain to do "battle" with us, after which both fleets returned to Gibraltar.

Apart from sports and other competitions between the two fleets, our stay at Gibraltar was a very peaceful one, then, one day before the Home Fleet sailed for home, there was an exchange of personnel between the fleets. Ratings due for courses at one or other of the schools at home were drafted from the Mediterranean Fleet to the Home Fleet for passage home, replacements being provided by Home Fleet ships. It was during this swap over that I found myself realizing my long awaited dream – for my name was on the transfer list to join H.M.S. *Queen Elizabeth,* the Mediterranean fleet flagship.

Fate had been kind to me, for there was no other ship I would rather serve in than this famous old veteran of the Dardanelles campaign and I was delighted with the drafting. A day before *Nelson* sailed for home, I transferred myself and my kit a hundred yards further along the mole and boarded *Queen Elizabeth.* As a further act of grace, Burge and Mo were transferred with me.

Thus ended a very happy year in H.M.S. *Nelson,* during which time I had been advanced to Able Seaman three months before my time and in which I had seen quite a bit more of this exciting world.

H.M.S. *Centaur*

H.M.S. *Nelson*

Len 18 years old – 22 August

Chapter Five

H.M.S. *QUEEN ELIZABETH*

<u>1931 – 1932</u>

I loved this old ship from the moment I first stepped onboard her. Here was 30,000 tons of history. This light grey warrior, with her brasswork sparkling in the brilliant sunshine, had led the British fleet in the attack on the Dardanelles forts in 1915. Around her wardroom table had sat the Allied and German naval officers to sign the surrender of the German Fleet. In her silver cupboard were gifts of magnificent silver ornaments from the grateful inhabitants of France and now she flew the flag of Sir Ernle Chatfield, himself a famous officer. I, her latest Able Seaman had a lot to live up to and I was conscious of the fact.

I was victualled in a mess, the members of which were mainly Irish or West Countrymen, since *Queen Elizabeth* was a Devonport manned ship. We were a happy-go-lucky lot and many were the times we had a mess sing-song, with a couple of our Irish members playing piano accordians. The Cornish and Devon types possessed a soft and pleasant accent which fascinated me, and one or two of them wore a single gold ring in one ear in the manner of gypsies. Some wore magnificent beards, black and smartly trimmed. As the only Portsmouth rating in the mess, I took a lot of ribbing from this gang of pirates, but I was glad to be of their number.

We had a fine skipper in Captain R.C. Davenport, and a positive gem for our Executive Officer, one Commander Charles Larcom, known to us all simply as Charlie. Of our Chief and Petty Officers, one stands out in my memory. He was a tall, well built West Countryman; ruddy faced with a beak like nose (in fact, his face startlingly reminded one of a seagull). He was the Chief Boatswain's Mate, or Chief Buffer as we called them.

The Buffer's outstanding idiosyncrasy was his insistence that the spit-kids (spitoons) were placed at the exact times laid down and that they were kept scrupulously clean. A few minutes before the appointed times, one could see him prowling about, waiting to pounce on the men responsible for this duty. Should they either be late or have dirty spit-kids, then down he would come like a load of bricks. He was known at both ends of the ship as the "Spitkid Pasha". For all his little whims, he was a loveable old rascal and well liked by all. He was always ready to help if one was in trouble and was a first class seaman.

We also had a feathered member of the ship's company, a large cockatoo belonging to the Commander. On Sunday mornings, Charlie would hang Cocky's cage under the mainmast to give him an airing. Charlie, although a most excellent officer, had one bad habit from the ship's company's point of view. He would always find something for the seamen to do a few minutes before dinner, with the result we usually went to dinner a little late, and so lost a few minutes of our dinner hour. This little failing earned him the title of "Nick-a-bit".

On Sunday mornings, when the bird was enjoying the Mediterranean sunshine, one could see a few sailors gathered around his cage teaching him to say "NICK-A-BIT YOU OLD BASKET" I have often wondered if the bird ever repeated this remark, and it would have been wonderful to be able to see the expression on Charlie's face if it had done so!

I soon settled down in *Queen Elizabeth* and was employed on the upper deck, painting and generally keeping the forecastle clean. The ship was kept in a spotless condition. In fact, so fussy were we regarding the cleanliness of our decks and paintwork that on Sunday mornings, when the skipper inspected the upper deck, we placed a seaman up in the bridge wings with a rifle and a pocket full of blanks. His duty being to scare away from the paintwork such irreverent seagulls wishing to excrete upon it, before the skipper had seen it in all its glory.

There was always plenty to do and before leaving Gibraltar, we painted the ship overall and I found myself sitting on a stage over the ship's side. A day or two later *Queen Elizabeth* with the rest of the Mediterranean fleet sailed for courtesy visits to the French and Italian Riviera.

Our first visit was to the French naval port of Toulon and, after a very rough passage through the Gulf of Lyons, during which I was nearly washed overboard, we arrived at Toulon on a glittering Spring morning.

Behind the City, partially shrouded in the early morning haze, were the Maritime Alps. Anchored in the harbour were units of the French Mediterranean fleet, most of them fairly modern cruisers and destroyers. Most of the forenoon was spent with salutes and official calls and all the necessary "Bull" connected with visits to a foreign country. During our stay here, we were the guests of the French Navy, and jolly fine hosts they turned out to be!

On the second day of our stay we were given an official dinner in our honour by the French Fleet. It was held in a hotel situated part of the way up the Maritime Alps. Burge, Mo and I were fortunate enough to be able to attend this function and, after tea, we boarded our launch and were taken ashore, where a motor coach took our party on a tour of Toulon first, then on to the hotel.

There must have been about 150 of us and a like number of French matelots, sitting down at the tables. There were seven courses, with wines served at each. It was a gigantic meal. We toasted each other's navies in Champagne. We toasted the King, the President of France, ourselves and Uncle Tom Cobbley and many were the speeches made, although due to the language difficulty, nobody knew what was being said or for that matter, cared, for we were sailors on a binge!

We thoroughly enjoyed ourselves but it was a different story returning to our ship late that night. A wind had sprung up and the water was choppy. We were all full of good cheer until the boat began to pitch about, then we were all fearfully and wonderfully seasick, aggravated by the dinner and wines we had just consumed. I wonder what Nelson would have said could he have seen us wining and dining with the French!

A week at Toulon was quite enough for we were feasted and taken on excursions and generally well looked after by our hosts who were more than generous, and despite the language difficulty, we got on famously. The rate of exchange too, was in our favour, being 125 francs to the pound, although later in the year, due mainly to the Fleet troubles at Invergordon, it fell to 85. We left Toulon with many happy memories and moved along the coast to Cannes and Monte Carlo.

Arriving at Monte Carlo we anchored off the breakwater, outside the harbour. Apart from the surrounding scenery, Monte Carlo was not for us. It was really a rich man's playground and judging from the large number of fabulous yachts in the harbour, there must have been a lot of rich people in Monte during the time we were there.

The ship gave a cocktail party for the English community ashore, including some of the big wigs from the Principality of Monaco. Whilst on this topic, we had our quota of well connected people in our ward room, among them was Lieutenant Commander Lord Louis Mountbatten, who at this period, was serving as Fleet Wireless Officer. He was an extremely able and efficient officer and a charming personality to boot, and was well liked by us all.

Our last call along the French Riviera was to a delightful little place called Villefrance-sur-Mer, close to Cap Ferrat, where the Duke of Connaught had a villa. The railway passed through a coastal tunnel here and we often saw the famous blue train, or Riviera Express, entering the tunnel.

During our stay at Villefrance, we landed a company of sailors, of whom I was one, to lay a wreath on the local War Memorial. I well remember this, because we had to march behind the famous French mountain regiment the Chasseurs Alpines and their band. This regiment is noted for their fast rate of marching, and one can well imagine our feelings when we had to keep up with them and the rapid music of their band! To put it mildly, the air was blue with well chosen nautical language.

That afternoon, Burge, Mo and I took a taxi to Nice, a few miles along the coast road. It was a hair-raising trip; we had heard a lot about French taxi drivers, now we were experiencing the doubtful thrill of travelling along a coastal road at over 60 miles an hour. It was with a feeling of great relief that we arrived at Nice, safe, but not unshaken.

As we stepped out of the cab we were accosted by a suave looking gent, dressed in striped trousers and dark jacket. He offered to show us some of the sights of Nice, for a consideration of course, but a word from the taxi driver in Burge's ear made us dispense with his services. It turned out he was a ponce and in his broken English, our taxi driver told us that he worked for a local brothel!

We spent an interesting afternoon in Nice, sightseeing, and finishing up with an amusing experience in a café in the Rue St. Michael. Burge wanted eggs and chips for his tea, but being unable to speak French, he began to demonstrate to the pretty young waitress. He dropped a box of matches from his behind and imitated the clucking of a hen. To our great surprise and amusement, the waitress in flawless English asked him if he wanted them boiled or fried. I can still see the look on Burge's face. He was flabbergasted.

After tea we returned to Villefrance, this time we got a bus. The rest of the evening we spent in the bar of the waterfront hotel where we were going to sleep. It was a pleasant evening, although we were not very keen on French beer. It tasted a little like sour vinegar!

We were up at 6.30 a.m. and made our way down to the boat. On the way we bought some of those long crusty loaves of bread for which the French are famous and made a hearty breakfast off them when we got back onboard. They were delicious.

Our next and last port of call of the Spring cruise was the Italian naval base of Spezia on the N.W. coast of Italy. The routine here was much the same as at Toulon. I did not visit the place personally, but it was famous for the excellent mandolins manufactured here and several of our ship's company purchased some really beautiful instruments during our week here.

Our stay soon came to an end and although enjoyed by most, it was generally agreed that the French part of our cruise was by far the best. This was the end of our Spring cruise and *Queen Elizabeth* sailed for Malta, the Mediterranean Fleet base.

It had been a most successful cruise, marred only by the tragic collision between our aircraft carrier *Glorious* and the French passenger liner *Florida* earlier in the cruise. In beautiful sunshine, with a sea as smooth as glass, the fleet had suddenly run into a typical Mediterranean sea mist. Neither the fleet nor *Florida* were aware of each other's presence in the area, and without warning, and at a speed of about 15 knots, *Glorious* struck *Florida* just before her bridge, almost cutting off her bows. As for *Glorious*, she suffered a concertina crushing of her bows and the loss of a young seaman, killed in the collision. *Florida* I believe, had some 30 odd passengers and crew killed and many more injured, but was able to limp into Malaga, escorted by our destroyers.

At the time of the collision, the carrier had a flight of aircraft in the air; running out of fuel, and now unable to land on the carrier, they were obliged to ditch in the sea as near as possible to our ships, who picked up all the pilots unharmed. The aircraft of course, were a total loss.

Malta, that glistening pearl of the Mediterranean, was now the target of my attention. I had listened to the tales of seamen during the past couple of years, in which Malta had formed the centrepiece. It was from all accounts, a sailor's paradise, but quite apart from this, it was a place of great historical interest. When one thinks of Malta, one conjures up visions of crusades, the Knights of St. John of Jerusalem, and the bastion of Christendom. Here, on this enchanted island, St. Paul was shipwrecked, and there is a wonderful Bay named after him. It is particularly linked with the Royal Navy, for it was Nelson who drove out the French and offered the Maltese British protection. They chose to accept this, and have been our responsibility ever since. Needless to say, on the morning we were due to arrive, I was up on deck eager to get a preview.

It was a beautiful morning in the middle of April. The sea sparkled in the early sunlight, the only disturbance on its surface being the wash from the bow waves of the fleet. Suddenly, fine on the starboard bow and lying low on the distant horizon, lay Malta, resting like a jewel on a deep blue carpet. As we drew nearer, I could see the tall slender radio masts of Rinella W/T station with the Royal Naval Hospital behind them. The low breakwaters with their stumpy lighthouses at Valetta harbour entrance came into focus, whilst high up on the right of the entrance was the Barracca and the Castille signal station. The whole scene was a three tone colour contrast; the pale blue of the cloudless sky, the light sandstone of the buildings, then the deeper blue of the Mediterranean sea. In the early morning sunshine, my first sight of this lovely island was one which I shall always remember.

As we got closer, the fleet split up. The destroyer flotillas turning to starboard, began to enter Sliema Creek, one at a time and in their usual spectacular way, stern first, manoeuvring in between their buoys like whippets. We, as fleet flagship, entered the Grand Harbour first. Stationed on the forecastle, I had a magnificent view of this wonderful harbour and I was thrilled with all I saw. Whether it was the flush of my youth, – for I was only 20, – or genuine interest in this historic old island, I do not know, but Malta at this moment captured my heart and has held it ever since.

Queen Elizabeth slowly passed the ancient Fort St. Angelo on our Port side, and sliding past Dockyard Creek, she turned completely round and secured between the flagship's buoys, close to the Customs House, with her bows toward the harbour entrance.

Gradually the rest of the fleet came in. *Revenge, Ramilles, Royal Oak, Royal Sovereign*; the heavy cruisers *London, Sussex, Shropshire* and *Devonshire* and a host of smaller cruisers, submarines and the netlayer *Protector*. Dodging in between the ships, like water beetles skating across a pond, were the Maltese dghaisas. These were small gondola like boats, rowed by a single crewman, standing up and facing its bows in the manner of a Venetian gondolier. These boats were the pride of their owner's hearts and were kept scrupulously clean. Painted in all sorts of bright colours, they looked very picturesque, with their highly polished brasswork flashing in the sun. We sailors made use of them when going ashore. A dghaisa would take about ten of us at a penny a head, and it saved us having to wait for the ship's routine boat.

At about this time, a vacancy arose in the Torpedo division for a seaman torpedoman and since it was the custom to train a seaman on an acting basis to fill these vacancies, I saw my opportunity to realise an old ambition to get into this branch of the service. I applied at once to become an acting seaman torpedoman.

Normally there was great competition to get one of these vacancies, but here I was lucky for our Torpedo Officer was an old shipmate of mine from *Centaur* days, Lieut. Commander C. P. Clarke, who, when going through the service certificates of the various applicants, noticed this fact, with the result that I was sent for and interviewed, after which I was transferred to the Torpedo division to my great delight.

My duties in the new division were the investigation and repair of faults in the 220 volt electrical distribution system and, in order to train me, I was attached to the High Power section and acted as mate to one of the fully qualified men. This was extremely interesting work which ranged from electric fans, motors, lighting, lifts, ovens and the simple renewal of fuses.

Every fourth day I acted as duty seaman torpedoman, and helped to rig up temporary lighting to illuminate the lower booms, lifeboat and quarterdeck which was lit by large brass ornamental lanterns. These were all switched "On" at sunset when the ensign was ceremonially lowered to the notes of a bugle.

My transfer to the torpedo division, meaning as it did a change of mess, also introduced me to new friends, among these was Mervyn, who because of his dark skin was popularly known as "Nigger". We were kindred spirits inasmuch that we were both 20 years of age and were both acting torpedomen. "Nigger" and I became fast friends. We learned our jobs together, and in the evenings swotted over electrical and torpedo subjects when we were not going ashore. During our training, we both had 3 months of switchboard watchkeeping, when, during our period of duty we had charge of all the electrical circuits of the ship. We learned a lot together, and as a shore going pal, "Nigger" shared the same likes and dislikes as myself.

Malta provided a happy hunting ground for sailors. One could buy beer at fourpence a bottle; a bed for the night cost only a shilling and a first class three course supper of soup, steak, eggs and chips with tomatoes, followed by a sweet was only one shilling and tenpence. Add to this the cost of a seat at the cinema which was one shilling, one could have a good run ashore for five shillings. Small wonder that Malta was popular with the fleet!

In those days, the fleet was paid monthly, on the last day of each month. On pay night, with the fleet in Malta, the island could expect and usually had, some nine to ten thousand sailors ashore, whilst the Naval canteen at Corradino, in the Dockyard had about another five hundred. The island literally swarmed with them, but these men and the business they brought were the life blood of the island, since there was very little industry apart from the dockyard.

One particular street, known as Strada Stretta, consisted of a long narrow thoroughfare sloping down to the sea. It was lined on either side with saloons, cabaret shows and restaurants. Because of its notoriety, it was popularly known to sailors the world over as "The Gut". On pay nights, The Gut was packed tight with matelots of all shapes and sizes and from all sorts of ships. To walk down this street was an education. Every bar and cabaret had its own honky tonk orchestra consisting of a couple of violinists, drummer and pianist. On a hot summer's evening, with the ear splitting music of a dozen different orchestras rending the air and the raucous voices of the sailors singing in their cups, was something to be seen to be believed. At this period of my service I avoided the Gut, but later, when serving in another ship, I came to love the place.

About the middle of June, the fleet left Malta for its summer cruise, which was to take us mainly to the Adriatic and Aegean areas and the far eastern end of the Mediterranean. I was longing to get started on this cruise, to visit Greece and the Aegean islands. Home of the Immortals! Land of legend and mythology. The happy hunting grounds of Heracles, of Zeus, Jason and the Argonauts, Mount Olympus and its golden thrones and, more factual, the glorious Acropolis and Parthenon at Athens.

We visited Corfu, Navarin, Salonika, Athens and most of the islands forming the Greek Archaepeligo. We paid visits to Durrazo in

Albania, Kotor and Split in Yugoslavia, Famagusta and Limassol in Cyprus and the island of Mudros.

Whilst at Mudros several of our ship's company, including myself, went on a day's tour of the Dardanelles battlefields. Since the destroyer *Beagle* had a predecessor which had taken part in the 1915 assault, she was chosen to take us to Cape Helles.

We each took a packed lunch and boarded *Beagle* at about 7 a.m. and after a smooth passage we landed on the famous beach, close to Fort Seddl Bahr, still in ruins after *Queen Elizabeth's* bombardment 16 years earlier. To our surprise, the beach was still littered with empty cartridge cases, clips, barbed wire and all the paraphernalia of war. There was also a large number of rusty, but otherwise very live shells lying about.

Up on top of a hill, and overlooking the entrance to the Dardanelles was a tall war memorial, at the foot of which we laid a wreath. We also toured the actual battlefield, still cluttered with wire and rusting relics such as empty food tins, helmets, etc. We saw a Turkish gun emplacement, the gun leaning over drunkenly, just as it had been damaged in 1915. On the concrete walls were some initials and ribald remarks, written by some Cobber or Tommy.

One thing stood out in my mind, looking at the terrain, the barbed wire and the Turkish defence system on the hill slopes behind the beach, I wondered how on earth our troops ever got a foothold on this beach at all! It must have been sheer suicide. However, we were all very glad to see how beautiful the war cemetery was kept. It is to the everlasting credit of the Imperial War Graves Commission that, amongst all this rusty desolation, there is a piece of green land that is, in the lovely words of Rupert Brooke – "Forever England."

After a most interesting day, we returned onboard *Beagle* and began our journey back to Mudros and *Queen Elizabeth,* with food for thought and many proud memories of our forebears.

During the cruise we held the fleet regatta at Corfu. I rowed port stroke in the torpedomen's whaler, but among such vast competition our chances were slim. I think we finished about fourth or fifth, but it was exciting and I loved racing in Fleet Regattas.

Sometimes we torpedomen would challenge another mess to a whaler race, the losers to pay for the supper of the entire winner's mess. This usually happened towards the end of the month, when mess funds were low and all we could afford would be, perhaps, bread and cheese. *Queen Elizabeth* was a canteen mess ship which, unlike General Mess ships, members bought their own food from the canteen or shore and, preparing it themselves, all the cooks had to do was cook it. These boat races, therefore, caused great excitement, since the winners usually claimed a slap up supper; but heaven help the losers, all they got was a large mess bill for food they had not had!

Many are the tales that were bandied about in connection with Canteen messing. One in particular stands out in my mind and is supposed to be true. In one particular ship which was lying alongside a dockyard wall, the Chief Cook was a stickler for having the lid of the giant steamer closed sharp at 9 a.m. Any mess bringing up a pudding after that time was unlucky. It just did not get cooked. Now it was the practice of messes that, in order to be able to identify their puddings, a fork with the mess number stamped on its handle was tied to the neck of the pudding cloth. On one occasion, a hard up mess could not afford a pudding, having lived too well earlier in the month. However, one bright genius, spotting the snow on the dockside, took his mess's pudding cloth and stuffed it with a fair sized snowball. Attaching the customary numbered fork to it and waiting until it was almost 9 a.m. he dashed into the galley and passing some remark to the eagle-eyed Chief Cook about "having just caught the boiler before the lid closes", he popped his "pudding" into the boiler.

In ships using the Canteen messing system it was the rule that dinners spoiled or lost, had to be replaced by the cooks. Imagine therefore, the confusion that must have existed in that galley when an empty pudding cloth was yanked out of the boiler at dinner time complete with its fork. Such enterprise deserved a free pudding!

Towards the middle of September, the fleet returned to Malta and for about a month was engaged in gunnery practices of all kinds, after which we were dispersed to all parts of the Mediterranean. This was unusual, but at about this time the Government introduced economy cuts at home and one of these was to reduce the pay of

H.M.Forces, with the result that the Home Fleet at Invergordon, indulged in a passive mutiny.

A decision had been made to cut the wages of the Civil Service, and other departments, by ten percent, which was accepted under protest. When it came to the Forces however, a different technique was used. At this time in the Royal Navy, two pay scales existed and, using an Able Seaman's rating as an example, it compared as follows -

Men entering the service prior to a specified date in 1925 (I believe this to be the year) received a basic rate of pay of four shillings per day. All who joined after this date received three shillings per day. In order to effect their economies as far as the navy was concerned, the Government decided to put everyone on the post 1925 rate, i.e. three shillings per day.

Now when I went to school, to take one shilling away from four shillings resulted in a loss of 25%. If only one intelligent gentleman in the Government had stopped to work out that little sum, there would have been no mutiny at Invergordon. As it was, the seamen of the Home Fleet were quick to note that, whereas everyone else was getting a 10% cut in their incomes, they, the seamen, were expected to take 25%. Over double everyone else's and this on top of the fact that His Majesty's Forces were the lowest paid of any workers. From this time on I lost faith in politicians, no matter what their creed or colour. If this was the sort of intelligence required to be one of His Majesty's Ministers, it did not say much for Britain!

Having no Trade Union and realising that representations were getting them nowhere, they took the only course left to them. They embarked on a passive disobedience campaign, so well organized that the Government were compelled to hastily re-adjust the sailors' pay. The damage was done, however, for the pound sterling slumped overnight. In Paris, the pound, which was normally worth 125 francs, dropped to 85 and it was the same story everywhere. The country was paying dearly for the idiocy of its Government.

As I was on the three shilling rate, it did not directly affect me, but my sympathies were on the side of our "four bob" sailors. After all, I had signed on for 3/- a day and I was a single man. The older men however, were mostly married with homes and children to maintain, responsibilities which they had undertaken because they were, at the time, within their incomes. To try to inflict a 25% reduction on these men was not only downright unfair and stupid, but amounted to incitement to mutiny on the part of the Government itself! And who took the blame for the blunderings of these idiots? As always, a scapegoat had to be found to cover up the errors of the Politico. The Commander-in-Chief, Admiral Sir Michael Hodges had reported sick before the cruise had commenced, which left the Home Fleet under the temporary command of Vice Admiral Tompkinson. It was this able Officer who was placed on the retired list for something which was no fault of his and, in any case, for something which he could not have prevented anyway. History, particularly Naval History, is full of such injustices. Why Governments cannot shoulder their own blame I will never know!

We, in the Mediterranean fleet, were more fortunate, insomuch that our Commander-in-Chief, with very great foresight, scattered his command to the far corners of the Mediterranean, so that no two ships were together, with the result that the men had to rely on their bretheren of the Home Fleet to do what they could to put matters right. Had the Mediterranean Fleet been at Malta there would have been a much more serious state of affairs.

After the Invergordon affair was settled, we returned to Malta for two months winter lay up, when secured peacefully between our buoys, our ship's company indulged in painting, scraping and self refitting the ship and of course, we enjoyed the night life of the island to the full and dreamed of the coming Spring cruise.

During our spell in Malta we had severe gales. These were known as Gregales and they blew with great ferocity, the heaving seas breaking over the harbour breakwaters in huge yeasty-capped combers. It was very uncomfortable for routine boatwork inside the harbour, due to a heavy ground swell and therefore, boat traffic was restricted to a minimum. However, the more stout-hearted of the dghaisamen kept their boats running so we were able to have our runs ashore on these blustery occasions. One always knew when to expect a

Gregale, because at night the Castille signal station would hoist two green lights, one above the other. If a severe Gregale was expected, it would be three green lights. By day, of course, the lights were replaced by black balls.

January 1932 arrived and towards the end of the month the whole fleet once more left Malta and steamed westward, where we were to take part in exercises with the Home Fleet, after which we would return to Gibraltar for a few days before beginning the courtesy visits of the Spring cruise.

Before this happened, however, both Nigger and I were transferred to the aircraft carrier *Glorious* for immediate passage to Gibraltar where we picked up *Nelson* and sailed for home, in order to qualify as Seaman Torpedomen at H.M.S. *Vernon*, the Torpedo School at Portsmouth.

I was really sorry to leave the old ship, for it had been a very happy year and I had travelled all over the Mediterranean in her, and had seen many wonderful and interesting places. Once again I had that feeling I had come to hate, that of having to leave a ship I loved.

H.M.S. *Queen Elizabeth*

H.M.S. *Royal Sovereign*

Chapter Six

H.M.S. *ROYAL SOVEREIGN*

<u>1932 – 1935</u>

Returning to England, I reported to the Royal Naval Barracks, and, after storing my kit, was sent on a month's leave. One of the first things I did was to purchase a motor cycle, a long wished for toy. On this machine I toured and explored the byways of Hampshire and Sussex. It was very pleasant, but after a month or two of leave and Barrack life, the urge to be off abroad again began to gnaw at my bones. This urge became stronger when it was obvious that, due to the limited number of men being trained in the Torpedo and Gunnery schools, my immediate chances of qualifying torpedoman were very slim indeed.

During the summer, the R.N.R. did a training cruise, making use of the cruiser *Vindictive*, and the ship was brought out of reserve, and with a skeleton crew of regular navy men, of whom I was one, she was commissioned with reserves and sent on a cruise to Scottish waters.

This made a welcome change to the soul destroying routine of the barracks, but it was not the real answer to my problem. I loved the Mediterranean, particularly Malta, and this was where I wanted to be.

Vindictive returned to Portsmouth about the beginning of September, and whilst in the barracks Regulating Office, I discovered that the battleship *Royal Sovereign* was returning to the Mediterranean in October for a further two and a half years commission. Immediately my request went in to volunteer for service in this ship, and to my satisfaction, in the middle of September I received a draft note to the effect that since I was allocated to *Royal Sovereign* I was to report to the Sick Bay for inoculations etc. and to proceed thereafter on ten days draft leave.

It was a very happy me who went on leave. I got rid of my motor cycle, and for the rest of my leave mooned about, passing my time by either reading or visiting the beach and cinemas.

Since our return from *Queen Elizabeth* I had only seen Nigger on brief occasions. He lived in Horsham, and on every possible occasion, spent his leaves there, so for the most of my time on leave, I was on my own. Burge, and Mo I had left behind in "Q.E." This is Navy Life, friends are like ships, they meet and pass in the night, and the next time one meets up with them may be years later, in some remote part of the world, when the remark on meeting again would be, "Well, fancy meeting you here!"

At the beginning of October, *Royal Sovereign*'s new crew marched out of the barrack gates en-route for the dockyard up the road. The ship herself was high and dry in the floating dock at Fountain Lake. She was still painted in the light grey of the Mediterranean Fleet, but with the daubs of red lead paint here and there, she resembled a patchwork quilt.

We spent the morning getting our kit onboard, and generally settling in. On consulting the notice board I discovered that I had been allocated to the Forecastle Division and for my action station, was a member of S.1 six inch gun's crew. My normal job was to be Petty Officer's Messman with three others; our job being to keep the P.O's Mess clean, wash up after meals and lay tables etc.

Although victualled in the P.O's Mess, I also retained my membership of the Forecastle Division's Mess, where, after my duties with the P.O's were finished for the day, I would relax, read or write letters. It was in this mess that I first met Snowy Sanders, that curly headed, flaxen haired, happy-go-lucky young seaman who was to be my shore going companion, and to whom I have dedicated this story.

Herbert Sanders was 21 years of age, the same age as myself. Because of his unruly yellow thatch, he was automatically christened "Snowy" by all of us and nobody could ever be miserable in his infectious company. When he smiled his whole face lit up, and one automatically smiled with him. Nothing ever worried him, he was the sort of being who, if one was in his company, one dropped all cares and worries and began to really live. This was his wonderful gift, and it was to be my good fortune to be his particular friend.

By the end of October, the ship had left the dock and had begun dockyard trials. Among other items, an aircraft catapult had been fitted on the quarterdeck, and we proceeded to Spithead to carry out tests with it. We carried a Fairy Swordfish biplane, fitted with floats, and after firing a number of dummy shots successfully, the dockyard staff loaded the aircraft with its pilot on to the catapult and the live shot was fired.

The Swordfish shot into the air without a hitch, and after a circuit of the ship, landed on the water and was hoisted back on to the catapult. Twice more it was fired, and the tests brought to a successful conclusion, after which the ship anchored for the rest of the day and night.

Next day we returned to Portsmouth and after topping up with stores, food and oil, and painting the ship overall, the ship's company went off on their last week end leave. On Monday morning, an hour after flood tide, *Royal Sovereign*, fresh in her new paint, left harbour for Gibraltar and the Mediterranean.

We were a private ship, that is to say, we did not carry an Admiral; consequently we did not enjoy the privileges of entering harbour first, or of being allocated the best billets and anchorages such as flagships enjoy. We had Captain K. Creighton as our skipper, and Commander L. H. Bell as the executive officer. Both of these men were first rate officers, but the skipper we always referred to as "Daddy Creighton". He was small and slightly built, and by his attitude, gave us the impression of a father rather than a Commanding Officer.

The weather during that late October and early November was beautiful and we had a smooth and peaceful trip. We stopped at Gibraltar only long enough to re-fuel and pick up fresh vegetables and mail, then on to Malta.

Twelve days after leaving U.K. *Royal Sovereign* altered course to make the approach to Malta. Coming up on deck for a breath of fresh air, I looked around and there, dead ahead, was the Island.

I took in the now familiar landmarks and in the warm sunshine, I had a strange feeling of "coming home". Don't ask me why, for I could not explain it, but I have never experienced it in any other of the many places I have visited. Malta, I guess, had me under its spell!

As we slid slowly through the entrance to the Grand Harbour, we saw the crowds of Maltese, high up on the Barracca, waving to us as we assed and further up the harbour we saw the rest of the Mediterranean Fleet moored peacefully between their buoys. They had finished their programmes for the year. We, for the next four weeks, would be practising drills, Gunnery and other exercises to bring us up to fleet standard, which, in this fleet, was very high indeed.

This "working up" period, as it was called, was to commence on the following Monday morning, so we had the weekend to go ashore and follow our own pursuits. Snowy and I were in the watch ashore, so we made plans to land at 6 p.m.

Unlike myself, he had not previously been to Malta. The booming church bells, which seemed to ring endlessly, the Carozzins or Gharries as we termed them (those quaint horse-drawn cabs), the brightly coloured dghaisas, and the historic sandstone buildings grouped around Valletta harbour, were all new to him, and he was intrigued with all he saw. I do not think the place affected him in the same way as it did me, however, I was able to point out one or two places of interest. It soon became obvious to me that Snowy was essentially a creature of the bright lights. Here his bubbling spirits were at their best, and it was not long before we found our way to the famous "Gut".

During my previous service in Malta, I had specifically avoided this "street of a thousand boozers", but, as I have already mentioned, in Snowy's company one did as he did, and strangely enough one enjoyed the doing of it.

We started our tour of the honky-tonks with the "Egyptian Queen" at the top of the Gut but it was not until we reached the bottom that Snowy found two bars that both of us really liked. One was known as "The Silver Horse" and the other "The Morning Star".

The naming of these various bars and restaurants had both naval and western flavours. For instance, there were such famous ship names as *Illustrious, London, Queen Elizabeth, Ocean* etc. , whilst others went under such romantic names as *Silver Dollar, Silver Horse* (popularly known as The Galvanized Donkey), *Egyptian Queen* and so on.

Our favourite cabarets were finally sorted out and these were the two we always made for. They were similar places, with bat wing doors, a tiled floor for dancing, with tables and chairs around the edge and at the far end, a small stage with space for a small orchestra. Around the walls were highly coloured murals depicting scenes connected with the name of the bar.

On pay nights, when the beer was flowing fast, one could, and usually did, have a hilarious evening. The stage, between dances, was sometimes occupied by one or another of the customers, who, thinking they had some special talent, such as singing, or a dance act, would cause great amusement to the rest of the audience, which usually resulted in a lot of cat-calling and caustic remarks from the more particular customers. Mostly, the bars imported minor variety acts to entertain the men of the fleet, and some of these were very good.

Apart from the beer and wines, most of the cabarets employed hostesses to dance with the sailors, and of course, with his mop of yellow hair, Snowy was a riot with the girls from the start. Normally a bit of a Romeo, he was the centre of attraction from the moment he entered the bar. Since I did not dance, it was usually my job to mind the beer whilst he danced. This arrangement suited me very well, so we were both satisfied.

Of the two cabarets, we both liked the "Morning Star" best, and we usually finished up the evening there. Here it was that Snowy first met Annie Gardiner, one of the dance hostesses. An Anglo–Maltese girl, she was fair, slim and good looking and danced like a dream. Both of them had the good sense to realise that theirs could only be a dancing partnership, consequently nothing serious developed between them. For one thing, Snowy was a high spirited animal who liked his freedom and for another, the pay was not sufficient to entertain serious relations with the opposite sex.

In between dances, Annie would sit at our table with her friend, Carrie, and their quaint accent and vivacious spirits gave us many happy evenings ashore, although the management expected us to buy the usual coloured water drinks for the girls in order to boost sales and give the girls their commission. During that winter, Snowy and I really enjoyed ourselves, as friends we were ideally suited, and his gay, bubbling nature, brought me more to life than ever before.

In the late Spring and throughout the Summer, on Saturdays and Sundays when in Malta, Snowy and I would go swimming, taking a picnic with us. A dghaisa would ferry us over to the harbour break-water, the inner end of which terminated in a flat sandstone area, an ideal site for swimming, diving and picnicking.

About a hundred yards out, a buoy was moored and often, after a doze in the sun, Snowy would suddenly sit up and exclaim – "Race you to the buoy Bungy, loser pays for the first beer tonight." There would be an immediate scramble, and two large splashes followed by a hectic swim, accompanied by ribald remarks as we battled our way out to the buoy.

As my memory serves me, Snowy usually got there first, but there were occasions when I managed to pip him to it. We would heave our tired and dripping bodies out of the sparkling water, and sitting on top of the buoy we would chatter away like a couple of monkeys. Or more often, just remain silent, glad of each other's company and enjoying the peace and sunshine of the Mediterranean scene.

These were the fresh days of our youth. Untrammelled by responsibility or cares. Golden days that only come once in a lifetime. We can never recapture them, but the recalling of them brings a glow of pleasure.

Christmas came and went with the usual festivities onboard and then, early in January, we sailed for the customary combined fleet exercises with the Home Fleet, followed by our courtesy Spring Cruise.

We visited Palma, Le Lavandou, Santa Margharita, Rapallo and Monte Carlo. Snowy and I went ashore at all of these places, and whilst at Santa Margharita we walked along the coast road to Rapallo, where we had a swim.

Returning to Malta in early April we carried out our quarterly firing programme. As a member of a 6" gun's crew, I had not yet taken part in a full calibre shoot. About a week prior to the actual firing, guns crews had to carry out loader practice. This consisted of using a device fitted with a full size breech block which allowed dummy projectiles and charges to be loaded, and gun drill to be carried out under realistic conditions. The aim was to load and fire ten rounds per minute. The whole drill was timed by stopwatch and each crew in turn had a loader practice session each day. We also ran a loader competition in which teams from all branches could take part.

On the actual day of the shoot, all loose glass fittings, mirrors etc. were taken down and at the appointed time, the ship's company would be closed up at "Action Stations". The target, towed about 600 yards behind the tug, would be at approximately 10,000 yards range and proceeding at about 7 knots. There was always a tense atmosphere about a full calibre shoot, until the first salvo had been fired, then, the first shock over, everyone settled down to the rhythm of the drill.

I will always remember my first experience of this. As one of the ammunition numbers of S.1.6" gun, my job was to stagger to the open breech with a 100 lb shell in my arms, and resting it on the loading tray, help the ramming number to ram the projectile hard into the chamber until the driving band bit into the rifling of the barrel. The cordite charge was then put into the chamber behind the shell and the breech closed, the breech worker having first inserted an electric tube into the lock. As the breech closed it brought two electric contacts into marriage; it then only remained for the breech worker to complete the firing circuit ready lamps by closing the interceptor switch at the side of the gun breech. The gun was then fired by the Director Layer in the control position aloft.

Before firing, a single stroke bell was rung twice to warn one that the gun was about to be fired and to keep clear of the recoil. This was always the moment when everyone's nerves were taut, and the atmosphere charged with expectancy.

The bell rang twice, a slight pause whilst the gyro firing mechanism checked that the ship was on an even keel, then a terrific roar and a flash of golden flame, with the gun viciously sitting back in its recoil, amid a cloud of dun coloured smoke. As the gun runs out into the firing position again, under the influence of the recovery springs, the breech is swung open, a jet of water under pressure is automatically shot into the breech and high pressure air helps to blow any smouldering residue out of the barrel, ready for the next reloading. It is always this first round which builds up the taut nerves, and it is quite a relief when it has been fired successfully.

The big danger in gun firing is the risk of a misfire and, if this happens, should all other methods to fire the gun fail, it is then left on a safe bearing for a period of 30 minutes before any attempt is made to open the breech. Failure to observe this safety precaution caused heavy loss of life in one of our cruisers, when, after a misfire in one of her 8" gun turrets, the breech was opened, presumably in error; (we shall never know, since the breech operator was killed). There happened to be a smouldering charge inside the breech which ignited when the breech opened, thereby causing an explosion which blew the roof off the turret and killed most of the turret's crew and injured many others. This is the sort of thing which helps to build up that tension before firing. Everyone is slightly worried until the first salvo is successfully fired. I have been involved in misfires from time to time, but on each occasion the drill was properly carried out, but it is a nasty situation, which has to be handled exactly right. There is no second chance.

After our firing practice, we went back to Valletta Harbour and during our spell in Malta, the whole of our ship's company did a rifle shooting course at Ricasoli Range. It lasted a week and we all had a most interesting time. To our surprise, both Snowy and I qualified as marksmen. These were halcyon days. We worked hard, life was very pleasant and in the evenings, under the star spangled, warm Malta nights, we had our cabaret shows and our fun.

At about this time (1933) Hitler came to power in Germany. To us, this news was of minor importance. We could not be expected, at this stage of Hitler's success, to be concerned with European politics. Berlin was a long way away and, although most of us realised that nothing good would come of it, we considered that it was not much good worrying about it, and as yet, all was peaceful in Malta and the

Mediterranean. We matelots, whilst practising the arts of war, were more concerned with our existing way of life and Malta, in the Spring and early Summer was very beautiful.

About the middle of June saw us leaving the Grand Harbour and commencing our Summer Cruise which was to take us to the Aegean, Adriatic and the eastern basin of the Mediterranean; calling at Haifa, Jaffa, Port Said, most of the major Greek Islands, Albania, Yugoslavia and a host of other ports large and small.

Yugoslavia and the Greek Islands were beautiful and romantic places. Well do I remember our visit to Breno Bay in the Adriatic. Snowy and I joined a party going to a nearby resort, which was a coach ride through the hills from where we were anchored. We found a beer garden on our arrival, and sitting at a small table, we ordered iced beer.

The Beer Garden was typically "Student Prince" style, with strings of coloured fairy lights hung between the trees. At an adjoining table, a smartly dressed young lady sat sipping a drink from a tall glass. It was a warm night, with a large yellow moon riding above the scented trees. A stringed orchestra was playing selections of popular music from the current world shows, and we were greatly taken by the romantic setting.

We were further impressed as we saw a tall Yugoslav army officer, complete with sword, come up to the lady's table and with a click of the heels and a courteous bow, he said something to her. She nodded, and gathering up his sword, he sat down opposite her and called over the waiter. It was like something out of the world of Johann Strauss, and we greatly appreciated having seen it.

Later, we enjoyed a wonderful moonlit trip back to the ship in an open coach. The tree scented night air and the hilly scenery, bathed in moonlight, made it a most memorable trip which Snowy and I thoroughly enjoyed.

During the warm summer nights, most of the ship's company slept on deck. We two used to sling our hammocks between the bridge superstructure and an awning stanchion at the ship's side, so that we could look out over the water. Long after most of the others were asleep, Snowy and I would be talking. Going over our jaunts ashore, our hopes for tomorrow or the current news, until we had exhausted our conversation. In that moment before sleep overtook us, gazing up at a thousand brilliant stars pulsating on their indigo blanket, I thought of the new places we should visit, the fresh exciting experiences we would have, for we were young together, and Navy life was exceedingly good.

Our last call of the cruise was Port Said, and of course we went ashore in the evening. We found a bar called the "Liverpool" and in the company of a couple of our stokers, we went inside and ordered iced beer. The owner, despite the fact that he wore a tarboosh, spoke excellent English. Prawns and salted peanuts were provided at our table free of charge, and we thought the owner extremely generous. After spending a small fortune on iced drinks, we woke up to the cause of our thirst. Crafty people these Egyptians!

We also got inveigled into taking a taxi tour of Port Said and the notorious Arab Quarter. Since it was night, we did not see much of it, apart from lights, but we heard the wailing voices and other peculiar noises which the local radio station was churning out, via the many café radio sets as we passed by. We found out later, when back onboard, that it was a dangerous pastime, since the taxi drivers had been known to drive their fares to some out of the way spot, where their pals would help to rob the passengers. We were lucky, we had an honest driver.

My own feelings about Port Said were such that I would have liked to have spent a great deal more time looking around the place. The desert beyond intrigued me, and I wanted to take a trip through the Suez Canal, but this was a dream I was to realize many years later, after I had left the Navy.

Royal Sovereign arrived back in Malta during the latter part of September, and was placed in the floating dock to have the periodical bottom scrape, and to have her rudder removed for repairs. During this month two changes were made which were to have far reaching effects. One affected the whole ship's company and the other me personally.

In the first place our "Daddy Creighton's" period of command had come to an end and he was promoted Rear Admiral and placed on the retired list. Secondly, I changed my job from Petty Officer's messman and was now a member of the 1st Picket Boat's crew.

This new job I viewed with mixed feelings, mainly because it meant that since it was a 24 hour about watchkeeping duty, my chances now of getting ashore with Snowy were almost non-existent. With the normal run of jobs, one could always manage to arrange a substitute, but in the case of a boat's crew this was virtually impossible. Apart from when we met in the mess or when our boat was hoisted in for boiler cleaning or painting, we did not see a great deal more of each other. However, we did snatch a run ashore together when the rare opportunity offered. Such is service life!

As for Captain Creighton's retirement, we were all extremely sorry to see him go. Under his command, we had jogged comfortably along and were a happy ship's company. A few days later a "bomb" arrived onboard in the shape of Captain B. H. Ramsay, who later was to become famous as C.-in-C. Dover and Allied Naval Commander-in-Chief at the invasion of Europe in 1944.

He was known throughout the service as "Dynamo Ramsay" and we in *Royal Sovereign* were soon to know why.

Whilst the ship was in dock, we saw and heard little of "Dynamo". He appeared to be well connected socially, and was a personal friend of the Second-in-Command of the fleet, Vice Admiral Sir Roger Backhouse. However, once the ship moved from the dock and moored between our usual buoys "Dynamo" descended on us like a load of bricks.

He cleared the lower deck of every living soul that could be spared from duty, and had us fallen in on the quarterdeck, officers as well. Then he began to tell us in some nicely chosen phrases, exactly what he thought of the *Royal Sovereign* as a ship and of us as her company. The gist of his remarks are best summed up in the remark of one of our seamen, who, turning to me said "You know Bungy, that bloke isn't nice to know".

"Dynamo" had told us that from now on we were to be the

smartest and cleanest ship in the fleet; and that in about two months he wanted, and was determined to have, a show vessel to which he could invite the captains of the rest of the fleet in order to show them what a ship should really look like. He also stated that he expected us to win the annual 15", 6" and 4"AA firing trophies. Not one, mark you, but all three! It is to his great credit and to our sweat, toil and heartbreak that he succeeded in all he undertook, for within the time he had laid down, the ship was looking like the Royal Yacht and when the Fleet Firing Competition came around, *Royal Sovereign* won all three trophies, an almost unheard of event!

I must mention that in the doing of all these things, on more than one occasion, "Dynamo" almost drove the ship's company to disobedience. Only the loyalty and good sense of the men prevented it.

Most of our winter lay up in Malta was spent in drills and practices, frequently lasting well into the evenings , which of course, robbed the crew of some of their precious shore leave time. This was a bitter pill, particularly as we could see the liberty boats of the rest of the fleet chugging shorewards at 4.30 p.m. We were not very pleased with "Dynamo Ramsay" at this stage of our acquaintance.

I had taken up my new duties as Picket Boat's crew and began to enjoy the job. Ours was a 17 ton steam boat, oil fired, with a short funnel which was fitted with a brass bell top. A navy blue enamelled hull, white upperworks, with two large brass ventilators completed the general outline. On either bow was the ship's crest, a gold crown surmounted by a lion, with a scroll below containing our motto, Pro Gloria Quid, which I believe means For our Glorious Sovereign, although we interpreted it as "If you want a quid, borrow one!"

There were eight of us in the crew:- Two bowmen, of whom I was one, a sternsheetman, fender boy, Leading Seaman as Coxswain, Midshipman as trainee coxswain and Officer in charge of the boat, Stoker Petty Officer and a Stoker. We had two complete crews, one working the 24 hours on, whilst the other had the day off.

The duty ran from 8 a.m. one day to 8 a.m. the following day, when it was the responsibility of the off going crew to turn the boat over to the new crew in a spotless condition. We all wore white rubber-soled shoes to avoid damage to the deck, and when leaving or coming alongside a gangway or jetty, we had a system of boathook drill, which, when properly carried out, enhanced the smartness of the boats crew and the good name of the ship she belonged to.

"Dynamo" had already instilled into us that a ship was known by the smartness and cleanliness of her boats, and he saw to it that ours reflected his ideas on the subject. Without doubt our First Picket Boat was a show boat of snowy white decks, shiny paintwork and glittering brasswork, whilst the stern cabin consisting of spotlessly white cushions, trimmed with navy blue piping, floral curtains at the windows, fancy white rope work and two highly polished brass dolphins, one at each end of the cabin, was a joy to behold!

As a member of its crew, I have to admit that our boat was a picture, lying moored at the lower boom, with its white sharkskinned decks and sparkling brasswork glinting in the sun.

Sometimes "Dynamo" would pay an Official call on the flagship or other vessel. On these occasions we put up his pennant on a short staff in the bows. This indicated to all and sundry that the Captain of H.M.S. *Royal Sovereign* was making an "Official Call" and would be expecting the appropriate mark of respect to his rank. On these occasions we would give the boat a bit of extra spit and polish, since all the eyes of the fleet would be upon us, and some of those eyes were very critical!

We had one or two severe Gregales during that winter which made boatwork rather wet and unpleasant, but taking the rough with the smooth, life as a member of the Picket Boat's crew was quite pleasant. We were a happy-go-lucky lot, and got on famously together. We had our exciting moments, such as trying to get in and out of the boat via the Jacob's ladder at the boom, when the weather was really rough. This was always a dangerous and sometimes difficult job, but if one wanted one's breakfast or dinner, one just had to get out of the boat.

In January, 1934, we once more sailed for combined manoeuvres with the Home Fleet. This time they were to be held in the Atlantic and were to last for 14 days. It was very noticeable that since the Nazi Government had taken over in Germany the year previous, our fleet practices had become more intense. This may have been coincidental, but I have sometimes wondered about this.

These exercises were carried out in some of the worst Atlantic weather I have experienced. We had heavy seas and high winds for the whole of the period, and everything and everybody was wet and uncomfortable. The ship was thrown about like a cork and many of us were violently seasick for days on end. We were all heartily glad when it was over, particularly the destroyers. As it was, one of the aircraft carriers had her hanger doors smashed in by the high seas.

Thankfully we returned to Gibraltar where we had a week's rest. Whilst there we had the annual Parade and March Past in the Alameida Gardens, but this time, as a boat's crew member, I was not on parade.

Leaving Gibraltar, we began our courtesy visits to France and Italy, calling at Monaco, Cannes, Juan-les-Pins and most of the Riviera ports. Whilst at Monaco the ship, which was anchored outside the breakwater, had to put to sea due to a heavy gale blowing up, causing *Royal Sovereign* to drag her anchor. It was considered too rough to attempt the hoisting of our Picket Boat, so we were sent into the harbour and told to report to the British Consul at the quayside. He had been briefed as to our predicament by radio.

After a staggering trip inshore, we finally moored the boat alongside the jetty in Monaco Harbour, and were met at the top of the jetty steps by the Consul. He informed us that we had all been booked in at the palatial Hotel Bristol and advanced us three pounds each in francs against the ship's account.

We spent a very pleasant evening and had an excellent meal in the hotel. Tubby, our stoker, who had to stand by the boat to keep steam, was not forgotten either, for the Chef sent down a picnic basket containing cold chicken, bottle of wine and other tasty morsels.

During the early part of the evening, a yacht belonging to a Swedish millionaire, broke loose from her moorings and was drifting towards the rocks outside the breakwater. The seas running were really mountainous, breaking viciously over the breakwater in huge cataracts of wild yeasty water. Our coxswain asked us if we would risk taking the boat out in an effort to save the yacht, which was now heading for certain destruction. Although we knew that there was nobody onboard it, we realised that the salvage money would be considerable if we were able to save her. We decided to have a go, and donning our life-jackets and with a full head of steam, we cast off and steamed towards the breakwater exit. We were thrown about considerably as we surged along on the crests of gigantic waves. The seas were steep and our puny little steamboat almost stood on her nose. Our Stoker Petty Officer and Tubby, his mate, down in the tiny engine and boiler room must have had stomachs of cast iron to be able to withstand the giddy motion. We were almost thrown through the narrow gap between the two breakwaters and turning to port, we buffeted our way towards the deserted yacht.

Finally we came close enough to get a line aboard, but by now, the yacht was so close to the rocky coast and the high sea running made it dangerous to life and limb to proceed any further with the idea of trying to save her. Our coxswain quite rightly decided to abandon the idea. After what seemed an age, we finally managed to turn our boat around without capsizing her and hightailed it back to the harbour. The yacht went to pieces on the sharp rocks and as we were securing the boat for the night, the owner came down to thank us for our efforts, pointing out that had we succeeded, we would have had a considerable amount of salvage money. We thanked him kindly for calling, but privately thought that our lives and our old picket boat were worth a lot more than his yacht.

After a luxurious night and a fabulous breakfast in the hotel, we looked out over the harbour and noted that the gale had blown itself out. Further we could see *Royal Sovereign* approaching her anchorage from seaward. Thanking the Maître d'hotel for all he had done for us, we bade him farewell and made our way down to the boat where we found Tubby waiting with a full head of steam.

We nosed out of the harbour into a much smoother sea, and after the ship had anchored, we secured to the lower boom and turned the boat over to the relief crew after a very exciting and pleasant 24 hours in Monaco.

After a successful cruise, we made our way back to Malta, which despite its general reputation for bells and smells, was welcomed by the men of the fleet for its hospitality at a reasonable price. For myself, I always look forward to entering Valletta harbour.

During our stay, I decided to take an acting seaman gunner's course, since I was already performing the duty of Breechworker on our gun. This course occupied the full two months stay in Malta, and successfully passing the examination, I began to receive the pay for it, which was 3d. per day!

I was temporarily relieved from the Picket Boat to enable me to take this course and to my delight, was able to go ashore with Snowy again. Like a couple of long lost pals, we visited our old haunts down the "Gut" and we took in a fair amount of swimming as well. We both thoroughly enjoyed this break together but by the time we began our Summer cruise I was back in the Picket boat again, a job I really loved. It was a job away from the main hubbub of ship life, and I look back with pleasure to those fresh early mornings, secured to our boom, all of us busy washing down our boat and polishing its brass, with the early morning Mediterranean sunshine warming our bodies, and the sea like a mirror. Now and again one would get the smell of frying bacon wafting out from the galley exhaust fans, to start our gastric juices working.

During the summer months we had optional swimming periods during which the ship's company could enjoy a dip in the cool Mediterranean. These sessions were usually between 7 to 7.30 a.m. and 5 to 5.30 p.m. daily. I never missed these, it was delicious to come up on deck from the clammy atmosphere below and to dive into the sea, particularly in the morning, when the sea was usually flat, like a sheet of glass. We could swim well away from the ship, although a lifeboat was always in attendance during the swimming period.

We also held water polo matches alongside, and these provided endless entertainment for the ship's company right throughout the summer. These swimming and Polo sessions were common throughout the fleet and were held, weather permitting, wherever the ships happened to be. Once a year, the sea going swimming test was held, when all those who had not passed it would have to swim from the lower boom forward, to the after accommodation ladder and then float around for 3 minutes. This test had to be performed whilst wearing either a duck suit or an overall. Everyone had to pass this test before becoming eligible for promotion.

On our way from Valletta to the Adriatic the ship stopped, dead in the middle of the Mediterranean, then lowering the sea boat, the order was passed "Hands to bathe". It was a warm evening, even at sea, and the sea was calm. Without more ado, we soon changed into trunks, and in no time at all more than half of the crew were over the side enjoying this welcome dip. It was a queer sensation to find one-self swimming in the middle of a sea with no land in sight anywhere. I enjoyed it, as did the rest of us. This was one of "Dynamo's" rare moments, and we all appreciated his gesture.

After this pleasant interlude we continued on our way to Dubrovnik, a Yugoslav seaport, which was our first port of call on the Dalmation coast. There is not a great deal to say about this cruise that has not already been said, since it was similar to the previous year; however, *Royal Sovereign* had one sad duty to perform ere we returned to Malta. During our cruise, King Alexander of Yugoslavia was assassinated whilst on a state visit to France. He was shot at close range in the streets of Marseilles. *Royal Sovereign* helped to escort the Dalmation destroyer *Dubrovnik*, carrying the King's body back to his homeland. It was a sad duty for us, since we had just enjoyed the hospitality of the late King's country. We then called at Famagusta in the island of Cyprus, where we had a route march through the town finishing up in an orange grove where the owner gave us permission to eat what we liked. After a hot, dusty march, his kind offer was accepted with alacrity, for we were very thirsty. Leaving Cyprus, we returned to Malta.

Our commission was now coming to an end. The following April we would have completed our two and a half years on the station. Most of the ship's company were beginning to have thoughts of home, besides which, it was almost Christmas.

During our lay up in Valletta, I applied for and was granted, an acting Rangetaker's course, since I was determined to qualify in one or the other of the specialist rates. This course involved instruction in Optical instruments, lenses and the operation of Rangefinder Instruments and Inclinometers. One had to undergo a very rigid eyesight test in addition to the technical instruction I successfully passed the examination and was rated Acting Rangetaker 3rd class.

This latest course must have made me almost unique because I now held three acting rates, and had not, as yet, passed through the Gunnery or Torpedo Schools to qualify in either of them.

The First Picket Boat was hoisted inboard for boiler cleaning, so we of its crew, had a welcome break from the 24 hour about duty, with the result that Snowy and I were able to have a few trips ashore together. The ship was dry docked again for bottom scraping and painting and our routine was allowed to relax slightly.

After the Christmas and New Year celebrations were over, the fleet sailed for the Western Mediterranean and the usual combined exercises. On our return to Malta in April, *Royal Sovereign* stayed but a short time. We had now finished our commission and, on the last Sunday before sailing for home, we hoisted our paying off pennant; which is a long narrow white pennant with a red St. George's cross close to the mast end. This pennant, flown from the mainmast, is almost as long as the ship herself, so long, in fact, that its free extremity has to be supported by a gas filled meteorological balloon.

As the snow white pennant floated lazily in the light air currents I went back over the past two and a half years. They had been good years in which we had experienced our ups and downs, but we had profited a lot as well. We had visited most of the Mediterranean sea ports, we had worked and played hard and I, in particular, had enjoyed every moment. I had taken part in the annual regatta during both years and with Snowy, had enjoyed the fruits the land had to offer.

In winning all three Gunnery trophies, we had proved ourselves the most efficient unit in the fleet. Good companions, happy runs ashore, swimming picnics, and sparkling nights in the Silver Horse and Morning Star. Altogether a most satisfying commission! Now we were going home. First to take part in King George V's Coronation Review at Spithead and afterwards to pay off.

The day we left Valletta for home we once again hoisted our paying off pennant. As we slipped our buoys and slowly moved towards the entrance of the harbour, we were cheered by all the ships we passed. Our band played 'Auld Lang Syne" and "Rolling Home to Merrie England", whilst the population of Valletta, or a goodly proportion of them, crowded the high ramparts of the Barracca waving scarves and handkerchiefs. These paying off farewells were always very touching and I had difficulty in swallowing on more than one occasion, but I knew in my heart that I would be back one day soon, for I loved the Mediterranean and Malta in particular.

We cleared the entrance and looking back, I watched the Island slowly getting smaller until finally it vanished below the rim of the horizon. All that was left was the creaming foam of our stern wake as we began to pound out the miles towards Gibraltar. I slowly turned and went below, a little sad at having to leave this island where I had spent so many happy hours.

Arriving at Portsmouth, we gave Foreign Service leave, after which we painted and cleaned up the ship for the Fleet Review. When the pomp and circumstance of the celebrations was over, we returned to Portsmouth harbour and paid off. And so ended a momentous commission, my happiest to date!

H.M.S. *Royal Sovereign*

H.M.S. *Windsor*

Chapter Seven

H.M.S. *WINDSOR* and H.M.S. *VERNON*

<u>1935 – 1936</u>

Being drafted from a ship one has happily served in for long periods was always an ordeal for me. When that draft happens to be to the R.N.Barracks it is doubly so. In a ship one knows almost everyone and once you have settle down it is a grand life. Soon the motley crowd become an orderly, well trained, happy crew. This can never be the case in a depot.

To begin with you are one of thousands without ship, job or purpose. You become an odd job man, whilst awaiting the whim and pleasure of the Drafting Office. Never knowing, and half fearing where you will be ultimately drafted.

I always hated barrack life and did my best to avoid it. Where possible I liked to pick my own ships, then apply to be drafted to them, which in the case of foreign service, one was able to do. This time, however, Mussolini, the Italian Dictator took a hand, and because of the Invasion of Ethiopia by Italy, I found myself drafted to an ancient destroyer, H.M.S. *Windsor* which, with numerous other craft, was taken out of reserve and put into commission.

Destroyer service had never, at any time appealed to me, and consequently I was not overjoyed at receiving this draft, but it was a case of having to accept it and so, complete with kit I was duly delivered to *Windsor* by lorry.

Of 1918 vintage, she looked a picture of dejection. Her salt encrusted paintwork, caused by years of lying up the creek in reserve, was enough to break any sailor's heart. I could see that for some time to come, we were going to be busy getting *Windsor* back into shape.

These "V" and "W" boats, as we called them, were of a familiar silhouette, with their tall slim woodbine forward funnel and the squat fat one behind. They were armed with four 4" semi-automatic guns and six 21" torpedo tubes. With a speed of some 32 knots, they were formidable fighting craft.

One big snag with them was the rather primitive bathing facilities for the crew. Whereas in modern destroyers a bathroom is fitted, in *Windsor* and her sisters, one had to scrounge a bucket of hot water from the cook, then go and find a quiet place to have a bath, if you can call it that! I mainly used the depth charge store aft, when, placing a piece of coconut matting over the top of the depth charges to help absorb the water, I would have a wash down.

Another pain in our necks was the position of the steam capstan engine in our forecastle mess-deck. Whenever steam was required on the capstan to heave in the anchor, our mess-deck would be lost in a fog of steam, which, combined with its vile smell, almost turned one's stomach over.

Our skipper was Commander J. A. McCoy, who lived, talked and ate destroyers, and did his best to make us do the same. He was an extremely able officer, and all of us liked him immensely. He was known to us simply as "Tim". On one occasion, when we were at Portland, he entertained a brother Captain to dinner one evening. During the night it suddenly blew up rough and our small motor boat, of which I was the bowman, was bucketing about alongside the gangway, waiting to take Tim's guest back to his own ship. We were plunging about badly and our crew were getting very wet with spray, when suddenly our stoker, lifting the canvas flap of the engine room, remarked in an irritated voice "When is that silly old basket going to arrive?" It so happened that the scuttle of the skipper's cabin was immediately above us, and about ten minutes later, Tim and his guest clattered down the gangway, and before entering the boat he lifted up the engineroom flap and remarked in an Oxford accent "Stoker, the silly old basket has arrived," to the complete embarrassment of our stoker, but to the delight of the rest of us.

Since the Italian-Ethiopian affair partially involved us, we lost no time in storing and ammunitioning the ship and after painting and cleaning, she looked more like a naval vessel than the dirt barge we had first seen. Then, when all was ready, we sailed for Portland for working up.

I will not dwell on my service in *Windsor*, because within three months of joining her, the emergency had subsided without Britain becoming involved in hostilities and so it was back to the hated depot for me. Not for long, however, since within a day or so I received a draft note to join H.M.S. *Excellent*, the Gunnery School, to qualify as Seaman Gunner.

This was a bitter blow to my dream of becoming a torpedoman. I hated drill and "Bull" of all descriptions and *Excellent* was the last place on earth I wished to go to. In view of the fact that I had taken an Acting Torpedoman's Course whilst in *Queen Elizabeth*, I tried to get the draft stopped and a torpedo course substituted. It was pointed out to me that my marks received for the Acting Gunnery Course in *Royal Sovereign* had earned me a "Higher" recommend and that therefore the draft must stand.

The bird was coming home to roost! My past was catching up with me. I felt that I was being pushed around and this made me determined to have this draft cancelled by hook or by crook. Not out of any vindictive sense, but because my career was at stake, and I did not want to be forced into doing something that I knew I would hate.

It so happened that my elder brother was serving in the barracks as a Boatswain, which is Officer rank, and he himself had been a Torpedo Gunner's Mate before being promoted. He was the depot clothing officer at the time I write of, so I paid him a visit and laid all my troubles on his plate. The following day I was sent for by the Drafting Office and was informed that my draft to *Excellent* was cancelled and that I would now be going to *Vernon* for a torpedo course. I was highly delighted, because the draft was leaving next day. This was the first and only occasion that I made use of my brother for service purposes, but he certainly saved my bacon that time!

Next afternoon, which was Friday, I was on my way to the Torpedo School, where, after the weekend to settle in, I started the course on the following Monday morning.

We commenced with the necessary mathematics connected with electricity. We learned all about Ohm's law, Lenz's law, Volts, Amperes, Joules, etc. The theory of Magnetism and Electricity was stuffed into our brains, and we were busily engaged in working out electrical problems. By the end of the week we had a fair knowledge of what it was all about.

Our second week proved more interesting for we had the theory and practical side of motors, dynamos, circuit breakers, lighting systems, searchlights etc. This was followed in the succeeding weeks by instruction in batteries, bells, buzzers, telephones and the location and cure of faults. We went on to electrical distribution systems, earth finding and the thousand and one things, and complications, connected with a ship's complicated installation.

At the end of this first part of the course, we took the examination which consisted of three parts… (a) Written papers, (b) Oral Questions and (c) Practical Fault finding and Maintenance. It was one of the most interesting periods I'd had to date, and I enjoyed it very much.

The next part of our course was the torpedo section, which we commenced on the Monday following the completion of the electrical section. Before we started this, however, those who had failed to make the grade thus far were weeded out and returned to the depot. We also had one rejected because his general conduct and character did not come up to standard.

In those days, the torpedo branch was considered to be an "Elite Society" in the service, and was not easy to get into. Consequently, one had to be of the "cream" so to speak. There will be those of other branches who will 'pooh pooh!' this, but I had evidence of more than one occasion that this was so. However, on with the story.

On Monday morning, after the usual Divisions and Prayers on parade, we were marched down to the torpedo workshops and lecture rooms which ran parallel to the jetty and which bore the word "Vulcan" in letters of blue and gold over the doors. We carried our overall suits under our arms, for messing about with torpedoes was oily work.

At one end of the building were the lecture rooms and the other end consisted of a large torpedo workshop, fitted with an overhead travelling crane and work benches around the walls. Outside, on the edge of the jetty, were a couple of small cranes for hoisting and lowering the torpedoes into the boat.

First of all we were taken on a tour of the building and shown everything, but the torpedo shop captured our hearts. There were 21" torpedoes all over the place. Some complete, some in various stages of assembly and a class, dressed in overalls were gathered around a torpedo, assisting the instructor to carry out a quarterly testing routine. Over all, hung the smell of the shale fuel oil, which the torpedo engine used as fuel, and which was the "tinfishmen's" trademark.

Torpedoes are intricate, delicate and extremely expensive weapons. If one was lost during a practice firing, it resulted in a Court of Inquiry, and about a week's sweeping of the area in which it was lost, consequently great care was always taken to thoroughly test the torpedo and make sure that the balance and buoyancy chamber doors were fitted with a new rubber washer, and the necessary airtightness test carried out before loading the "fish" into the tube.

Many are the tales that can be told about lost and contrary torpedoes. I myself, was involved in a Court of Inquiry over a lost torpedo fired by a submarine. Since I had prepared and tested the "fish" myself, it was my job to prove that its loss was not my fault. By consulting the chart and the area in which it was fired, and checking the submarine's depth when she fired it, I was able to prove that the fault rested with the submarine's captain. He had fired the torpedo with too little water beneath his keel, with the result, the "fish" on taking its initial dive before taking up its depth line, had dived into the mud at the bottom of the sea and had stuck there. It was eventually salvaged and further testing proved my point.

Then there is the story of a certain Torpedo Gunner's Mate who, after his torpedo had been fired, found its buoyancy chamber door lying on the deck beneath the tubes. When the torpedo was eventually located by sweeping, he is supposed to have bribed the diver to take down the door, screws and spanner and to fit the door on. The tale goes on to relate that when the "fish" was finally recovered and tests begun to discover why it had failed to surface, on removing the buoyancy chamber door, in addition to a deluge of water, a live fish also dropped out! Which landed both the Torpedo Gunner's Mate and the diver in the soup...

After the first few weeks of the course I knew that this was the life for me. I became deeply absorbed in the work and was greatly interested in the lectures, and the practical work on the "fish". We would have a lecture in the morning, then, after lunch, put it into practice on the actual torpedo. Dressed in our overalls, we would strip down, clean and re-assemble various parts of the complicated weapon, then test the completed job.

This was our routine for the next six weeks. We were thoroughly grounded in both theory and practice until we had a good idea of the weapon, its method of firing and recovery and the tubes it was fired from.

We did actual preparation on torpedoes, then, loading them into a launch, we took them out to a destroyer and loaded them into her tubes, then, steaming out to Spithead, we fired and recovered them. After all this, we had the examinations.

As before, it was in three parts. Written, Oral and Practical. The Practical test consisted of carrying out a quarterly test on either a balance or buoyancy chamber, or perhaps stripping and re-assembling a tail unit and propellers, and usually a deliberate fault was introduced so that the candidate had to carry out the tests correctly in order to find the fault. It was a most interesting and instructive course, and I took to the work like a duck to water.

Our next and final hurdle was the Mines and Explosives section, which we commenced on the Monday following our Torpedo examinations. Here we learned all about the mysteries of mines, depth charges, T.N.T. Gun Cotton, detonators etc.

We had a practical period allocated, when, loading a lorry with charges, primers and detonators, we set off for Horsea Island at the back of Portsmouth Harbour. Here we fitted and fired charges all the week. It was great fun, but it taught us to respect explosives and to treat them delicately. After a fortnight of this subject we had the examinations, the last of our course. As usual, we had to wait until Monday to hear the result, leaving us with the weekend to sweat and worry.

I did fairly well and managed to qualify with 86%, and drawing my torpedoman's badges from the store I was soon busily engaged sewing them on my uniforms. We had finished the course in April and now found ourselves employed as gardeners, cleaners and odd job men whilst awaiting draft. It was during this period that I first came into contact with the Royal Navy Polo Team and was inveigled into attending some of their matches at Hurlingham, as a field attendant.

Whilst trimming a hedge one sunny morning, *Vernon's* executive officer, Commander Charles Lambe (who was a member of Lord Mountbatten's Polo team) stopped and spoke to me for a few minutes. He asked me how I liked *Vernon* and what I thought of the course etc. During the course of our conversation, he asked me if I was free on the coming weekend, and on learning I was, asked me if I would kindly help the Polo team at Hurlingham.

Commander Lambe was a very charming man and a gentleman to boot, and I felt rather pleased that he had asked me. He pointed out that there would be one other, and that all our expenses would be paid and a tea provided. I accepted his proposition with alacrity and never regretted it, for I had several such interesting trips to Hurlingham and met the team, including Lord Mountbatten, who had been an old shipmate of mine from *Queen Elizabeth* days.

During that summer *Vernon* held its annual Gymkhana and I took part, winning a small cup in the wall race. We had to run 50 yards, scale a ten foot wall and run a further 50 yards. It was great fun and a good time was had by all.

By the time August arrived, I was beginning to feel that I had been on shore long enough and commenced to search around for a ship which might be going to the Mediterranean area.

There were rumours (or buzzes as we called them) to the effect that H.M.S. *Hood* was being prepared for service in that particular area and that with *Repulse* a Battle Cruiser Squadron was to be formed and attached to the Mediterranean Fleet.

Now there is only one way to scotch a "buzz" and that is to make some effort to verify it. With this end in view, I applied for a draft to *Hood* and service in the Mediterranean. If the "buzz" was false my application would have been refused on the grounds that one could only volunteer for foreign service. As it was, the "buzz" was correct and my draft to *Hood* came through in due course. I was delighted for I was going back, to what was for me, the enchanted island of Malta. And so, in October 1936 I joined H.M.S. *Hood*.

Chapter Eight

H.M.S. *HOOD*

<u>1936 – 1939</u>

In joining *Hood* I knew that I was joining the pride of the Navy. This 42,000 ton monster, 860 feet long and with a speed of 32 knots, was the most beautiful ship in service. When it came to her hull and superstructure, her designers had excelled themselves. Her long sweep of forecastle, the identically sized funnels, the armoured tower, masts of exactly the same height and her long, low quarterdeck, sweeping up to the stern, made her the finest looking ship in this, or any other navy. She was probably the best loved ship in the service, and I, her latest and very humble torpedoman, was very proud to be of her company.

Hood's torpedo division were a happy-go-lucky lot; we were about 90 to 100 strong and by age and service were the oldest division in the ship. Over 50% of us were three badge men, which meant that they had at least 13 years service to their credit. At this period, most torpedomen were fairly senior men due to the great competition to get into the branch to begin with.

My first job in *Hood* was with the torpedo maintenance section. We had four tubes, mounted two each side between decks, but above the water line, with armoured doors fitted on the outboard ends of the tubes. We carried eight 21" Mark IV★ torpedoes, one in each tube and a spare in the racks above each tube. These torpedoes were almost obsolete, since the more modern Mark IX★ was now being widely used throughout the fleet. However, we were not a new ship, and since our tubes were only adapted for use with the older type torpedo, these were the mark we had to have.

I had only touched but very briefly on the Mark IV★ in *Vernon*, most of our training having been with the newer weapon. However, one soon became familiar with them, and I began to like my new surroundings.

Our first job, soon after commissioning, was to change the colour of *Hood*'s paintwork. Almost from the time she was built, her colour had been dark Home Fleet grey and I think we all enjoyed slapping on the Mediterranean light grey, and when completed, the old lady looked more like a ballerina. I have never seen a ship look so different!

We also had to paint a red, white and blue tricolour flash across the roof of "B" turret. This was to identify us from the air when undertaking Spanish Patrol duties, since Spain was indulging in a civil war at this time.

We carried an Admiral too! And flew Vice Admiral Geoffrey Blake's flag at our Fore masthead and took over the duties of second-in-command, Mediterranean Fleet, so we would now be enjoying the berthing and other little privileges that went with a flagship. Our Commanding Officer was Captain F. Pridham, and the Executive Officer, Commander D. Orr-Ewing, who, after a short while, came to be affectionately known as "Big Hearted Dave" on account of his nibbling at our spare time!

In October, after provisioning, storing and amunitioning, *Hood* left Portsmouth for Gibraltar and so we began our commission. Our passage across the Bay of Biscay was calm, although there was a con-siderable ground swell, which caused the ship to develop a slow roll. This roll, among other things, swept the Wardroom breakfast table bare, smashing a considerable amount of crockery.

Three days later the familiar hump of Gibraltar loomed up over our port bow and in an hour or so we passed through the Mole entrance and secured alongside the jetty. It was here that we had our first casualty of the commission. As we were warping our stern into the jetty by means of a wire around the after capstan, a sudden gust of wind caught the stern and tautened the wire, which became jammed on the capstan. The wire started to "sing" and everybody jumped clear as the wire hawser snapped like a piece of thread, but one un-fortunate seaman did not move fast enough and the wire whipped back viciously and amputated both of his legs. He died the same day in hospital. One always had to be careful when using wires in con-junction with moving the ship. You had to be ready to immediately ease the wire when the strain became too great.

From the moment we arrived *Hood* took over Nyon Anti Piracy Patrol Duty off the Spanish Coast. There had been several incidents when torpedoes had been fired at vessels of all nations by unknown submarines. Also, Spanish gunboats, cruisers and destroyers, occasionally interfered with our merchant ships. To combat this, France, Italy, Germany and the United Kingdom, formed this anti piracy patrol, named after the Nyon Conference.

Operating with *Hood* on alternate patrols was *Repulse* also we had a few destroyers seconded from the Home Fleet. I believe they were the *Firedrake, Fortune, Fame* and *Fury*. The Germans had two of their pocket battleships, *Deutchland* and *Graf Spee*. One or other of them being either in Tangier, Gibraltar or on patrol. Whilst performing this duty, we had warheads fitted to our torpedoes and our shell was fuzed, ready for instant use. During one of these routine patrol trips, the destroyer *Hunter* struck a mine which blew a huge hole in her bottom and side, in the vicinity of the bridge, killing some 30 of her crew. It was a sad affair and we were really wild about this. Of all the vessels belonging to the opposing sides in the civil war, it had to be one of our ships to be caught by their wretched mines.

I watched *Hunter* being towed into dock. She was in a sorry mess, with decks awash and a burned and blackened hull and bridge. After she had docked and the water had been pumped out, the sad job of removing her dead began. After this had been completed, I walked over to the dock to have a look at her damage. There was a huge hole in her bottom just beneath the bridge, and another in her side. One could have driven a double-decker bus through them. It speaks volumes for the builders of *Hunter* that she managed to remain afloat at all!

Our patrol in *Hood* was between Gibraltar, Tangier, Palma and Marseilles. Occasionally it would be brightened by an odd incident such as the time when "Potato Jones" ran the Spanish Blockade to land his cargo of potatoes to the besieged population of Bilbao. On this occasion *Hood* was in Gibraltar and half of us were ashore on night leave. We received an urgent signal from the Admiralty to proceed at full speed to the Bilbao area to give protection to "Spud

Jones" and his ship which was being threatened by a Spanish cruiser. The recall flag was flying from the yard arm and periodically *Hood* blasted her syren to attract the attention of the men still onshore, of whom I was one. We libertymen hurried down to the harbour and got back onboard. The ship sailed at 5 p.m. and, at 25 knots, we belted out of the Mediterranean and turning northwards, headed for Bilbao, arriving off the port at 7 a.m. next morning.

On arrival we found a large Spanish cruiser and "Spud Jones's" steamer, within hailing distance of each other. Spud himself always wore a bowler hat and we could see him on his bridge gesticulating to the Spaniard. We received a signal from him to the effect that the "Blankety blank" cruiser was stopping him from going in to Bilbao to unload his potato cargo, which by this time, was beginning to go rotten.

Attached to *Hood* at this time were the Home Fleet destroyers *Firedrake, Fortune and Fame* and we informed Jones that he could proceed into Bilbao, and that the three destroyers had been detailed to escort him in. Thumbing his nose to the Spanish cruiser and with a puff of dirty black smoke from his steamer's funnel, "Spud Jones" went on his way with a destroyer on either side of him and another leading the way. *Hood*, with her crew at action stations, circled the cruiser to prevent any further interference.

"Potato Jones" was a persistent old cuss and on more than one occasion he and his ship had to be got out of scrapes; but he and his ilk were the salt of the earth. He had the freedom of the ocean and he wasn't going to be kicked around by Spaniards or anybody else! Leaving the victorious Jones, we returned to Gibraltar.

My shore going pal at this time was an old shipmate from *Royal Sovereign* days. We had shared the same mess then, and on joining *Hood* it was natural that we teemed up, since we knew each other. Harry was a gunnery rating, so we did not, on this occasion, share the same mess; but we went ashore together, both on swimming trips and on the rounds of the bars. He was a quieter sort of chap than Snowy had been, preferring the less patronized bars. However, we got on very well and had some enjoyable runs ashore.

Eventually *Repulse* arrived at Gibraltar and relieved us of our patrol duties, and we quietly slipped our wires and shaped course for Malta. On the way we did our quarterly full power trial, which was designed to produce the makers guaranteed speed.

To be in *Hood* when she was at speed was quite an experience. At about 28 knots or over, the bow waves caused fountains to shoot up each anchor hawsepipe; while the wash from her bows broke on-board at the forward end of the quarterdeck and washed aft to join the high pile up at her stern. In the bright Mediterranean sunlight, these fountains gave off the brilliant rainbow effect of the spectrum, in a kaleidoscope of colour, the falling water bouncing off the deck like a shower of diamonds scintillating in the sun.

The ship reached 31.5 knots and it gave one a thrill to see the deep blue of the sea thrown up into boiling, brilliant white foam as we sped along. After four hours, we began to ease down until our speed had dropped to 15 knots, and we resumed our more leisurely way towards Malta.

Passing the island of Pantalleria, we entered the last leg of our passage to Valletta and soon we saw the familiar slender masts of Rinella W/T Station and the dreaming spires and domes of the many churches in the island.

Due to her length, *Hood* had a special problem in entering the Grand Harbour. We had been allocated a berth in Bighi Bay, just below the R.N. Hospital. As this billet was almost a sharp left turn inside the entrance, and since the entrance itself was rather narrow, the ship had to enter bows first, then turning to starboard in her own length, proceed dead slow ahead towards the shore, until her stern lined up with the stern buoy; then, reversing engines, she would go astern gradually bringing her bows around to starboard until she came to rest dead between her mooring buoys.

It was a masterpiece in big ship handling in a confined space. We expected that at our first attempt there would have been some difficulty in manoeuvring so long a vessel, but our skipper brought *Hood* in as if she had been a destroyer with all the room in the world to play with. We were most impressed with his skill at ship handling.

We spent the next few weeks working up to Fleet standard, and carrying out firing programmes, then we were detached from the Mediterranean to attend King George VI's Coronation Review at Spithead. This made a welcome break for the ship's company as they were able to visit their homes for a brief spell.

During the review, *Hood*, in common with the rest of the fleet, illuminated ship each night. As torpedomen, responsible for the electrical installation of the ship, this job was dropped in our lap. We outlined the silhouette of the ship with lamps, and a large Royal Cypher GV1R was constructed and suspended half way between the after funnel and the mainmast. We also created our Vice Admiral's flag in lights and this was hoisted to the top of the mainmast. The whole effect was like something out of Fairyland. *Hood* cast her reflection on the water like jewels on rippled velvet. We also gave a searchlight display in company with the whole fleet and followed it up with a gigantic firework display.

After the review, *Hood* returned to the Mediterranean, when, completing a further period of Spanish Patrol Duty, we sailed for Malta. Harry, my shore going pal was drafted to *Barham* so I saw little of him, although we kept in touch by means of fleet letter whenever our two ships happened to be in company, and in this way we managed a few trips ashore.

About this time I became on friendly terms with Doug, who was a wireless operator. The "Sparks" mess was on the same messdeck as ours, and sometimes we would take a walk on deck together. Whether there was something about me which invited confidences I do not know, but Doug used to pour out all his troubles in my ear, and gradually we got on shore going terms.

He was more like Snowy than Harry had been, preferring the bright lights and cabarets to the quiet places. It was like old times again. We went swimming together at weekends, followed by an evening down the "Gut". In Doug's company I began to enjoy life again.

I changed my job onboard from Torpedo maintenance to ventilating fan maintenance which was a watchkeeping job, necessitating a visit to every running fan in the ship during one's period of duty. These large fan motors provide the forced ventilation between decks, some being supply fans and others exhaust. It was essential that the lubrication and the electrics of each fan be checked during each watch. As there were hundreds of these fans of all shapes and sizes and in various awkward positions, it took one the whole of one's four hour watch to get around them all.

With the watch-keeping job, one also enjoyed the privilege of watchkeeper's leave, which meant that, providing one returned on-board four hours before one commenced duty, one could lie abed late when on shore leave. Both Doug and I had watchkeeping jobs, so we were both able to enjoy this privilege.

In our runs ashore, Doug and I always included a visit to the "Forty Three" club in Floriana. We usually started here, before proceeding along the Strada Reale to the "Gut". This club was run by a man of about 40, known to all the fleet as "Charlie". He was a female impersonator, who when dressed up, resembled Mae West and took that famous lady off to a "T".

Charlie's pianist was a youth of about 19, named Jackie, whose ability on the piano must have put him among the concert pianist class, had he so desired. Both Doug and I were fond of good music, and between Charlie's tonsorial expeditions, we used to get Jackie to play the more serious stuff. It was an education to hear this lad render Beethoven's "Moonlight Sonata" or "Liebestraum", or perhaps, some of Chopin's delightful piano pieces. During the breathless magic of his playing, one could hear a pin drop, and when he had finished, the large room would echo with the thunderous applause from the men of the fleet, and there were many, for the "Forty Three" club was extremely popular.

Charlie's own *pièce-de-résistance* was a rendering of "September in the Rain" and "Pennies from Heaven". Dressed like Mae West, padded out around the bust and wearing a fabulous silver lamé gown and a blonde wig, he sang amid the cheers of the audience. Usually the lads quietened down as Charlie's voice came to be appreciated and he always received a tumultuous reception.

Sometimes we would take a bus or taxi over to Sliema, and visit one or two of the bars. These were mainly patronized by the destroyer men, since Sliema Creek was the destroyer anchorage. One bar in particular, the "Empire", staged a female boxing contest as their cabaret show, and we sailors would be treated to an orgy of boxing contests. The contenders, dressed in one piece swim suits, wore a coloured sash cross their chests indicating a "Miss England" or a "Miss Austria" or some other nationality. Although to watch two buxom wenches knocking each other about seemed pretty revolting to us, most of us cheered them on as we sipped our iced beer, but the atmosphere was so clouded with tobacco smoke that it was sometimes difficult to see the contenders at all!

Malta provided some pretty hilarious nights, which will long live in my memory and no doubt, in the memories of hundreds of thousands of sailors the world over. We owed a lot to the patience and kindness of "Joe", the average Maltese lodging house and bar keeper, who on numerous occasions, would help the worse for wear matelots to bed.

After a night ashore, we would both get up about 10.30 a.m. and after washing and dressing, go and have a rum and coffee and a light snack in a bar near the waterfront. Then strolling along the road to the Custom House, we would catch the ship's picket boat, which was sent in at 11.30 a.m. to pick up the stewards and postman. It was a grand life and we both appreciated it.

On nights when we were not ashore, Doug and I slept on the upper deck under the huge forecastle awning. We both had camp beds and we would lie and watch the signal lamp high up on the mast of the Castille Signal Station, flashing its messages to the fleet lying in the Grand Harbour. It was the limit of our vision, before the awning blotted out the stars. It was pleasant lying there listening to the bells of the horse drawn carozzins or gharries, as we usually called them and watching the lights of the waterfront bars and cafes ashore and the bobbing lights of the dghaisas going about their business. We would talk until the lights ashore began to go out one by one, and soon we ourselves would grow tired and fall asleep.

I was usually awake long before the hands were called. The angle of the early morning sun caused its brilliant rays to slant under the awning and bore into my eyes like a golden avalanche. One stirred and was wide awake immediately. The freshness of the early Mediterranean morning was intoxicating. The air was like wine and, like a rich vintage, one sniffed it appreciatively. In that half hour or so before "Reveillle", I would stretch luxuriously and let my thoughts run riot, while Doug and the rest of those sleeping on deck still snored.

I could hear the endless chatter of the dghaisamen as they cleaned and polished their boats and, in the distance, the deep tone of church bells calling their early devotees to prayer. The Maltese are a very religious people and the numerous church bells, with their varied tones, was a common everyday feature of life in the island. Most sailors hated the perpetual ringing, but to me they were Malta, Citadel of Christendom and home of the Knights of St. John of Jerusalem. But perhaps I was prejudiced for I loved this ancient island.

In due course we went off on our Summer Cruise around the Greek Islands, to Athens, the Adriatic and Palestine, calling at the French Foreign Legion base at Arzieu on the North African coast. We saw the glorious Acropolis at Athens, the modern towns of Haifa and Jaffa and the many glories of ancient Greece spread over the host of islands in the Aegean Sea.

We had our swimming and sailing parties and our trips ashore here and there, finally arriving back in Malta in early October, when *Hood* went into the floating dock for the periodical bottom scrape and paint and the overhaul of our underwater fittings.

Our story of Malta over the October – January period, followed the usual fleet pattern of refit, docking, painting and relaxation ashore in the cabarets, cinemas and cafes. Doug and I had a couple of pleasant months together, going ashore and enjoying ourselves before the Spring Cruise began, although for *Hood* this turned out to be another period of Spanish Patrol duty.

Shortly before we sailed, Doug was drafted to the destroyer leader *Hardy* and I saw very little of him afterwards. I missed him of course, but thereafter, when going ashore, I usually picked a casual friend to go with. It was not quite the same, since Doug and I had been together for a year and we each knew the other's likes and dislikes and we always got on so well together, but navy life is like this; friends come and go and one has to make the best of it.

We arrived at Gibraltar and relieved *Repulse*, who then proceeded on her courtesy cruise of the French and Italian ports. For the next six weeks we oscillated between Gibraltar, Tangier, Palma and Marseilles.

At Tangier, we were in company with the German *Graf Spee* and French and Italian naval vessels. It was interesting to note that when ashore, it was always the Germans and ourselves who seemed to fraternize and seldom, if ever, the other two nationalities. We maintained that it was because the Germans and ourselves were beer drinking types, whereas the others usually drank wine.

We had a party of officers over from *Graf Spee* to visit us. They lunched onboard and were shown over the ship. Whilst touring the vessel one of the Germans remarked on the absence of an armoured deck. Well he might, for this vital fact was to contribute, in my opinion, to *Hood's* downfall three years later and at the hands of the Germans!

After our spell of Patrol duty, we commenced our visit to the Riviera ports, visiting Mentone, Juan-les-Pins and other popular watering places before returning to Malta in April.

During our spell in Valletta, we went to sea on odd days for full calibre firing practices, using the radio controlled battleship *Centurion* as a target. On this particular occasion we took the C-in-C, Sir Dudley Pound out with us, to witness the shoot. As sometimes happens, when one wants things to go right, this time everything went wrong! But, after a series of irritating delays, we began the run in for the opening phase of the firing.

Centurion was controlled by the destroyer *Shikari* who took up her station some half a mile astern of her charge. By some error in the setting of the fire control instruments, our opening salvo of 5.5" shells passed between *Shikari's* funnels, causing a frantic exchange of signals.

I was on deck watching the firing, and looking at the direction in which the guns were pointing, it was obvious that it was not going to be *Centurion* who was going to receive our bricks. Why this simple observation was not also noticed by the gunnery people, heaven only knows, but it was a very long time before they lived it down. History does not record what the C-in-C might have said!

While we were enjoying the short stay in Malta, the international situation was building up in Europe. With Hitler's impossible demands, it was becoming obvious, even to us, that before long, Germany would be challenged into a position where she would either have to fight or back down.

At about this time the Italian Fleet paid a courtesy visit to the island. As the Italians had allied themselves to the Germans, they were no longer popular with either us or the Maltese people, and there were fears on the part of the powers that be as to whether there would be incidents when the Italians were ashore. However, sailors the world over, have a knack of conveniently sweeping under the carpet any political rumpus, as having nothing to do with them; and so it was with us. There was time to worry when a war actually started!

With their piano accordions and mandolins, the Italians spent quite a few happy evenings in the bars of Malta. I know, for I was in their company with a lot more of our men, singing away with them, and we all thoroughly enjoyed ourselves. On this occasion, Hitler and Mussolini were consigned to the dustbin!

The visit was a huge success, and in due course they left, leaving us with very pleasant memories, – International situation or no International situation! Not long after their departure, we too sailed for the Western Mediterranean and the Spanish Patrol.

During our stay in Malta we had a change in command. Our old skipper, Captain Pridham, returned to the U.K. and Captain H.T.C. Walker took over. He was a very much alive skipper, despite the fact that he had lost an arm at Zeebrugge in 1918. Naturally, he came to be known as Hooky!

We continued our patrol until the end of August, when the international situation began to burst at the seams, and by September the Government had begun to mobilize the Reserve Fleet and R.M.S.*Aquitania* was on her way to Gibraltar full of Naval Reservists for the fleet.

The German pocket battleship *Graf Spee* or *Deutchland* (I am not sure which) had slipped away from Gibraltar and was somewhere in the Atlantic. In order to protect *Aquitania*, in the event of hostilities, *Hood* slid quietly out into the Atlantic with a destroyer escort, and making contact with the liner, brought her safely into Gibraltar Bay.

All the world knows of how the Prime Minister, Neville Chamberlain, bought us a year of time at Munich, and so ended the September crisis of 1938. The ships dispersed and *Hood* returned once more to Malta.

We stayed in Valletta through October, November and December, enjoying the fruits of the land. Since Doug had left, I did not have a permanent friend, but nevertheless I had several trips ashore with this one and that.

Hood's commission was now drawing to a close and rumour had it that we were leaving for home in the New Year. I had now taken over another watchkeeping duty, this time in the ship's Main Switchboard, where for 24 hours at a time, in four hourly shifts, I worked with three others in controlling the ship's electrical installation. It was an interesting job, and I liked it, particularly as it also carried the late morning leave privilege with it.

Apart from our change of Commanding Officers, we also had a change of Flag Officers. Due to Vice-Admiral Blake retiring for health reasons, we had Vice Admiral Geoffrey Layton to replace him for a short while, then he too, in his turn, was replaced by Vice Admiral A.B.Cunningham, or "Cutts" as he was popularly known, and we managed to keep him until the commission ended.

Rumour proved correct about our supposed movements and in January, 1939, *Hood* left Malta for Portsmouth, where we gave leave to the ship's company. This was my last contact with Malta. To my regret, I have never returned; but my seven years in the Mediterranean I shall always remember, as possibly some of the happiest years of my life, and Malta I will never forget.

The Spring passed and our ship's company had all returned from their foreign service leave, and we were expecting to "Pay Off" and be sent back to the Depot. The international situation at this period was so tense and doubtful that it was decided to keep *Hood* in commission, and only a handful of ratings were drafted to the various schools to qualify for higher Gunnery, Torpedo or Signal ratings.

I had applied to qualify for Leading Torpedoman, but our Torpedo Officer had stopped me going on the grounds that I was considered one of the "Key" ratings, whom it was advisable to retain, since the switchboard required experienced operators. I had to accept this with the promise that my turn would come when circumstances permitted.

About June, we managed to get in some Summer leave for both watches of the crew, which took us into July. During this time, the Dockyard had seen to our defect lists, and we re-painted the ship in dark Home Fleet grey, to the disgust of most of us, me in particular. We topped up with stores, oil, provisions and ammunition and, at the end of August we sailed for Northern waters, during which journey we conducted a shadowing exercise in the area between Scapa Flow and the coast of Norway.

We were under no illusion as to the prevailing situation. There was little doubt in our minds that within days we would probably be at war, but it was hard to believe that it could happen to us. A few months ago we were enjoying ourselves in Malta now we were on the verge of a holocaust. After the exercise, we and the rest of the fleet passed through the boom defence gates of Scapa Flow, where 25 years earlier, another, but mightier fleet had taken up its war station.

On almost the last day of August, *Hood* and her destroyer escort of three, sailed from Scapa Flow, out into the westering sun; and, as we watched the low hills of the Orkneys turn to purple and slowly dip below the horizon, we knew in our hearts that when next we saw them, we would be a country at war.

On September the first, while cruising somewhere in the North Atlantic, we received news that Germany had invaded Poland at dawn, and that Britain had issued her ultimatum which expired at 11 a.m. on the 3rd September.

On receiving this information we realized that it could now only be a matter of hours before the balloon would go up. Our ship's company had taken up cruising stations and our shell was fuzed. Our torpedoes had their war heads fitted, and in all respects we were ready. We did not have long to wait. On Sunday morning, the 3rd September at about 11.20 a.m. we gathered around the loudspeakers (I, with a few pals and our Torpedo Officer, was listening to a portable radio belonging to one of our torpedomen) and heard the weak and utterly weary voice of Mr. Chamberlain bring Britain into war with Germany.

It was a relief. Now we knew where we were going. However long and difficult the road ahead, we had to get to the end. And so *Hood* and her company went to war.

H.M.S. *Hood*

'*Torpedoman*', H.M.S. *Hood*

H.M.S. *HOOD* 1939 – 1941

Part 2.

Latitude 63 deg. 20 min North

Longitude 31 deg. 50 min West

To a shipmate

"Yours were the stars, the sea, the earth,
The soft warm winds, and the Northern Lights.
Now your fair substance lies in tidal waters clear
Trapped in flooded steel for all eternity."

"You had your dreams, your youth, your hopes.
Ere ship met ship at dawn off Cape Farewell.
Forever now, your body, washed by northern seas
Shall rest, a priceless jewel in Neptune's crown."

"One day, perhaps, a saner world will find your ocean grave.
A torn and riven hull; and wonder at the madness of an age
Which squandered youth and brilliance such as yours."

Chapter Nine

H.M.S. *HOOD*

<u>1939 – 1941</u>

After hearing the declaration of war, we sat for a while around the portable radio. We were sitting on ventilators, boat's crutches or anything else available, for we were up on the boat deck.

It was a fine morning, with the ship lazily lifting her bows to the long Atlantic swell. Over on the port beam steamed one of our escort. I watched the thin spiral of smoke languidly rising from the destroyer's galley funnel, while the brilliance of this September morning warmed my bones.

I saw her crew going about their duties on the upper deck, and the forecastle gun's crew huddled behind their gun shield. Every now and then she would dip her bows to the swell and, occasionally, a sea would break onboard to sweep aft in a shower of spray which sparkled in the sunlight like cascading diamonds. It was a day to be at sea. Only one thought marred the peaceful scene and beauty of the morning. Somewhere beneath this heaving ocean, enemy submarines were at their war stations, and we were a prize target.

As a single man with no responsibilities, I received the news with a certain amount of indifference. I was annoyed, of course, because the tenor of my life was now about to be disturbed, which was, I suppose, a selfish way of looking at it. There was the other side to be considered too – for years we had trained for just such a possibility as this, now it was up to us to see that the taxpayer got a return for his money.

I tried to assess my ability to face up to the new situation. I knew my limits under normal conditions, but how would I react under war conditions, possible action, with all it could mean? I tried to detach myself like a shadow, and study myself from a position outside. "Will you be afraid", I asked myself, "Or will you be the stuff of which heroes are made?" I am afraid all of us asked ourselves similar questions and, like myself, received the same answer – "Wait and see!"

After all the bulletins on the radio had finished, there was a long silence, then we began to discuss our possible part in the war. We went on talking until the hands were piped to dinner, then, going below, we partook of our first war time Sunday dinner. At least the news had not affected our appetites.

Now the war had started, each of us took stock of our situation. From now on we had to be very particular about closing and properly clipping all watertight doors and hatches behind us. There was that little extra alertness and awareness about us as we went about our tasks. We all carried inflatable lifebelts everywhere we went. These were like motor car inner tubes, covered with a light canvas material and fitted with a harness and a non return valve for inflation purposes. It was advisable, if one was obliged to abandon the ship, to blow up the lifebelt first, as it was almost impossible to do so when in the water.

One of the first things I did was to provide myself with an electric torch and a whistle, the latter I tied to my lifebelt. It was obvious to me that if the ship received damage sufficient to sink her, then it was practically certain that all the lights and power would fail, therefore one had to find one's way out of the ship. Then, once in the water, particularly at night, it was essential to attract attention. Hence the torch and whistle.

My job was still at the Main Switchboard, although my action station was in the engine room attending one of the dynamo supply breakers. It was not a comforting thought to realize that the switchboard was well down in the bowels of the ship, and directly over the forward 15" magazines; and that in order to get out, one had to squeeze through numerous manholes, (fitted in the armoured hatch covers) just large enough to pass one's body through. But we did not think long about such things. We just hoped that nothing unpleasant would happen to us.

Whilst the phoney war was going on in France and the R.A.F. were plastering the Germans with leaflets, the war at sea began immediately, and before the first day was over the liner *Athenia* had been torpedoed and sunk in the Atlantic. Our new Captain, Irvine

Glennie, broadcast the news to us over the ship's loudspeaker system, with a few choice comments of his own.

Athenia's loss served to bring us all down to earth. We now knew that we were dealing with the same old Hun that our fathers had known. These people were inhuman monsters. There was no possible excuse for sinking *Athenia*. She was carrying passengers, of whom a large percentage were women and children. We were very bitter about this outrage, and it left us resolved, more than ever, to settle Germany's hash once and for all.

After about two more days we returned to Scapa Flow to re-fuel. I think the only reason we had gone to sea was to keep clear of Scapa Flow when war was declared, in case of a concentrated air attack on the anchorage. Whilst at Scapa we had several air raid alerts, but apart from one of our own aircraft which was fired on by shore batteries for approaching the Flow from the wrong direction, we had little interference at this time.

Towards the end of September, one of our submarines, H.M.S. *Spearfish* was heavily depth-charged whilst on patrol in the Heligoland bight. The damage sustained was such that she was unable to dive and could only proceed on the surface at a reduced speed.

The Commander-in-Chief, Admiral Sir Charles Forbes, decided to take the entire Fleet to Heligoland on a rescue operation, presumably also, in the hope of catching any German vessels who may be tempted to interfere with *Spearfish*.

It was a big decision to take, for the area concerned was right on Germany's doorstep. However, we in the navy have a reputation for looking after our own, and we soon found ourselves headed in a south easterly direction towards *Spearfish*.

When the fleet first arrived in the Bight, *Spearfish* was slowly struggling homewards but was constantly in danger of air attack. Whereas a solitary submarine could possibly have avoided detection, a fleet, spread over several miles of ocean, certainly could not. It was not long, therefore, before we were spotted by a German patrol aircraft and our position duly reported to its base. We could now expect severe air attacks. We were not disappointed! Within a short space of time the fleet was attacked by bombers coming down out of the sun, for it was a beautiful day, with a smooth sea. *Hood* being positioned well out on the screen, was not immediately involved. The carrier *Ark Royal* was severely bombed, and at times, was completely obliterated by smoke and bomb splashes. Because of her virtual disappearance in smoke and spray, the pilot of the aircraft concerned, claimed *Ark Royal* as sunk, and we later learned that he was awarded the Iron Cross for his "brilliant feat", and made a national hero. The truth was, *Ark Royal* was not even hit, and suffered no damage whatsoever. For months afterwards, the enemy maintained that she had been sunk and repeatedly asked over their propaganda radio, "Where is your *Ark Royal?*"

Our AA gunners in *Hood* had a grandstand view, since we were some five miles away from the main attack. Then quite suddenly, without any noise or other warning, a Dornier bomber approached *Hood* from astern, and out of the sun. As it passed over our mainmast, it dropped a fair sized bomb. Not satisfied with this, the pilot waved his hand as he sped by. Fortunately, the missile bounced off the ship and struck the water about fifteen feet off our port beam. It blew a hole in our torpedo protection bulge, but apart from scattering the tiles in the stoker's bathroom and covering with debris and dust the repair party stationed there, it did little damage and no casualties were incurred.

So sudden had been the attack, we had not even been able to fire a shot. Captain Glennie immediately broadcast orders that the gun's crews were, in future, to open fire without awaiting for orders. This had been a lesson to us. We were still versed in the peacetime practice procedure, where one waited for orders before opening fire on the target. We had got off lightly on this occasion but there was to be no further dallying and the skipper made this point quite clear.

The attacks on the fleet eased off on the approach of darkness, and finally ceased altogether, and we made our way homewards, escorting the badly damaged *Spearfish.* We had been very lucky this day, for we were all intact. It had been our first brush with the Luftwaffe and, whilst we now knew their fibre, we had also found the chinks in our own armour.

Returning to Scapa, *Hood* re-fuelled and after a day or so, sailed for what was to become our regular patrol area; that cold, sometimes misty stretch of water between Greenland and Iceland, the Denmark Straits. Here *Hood* enacted most of her war service and finally found her grave.

We always hoped that sooner or later, we would catch an enemy raider trying to break out into the Atlantic, and in the effort of doing this, we spent countless hours on watch, in exposed positions, in all sorts of beastly weather, straining our eyes due to long periods of looking through high powered binoculars.

At night the crew went to Defence Stations and my station in this particular organization was the searchlight control sight on the starboard wing of the bridge. Two of us shared this duty and high up on the open sweep of the bridge wings, we felt the full blast of the icy wind. Muffled up to the ears in woollies, we braced ourselves against the bitter elements and swept the tumbled horizon with our binoculars.

For four hours at a stretch we shared this duty, working in conjunction with each other so that one of us could squeeze under the bridge platform for a cup of hot cocoa and a temporary respite from the freezing wind. Always we had to be in the immediate vicinity of the searchlight control position, and always it was bitterly cold.

Far below us we could hear the swish of the sea as it broke against our huge hull, whilst above us, the heavens spread wide in a black velvety void, on which lay a million brilliant, scintillating stars; bigger and brighter than any I had seen before.

Those short, star spangled nights in the Denmark Straits will always live in my memory. The sharp, biting, salty wind, beating relentlessly against one's face, and finding every loophole in one's clothing; and the brilliant display of the Aurora Borealis, weaving across the heavens like a gigantic silvery fan, was an artistic feast to delight one's red rimmed eyes.

After four hours in the crisp, cold night air, one's watch is over and, still wide awake – for the air is like wine – we are relieved by the morning watch, and we tumble down below to get a cup of thick steaming cocoa before retiring on the mess table for what is left of the night.

We had our false alarms, like the occasion when we almost sent a 15" broadside into a peculiar cloud formation on the horizon, which looked for all the world like a squadron of ships.

Patrol after patrol we endured this existence, until, with the approach of summer and the entry of Italy into the war, we were transferred to the Mediterranean and to better and warmer operating conditions. But this was to come later.

Returning from this patrol, *Hood* was diverted to Loch Ewe on the north western corner of Scotland, where, on our arrival, we found the rest of the fleet. It appeared that, whilst we had been away, a "U" Boat had managed to penetrate the net defence of Scapa Flow and had sunk the *Royal Oak*, with the loss of approximately 800 lives. The fleet therefore, found an alternative base whilst the defences of Scapa were overhauled.

Loch Ewe, while being a fine natural harbour for the fleet was far from being ideal for the personnel. The only civilization was a small village containing one small pub to cater for the whole of the fleet! In view of this, leave was restricted to only 25% of each crew per day and then only for about five hours.

Since the tiny pub could only hold about forty people, it was allocated for the use of Chief and Petty Officers only, but junior rates could buy their beer through a side window and sit on the hillside and drink it. Glasses were at a premium, so Jack, not to be denied his beer, bought up all the galvanized buckets in the local hardware store and men could be seen tottering up the hill carrying bucketfuls of beer, until stocks exhausted, the publican had to frantically telephone to the nearest town for further supplies. Some months later, NAAFI erected a temporary canteen, but those first few weeks at Lock Ewe were murder.

After a few days break, *Hood* again sailed north for the Denmark Straits, and with the winter on us, we experienced icy gales and fog, which made night watches in the open positions extremely uncomfortable. To combat the bitter weather, I wore on top of my overall suit, a sweater, overcoat and an oilskin over the top. Balaclava helmet and gloves finished it off.

Most of these woollen garments were knitted and sent to the fleet by kindly souls at home, who, by so doing, were helping the war effort in the only way they could. Let me assure them that we seamen, blessed them for their efforts. I know I did, for the Denmark Straits in winter is not a nice place to know.

Our patrol lasted fourteen days and we returned, this time to Greenock on the Clyde. It seemed that every time we returned from a patrol we saw *Rodney* and *Nelson* peacefully at anchor in the harbour. This would irritate the ship's company no end. However, we all realized that there was no point in these slow vessels sharing our patrol duty, since high speed would be required against any enemy vessel trying to break through the Denmark Straits and both *Rodney* and her sister were only capable of about 23 knots flat out. Most of their work consisted of convoy protection. Many is the time I have heard one or the other of our crew remark, "I see those two fat baskets are swinging around on their milk tins again!" It is rather ironic, therefore, that it was *Rodney* more than any other ship, which finally battered *Bismarck* into a flaming wreck, thereby avenging *Hood*, and that she had left a convoy to be able to do so.

After a further trip, this time half way across the Atlantic to escort the Canadian Troop convoy home to Britain, *Hood* was detached with orders to proceed to Devonport for a brief refit and boiler cleaning. Proceeding down the Irish Sea, we arrived in Plymouth Sound and went into the Dockyard. Our ship's company being able to snatch ten days leave, one watch at a time.

This was our first visit south since the blackout came into being and to find one's way around Devonport at night, when not very familiar with the place, was quite an experience.

I was in the second watch for leave, but was recalled to the ship when only half way through it. This was due to the Armed Merchant cruiser *Rawalpindi* being sunk in an engagement with German cruisers.

I was in a Portsmouth cinema when the telegram was received by my mother, who arranged with the manager to have my name and address projected onto the screen. The slide was superimposed on the film being shown, and to my surprise, I saw it appear on the side of a flying boat, which, on the film was being launched down a slope. Leaving the cinema, I met my mother at the Box Office and she handed me the recall telegram.

I hastily packed my few things, and taking a packet of sandwiches with me, I kissed mother goodbye and took a bus to the station, where I found about two hundred others from *Hood* and a special train laid on to return us to Plymouth.

On arriving at Plymouth, we discovered that *Hood* had already been moved out from Devonport Dockyard and was anchored in the Sound with a full head of steam. We sailed with about a hundred and fifty of our crew still on leave, most of them key gunnery ratings. The local depot hurriedly drafted a like number of men to us before we sailed, but, on sorting them out we found they were mostly stokers.

We left Plymouth Sound in what, in my view, was some of the worst weather I have ever experienced. It was vile, with high winds and mountainous seas which for all her forty two thousand tons, threw *Hood* about like a shuttlecock.

In this operation, we were accompanied by the French battleship *Dunkerque*, one or two French destroyers and our own destroyer escort, which in the prevailing weather, were having a bad time of it; so much so, that the French Admiral, who was in charge of the operation, ordered them to return to base until the weather moderated.

Our job was to hunt down and destroy the *Rawalpindi*'s adversaries, but in weather like this, it was a hopeless task; besides which, we did not know whether they had broken out into the Atlantic, or returned to Germany, which was more likely on account of the alarm raised by their sinking of the *Rawalpindi*.

Unknown to me at this time, *Hood* was being filmed by a news-reel cameraman on one of the escorting vessels, showing how we were being buffeted by the high seas. I mention this, because when the film was shown in the cinemas later on, it was seen by a certain young lady, who, taking pity on we poor sailors, wrote to our Paymaster and asked for the name of a sailor to whom she could send magazines and sweets etc. Out of our company of some one thousand and four hundred men, he picked my name. That lovely girl is now my wife and I have been happy ever since, KISMET!

The search for the enemy vessels proved fruitless, and after a week we returned to the Clyde for a few days rest and to have a temporary degaussing circuit fitted to counter magnetic mines.

During our brief stay at Greenock, our ship's company were allowed ashore until about 10.30 p.m. one watch each night. It was an education to watch the scramble back onboard, particularly in the black-out. The landing place for libertymen was the inner harbour, and the motor fishing vessels, used to convey libertymen ashore, had to tie up alongside the jetty wall, and large wooden ladders were then laid against the wall and the men climbed out of the boat. There was a considerable difference in height between high and low tide in the Clyde area, and when the lads began to come back from leave, some of them the worse for wear, and singing their heads off, it proved quite an evolution to get them safely down the steep ladders and into the boat.

Captain Glennie, being a wise gentleman, and knowing the ways of sailors, had told the ship's company that he did not mind how his lads got back on board, provided that they DID get back. "I do not wish to go to sea in an emergency with any of my crew missing" he warned us. Consequently, many and varied were the conditions the sailors were in when we finally got them onboard. On one occasion we lowered a steel provisioning net into the liberty boat and, loading the helpless ones carefully into it, hoisted them inboard with the main derrick. However, I cannot remember us ever letting the skipper down, we always sailed with a full crew.

As soon as our degaussing circuit was fitted, we once more sailed for the Denmark Straits. During this patrol we received the news of the brilliant River Plate action, which bucked us up no end. Apart from the atrocious weather; snow, blizzards, fog and rough seas, the patrol was uneventful, although we had to keep a sharp lookout, because it was during such weather that escapes through the Straits were most likely.

Living as we did, cheek by jowl, in close contact with each other, often led to strong friendships. The sort of relationships not found amongst men in civilian life, where friends meet only occasionally and where lives are lived in separate houses. Here, we lived together as a giant family. We knew each other's failings and weaknesses, and liked each other in spite of them. We slept in close proximity, in swaying hammocks. We even bathed together in communal bathrooms. In fact we lived candidly with one another, accepting the rough with the smooth.

This sharing and living together, forged a comradeship which one can never find in civilian life. Nor was the ship herself left out of our lives, for everything we did was for her. On our smartness, the way we dressed, in fact everything we did, depended our ship's efficiency rating in the fleet. She was our constant taskmistress. While we could, and often did, call her all the rough names under the sun when things went wrong, heaven help those, not of our company, who tried to do the same.

This is the team spirit we miss when we leave the service, for it is something very fine. Something which, through countless ages, has scaled the highest mountains; fought and won the hopeless battles, and has made the Royal Navy the finest influence on international affairs the world has ever seen.

As one would expect, the first few months of the war revealed loopholes in our fighting efficiency. Reports were received by the Admiralty from various ships who had received damage in action. This information was thoroughly gone into by experts and various remedies were produced, which were put out in fleet orders. For instance, it was found that a "close by" underwater explosion caused messdeck steel ladders to jolt out of their housings, thereby crashing to the deck and preventing escape to the upper deck. To overcome this, we fitted all such ladders with wire strops, shackled to the ship's structure, so that if the ladder lifted out of its housing, the strop prevented it falling to the deck.

Other ships had reported that "Near Miss" explosions caused the dynamo supply switches to be automatically thrown off due to shock, thereby plunging the entire ship into darkness, and bringing all ventilation and auxiliary machinery to a standstill.

This meant that should it become necessary for the crew to abandon the ship, they would have extreme difficulty in finding the ladders and escape routes, apart from the additional hazards of falling kit lockers, loose equipment and the possible acute angle of the listing ship.

We adopted two cures for this trouble. First, we drilled the covers of all the dynamo switches and fitted a bolt into the hole, which penetrated the insulated part of the switch arm thereby locking the switch in the "ON" position. This of course, upset the overload safety arrangement, but the risk had to be accepted. Secondly, we fitted automatic electric battery lanterns, which, when the mains failed, the battery took over and automatically lit the lamp. These were placed in strategic positions throughout the ship, such as near ladders, hatchways and corridors.

At this period, I had recently been promoted to Leading Seaman, and was put in charge of all the electrical emergency circuits, which included these auto lanterns, temporary circuits, sick bay operating lamps etc. I had an assistant and it was a full time job, for we had some seven hundred of these auto lanterns alone to check over and maintain. They had to be kept charged up and periodically tested to see that the relays did not stick. In view of what happened later, it was heartbreaking to know that no opportunity was given to the ship's company to make use of these safety arrangements when trouble did come.

In a tremendous flash, a split second of searing time, *Hood* was gone, rendering all our efforts null and void. After serving for four and a half years in the ship I knew every compartment, nut and bolt in her. I can almost picture the terrible scene between decks when that fatal shell struck. The gigantic sheets of golden cordite flame sweeping through the narrow corridors and passages, incinerating everything in its path. The terrific hot blast, the bursting open of the armoured hull under the colossal pressure; and finally, the merciful avalanche of the cold sea, cleansing the charred and riven wreck, and bringing peace to those gallant souls I knew so well. On more than one occasion I have dreamed this scene and have returned to consciousness with the thought that "There, but for the Grace of God went I."

We continued the Northern Patrol duty into 1940, usually working fourteen days at a time on patrol with a week in port in between. Then, about the beginning of April, we again went to Devonport Dockyard to have our obsolete 5.5" guns removed and twin mounted dual purpose 4" guns installed in their place. We also gave our ship's company fourteen days leave. Once again I had second leave, and during the second week went to Wembley and met my "Girl of the Storm" and spent a wonderful week, becoming engaged before returning on board.

During this refit period at Devonport, life for those left onboard was most uncomfortable. The Dockyardmen were working day and night, getting the old guns out and putting the new twin mountings in. The clattering of the riveting hammers kept us from getting any sleep and it was a frequent occurrence to have a shower of red-hot fragments and sparks descend on one's dinner when sitting at the mid-day meal, where the white hot giant rivets, holding down new mountings, came through the deck head.

During this period, Germany was carrying out the conquest of Norway, and volunteers were called for to man our 3.7" howitzer and to take it over to Norway. In the confusion and the retreat, the gun was left behind and it was only with great difficulty that our men got back. So ended our efforts at playing soldiers.

As soon as our refit came to an end, *Hood* (complete with fourteen new 4" guns in seven twin mountings) sailed for the Mersey, and went into the Gladstone dock at Liverpool for a bottom scrape and the supposed fitting of an armour bomb proof deck. In actual fact, we only managed the bottom scrape, because in early June, Italy came into the war and we were hurriedly re-floated and sent post haste to Gibraltar, where we formed and became the first flagship of the famous FORCE "H", with Admiral Sir James Somerville as our Flag Officer.

"Force H", as far as my memory goes, consisted of *Hood, Valiant, Ark Royal, Resolution,* two cruisers I cannot remember, and the necessary destroyer escorts, the whole being based on Gibraltar. It was not an ideal base in war time, because Algiciras, being in neutral Spain and only about five miles across the bay from Gibraltar, still had an active German and Italian Consulate. With a pair of prismatic binoculars, one could spot every movement made by our ships, so we had to use every ruse and tactic to fool these Diplomatic gentlemen across the water. More than once, when leaving Gibraltar in daylight, we steered westwards through the straits, only to reverse our course after dark and re-enter the Mediterranean at speed.

Whenever we berthed in Gibraltar harbour, we always had a battle practice target moored alongside our seaward side. This was done to take the blast of any torpedo fired from such enterprising submarine as may risk a shot through the breakwater entrance.

Also at this time there were rumours going about that German engineers were installing 11"guns at Algiciras, with the view to placing a few well directed salvoes in our midst should Spain decide to abandon her neutrality. To enable us to make a quick getaway in the event of this happening, we arranged our berthing wires in such a way that they could be slipped immediately if the emergency arose. It never did.

After the weather conditions we had put up with in the Denmark Straits during the past winter, it was a relief to be in the Mediterranean. To me, it was very familiar territory, for I loved this inland sea. It was full of history and intrigue. There was not a mile of its coastline which could not, over the centuries, have told its own tale of courage, cruelty, adventure and romance. Now, here were we, to add further lustre to its story, or so we hoped, for we were thin in numbers, and our adversaries very fresh.

Whilst at Gibraltar the ship's company were allowed to swim in the harbour every evening between 5 and 6 p.m. Religiously, every night at 6 p.m. sharp, and just as we were finishing our swim, an

Italian spotting plane came over the harbour for a look around. After about ten minutes of circling the Rock, he would buzz off home. He came to be known to us as "George", and his regular appearances were our signal to get out of the water and back onboard, for we never knew what might follow his spying.

TRAGEDY AT ORAN

About this time, France capitulated, leaving the Allied naval situation in desperate straits. Our Navy would now have to cover areas normally protected by the French in addition to our own heavy commitment. There was also the very big risk that the Germans or Italians would take over the French Fleet, which consisted of some very fine modern and fast ships. To allow them to do this would be to change the whole naval balance of power in their favour.

As far as we were concerned, the French Vichy Government were an unknown quantity. We did not know if, under pressure, they would turn their ships over to German control, and we certainly could not afford to take chances on it. Mr. Churchill therefore ordered "Force H" to proceed to Mers-el-Kebir, Oran, where a large part of the French Fleet were based.

We were instructed to offer the French the choice of several options. I cannot remember the exact preamble, but it ran something like this:-

(a)   Come out and join your British Allies for the duration

(b)   Immobilise your ships

(c)   Proceed to Martinique and intern yourselves

(d)   Let us destroy your ships

(e)   In the event of failure to carry out any of the above conditions, we, the British Fleet would regretfully be obliged to open fire on your ships and destroy them.

At 5 p.m. on the 2nd July, 1940, "Force H" led by *Hood*, left Gibraltar and steamed towards Oran. We knew that the French had a considerable naval force in Mers-el-Kebir harbour, and as we slid through the quiet, starlit night, we hoped that our old comrades-in-arms would join us in the common effort against Germany and Italy.

We arrived off Oran at approximately 7 a.m. the next morning. It was a brilliant day, with a calm sea and blue skies. We could see the French Fleet ranged alongside the breakwater, and behind them, the white buildings, drowsing in the early morning sunlight.

"Force H" began cruising up and down outside the breakwater. Captain Holland, who spoke fluent French and who had recently been the British Naval Attache in Paris, was sent ashore to negotiate the terms with the Admiral-in-Charge, Vice Amiral Gensoul. The forenoon passed uneventfully and apart from the defence watch, the hands went to dinner.

After dinner "Force H" went to Action Stations as a precautionary measure; meanwhile the talks ashore seemed to be meeting difficulties, since no result had been forthcoming.

As the hot afternoon wore on, we hoped that the French Admiral and his staff would see reason, and that it would not be our miserable lot to have to fire on our old allies. With these morbid thoughts passing through my mind, I went back over the years to the wonderful times my shipmates and I had spent along the French Riviera. And that memorable dinner we had as guests of the French Navy at Toulon.

As these pleasant memories flooded back, I hoped against hope, that the ultimate tragedy would be averted. It was not to be, however, and once again in history, valuable lives were to be uselessly destroyed at the behest of idiotic political decisions.

At 4.30 p.m. the French asked for an extension of the 5.30 p.m. time limit. This was readily granted, and for another hour the haggling went on. It was noticed, however, that the French ships had been raising steam and furling their awnings, a sure sign of preparation for sea. We did not know whether this meant that they were contemplating coming out to join us, or whether they were preparing to fight us. We were therefore on the horns of a dilemma!

A further signal was sent to us asking for more time, but on instructions from London, and taking into consideration the approaching darkness, a final time limit of 5.55 p.m. was given. Beyond this, we would take such action as was necessary to render their fleet inoperable. Besides this, we had received reports that further French re-inforcements from Algiers were at sea, and we did not want further complications.

Captain Holland had managed to get back to *Foxhound* and, at 5.55 p.m. sharp, "Force H" opened fire on the vessels in Mers-el-Kebir harbour.

For the next ten to twenty minutes the bombardment continued, without respite, causing severe damage to the French Fleet. We, in our turn, received the attention of the forts behind Mers-el-Kebir, and the combined guns of the vessels in the harbour.

Our ships were fortunate, since none were hit. We, in *Hood* received only superficial damage from shell splinters. Our casualties amounted to two men wounded. It had been hot whilst it had lasted, and as darkness fell, we left the burning shambles and made our way back to Gibraltar. We returned, not as exultant victors, but as extremely sad allies, forced by circumstances beyond our control, to bring death and destruction to those we had called our friends. Never had the uselessness of war been brought home to us so starkly. It was a sorry squadron that finally berthed under the shadow of the Rock.

It had been our first involvement in a fleet action. It was not a pleasant experience to be fired on, particularly when it is known that the projectiles coming your way, weighed almost a ton. I, and most everyone else, was scared stiff. To begin with, my action station was three decks below in an electrical repair party, and although we could hear the shells passing over us like express trains, we could not see what was going on. We did see our two wounded men being helped down to the dressing station below us, and their blood-stained appearance did not help us any.

I had often searched my soul to try and analyse my feelings should I ever be faced with this sort of situation. How would I react? Would I show my feelings? Could I take it? Yes, fear was present without doubt, but I was consoled by the fact that none of the others looked very happy either! This made me realize that it was only a question of mastering it, and not breaking down under the strain.

Had we been given something to do, it would have helped. We just had to wait for a shell to come through the deck, and, if it did not either kill or wound us, we could then proceed to repair the damage. We talked, when we did not feel like talking and we walked up and down in the limited space at our disposal, and in this way we tried to forget what was going on above us. We were all very thankful when the gunfire ceased and we were told that the action was over. Our highly strung nerves relaxed and we began to live again. It was some time before the memory of Oran faded from our minds.

Our next operation was to escort *Ark Royal* on a bombing sortee against the Italian air base at Cagliari. This was cancelled at the last moment, but on the way back we were severely bombed by high level bombers. Although they did not hit any of our ships, they gave us some very uncomfortable thrills!

One gets a tingling sensation down one's spine when being deliberately bombed, which is not relieved until you see the splash of the missile striking the water. Then one heaves a sigh of relief, relaxes one's taut nerves and hopes that there won't be any more like that. It is one thing to be bombed in a city, where you are not the prime target, but in a ship, particularly a much sought after ship like *Hood*, it is not so funny, especially when you know it is your vessel they are after. We were glad when darkness descended and we were left in peace. Even so, one of our escorting destroyers was torpedoed and sunk during the night by some cute submarine, who, doubtless aware of our little jaunt, patiently awaited our return.

Admiral Somerville endeared himself to "Force H" inasmuch that he usually departed from the conventional. For instance, when we set off on the Cagliari mission, we received this signal from him:- "We are about to test the quality of the ice cream". From this terse message we deducted the rest. No doubt those most concerned with the operation were well briefed, but the rest of us had to be content with his ice cream message.

One other amusing signal which revealed the type of senior officer we were blessed with, came from Andrew Cunningham, who was C-in-C Mediterranean and stationed at Alexandria, which was at the other end of the Mediterranean. It so happened that James Somerville had received a second Order of Knighthood and Cunningham, being a bit of a wag, and unable to resist the opportunity, signaled, "Fancy, twice a knight at your age." These little quips helped to brighten things up a bit, at a time when we certainly needed it.

Our next trip was to convoy the first consignment of Hurricane fighters to within flying distance of Malta. These were carried in the old aircraft carrier *Argus* and flown off her deck when within reach of the Island. Since we had to come fairly close to Sicily we expected heavy air attacks. However, to our surprise, we were left alone.

Our time was occupied for the rest of our stay in the Mediterranean, in escorting similar convoys part way to Malta, fortunately without incident. Soon, our time came to leave this famous "Force H". It had come to be known as the "Force H Club" and we considered ourselves to be a cut above the rest of the service. It was an honour to belong to this famous squadron and we prided ourselves on having the finest Admiral in the navy as our Flag Officer. Sir James Somerville had welded us into a Flying Squadron to be reckoned with and we all thought the world of him.

About the middle of August, *Hood* left Gibraltar and "Force H", and returned to Scapa Flow, where we transferred the Admiral and his staff to *Renown*, who became the new flagship of the famous squadron. I had enjoyed my spell in the Mediterranean, but now we once more resumed our patrol of the Denmark Straits, which we continued to do periodically until Christmas. We maintained this patrol with a fast capital ship because the new German battleship *Bismarck* had moved up to Norwegian waters, and it was imperative that she should not be allowed to break out into the Atlantic. She was constantly being watched by our aircraft and every time she was reported missing from her usual anchorage, everyone immediately got into a flap, until such time as her whereabouts was known. She became a regular pain in the neck to our Naval Command and we were all heartily sick of her.

During our brief spells in Scapa, I managed to take the Petty Officer's examination, which involved power boat handling, boat sailing and numerous other practical and theoretical seamanship subjects. I had to read and send a message in Morse Code, using a flashing lamp, and due to those far off days when Doug and I lay on deck in Malta, watching the signal lamp on the Castille, I was able to do this with ease. This was how I first learned to read Morse. After a bit of swotting in my spare time, I succeeded in passing the complete examination and my name was forwarded to the Depot and placed on the Roster for advancement when my turn came along.

Christmas 1940, we spent at sea on another *Bismarck* alarm, and then carried on with our routine patrol, but this time we were cheered by the news that, on our return, we were to proceed to Rosyth dockyard for a short refit, and to have Radar fitted in the ship.

Apart from the customary snow storms, fog and rain, our patrol passed off quietly, and after fourteen days of this, we steamed south towards the Firth of Forth, finally arriving early in January 1941. We were taken into dockyard hands immediately, and were soon overrun with dockyardmen of all shapes and sizes, with their inevitable tool boxes, air lines and other paraphernalia connected with the yard.

Leave was given to both watches, and this time, I was in the first leave party. As my wedding banns had run out, I telegraphed my fiancée that I would be home on the 17th January and to go ahead with the wedding plans. Arriving home on Friday, I helped my fiancée to make all our arrangements, and next morning, we had to go to Westminster to obtain a Special Licence. We were married on Sunday, 19th January, and our reception was held to the music of the AA gunfire, although few of the guests were aware than an air raid was in progress.

On returning to the ship, we had to "de-perm" the hull and structure whilst she was in dry dock. This was done to remove the magnetism which had been put into the ship by our degaussing generators. In order to remove this magnetic effect, thick heavy cables were put around the ship in an opposite direction to the run of the degaussing circuit; i.e. the cables were run under the keel and up over the deck and bridge structure, and continued along the whole length of the ship until we were lying in the middle of a spiral of heavy cables. A heavy electric current was then passed through the circuit for a few seconds, thus de-magnetising the ship.

It was heavy, backbreaking work, hauling the cables across the bottom of the dock, and up the sides of the ship, and it took us a week to complete the job, and all for a few seconds flash of current!

During the re-fit, I thoroughly overhauled our emergency electrical system, and with the aid of some old motor car headlamps, was able to produce some fairly efficient emergency operating lamps for our action medical teams.

On the 28th February, I was promoted to Petty Officer, and at the same time received a Draft note to H.M.S. *Vernon*, the Torpedo School, to take the Leading Torpedoman's course, which I had been prevented from taking in 1939.

I received the draft with mixed feelings. Due to my long service in *Hood* I had grown attached to her. We had travelled many thousands of miles and had visited many distant places together; besides which, I liked my shipmates, most of whom, like myself, had served a very long time in the ship. On the other hand, I wanted, eventually, to qualify as a Torpedo Gunner's Mate and Instructor, and to do this, I must first of all clear the hurdle of the Leading Torpedoman's Course, which was the next step. Also, of course, I had recently married, and this course would give me a brief snatch of home life. Next day, I left the old ship with Bill Fairchild, who had been my Best Man, and Matt Reed, another messmate.

As our train passed over the Forth Bridge, we looked across to the dockyard and saw the "Old Lady" lying alongside the basin wall. I would not be honest if I did not admit that I was very close to tears as we watched her pass out of sight, as our train sped onwards towards Edinburgh. I had joined her a very humble Seaman Torpedoman, and had left, a Petty Officer. I owed *Hood* a lot and I was grateful.

Although I had now left the ship, in view of the short span left to her, I feel that this is the time to write her epitaph.

Events leading up to the destruction of *Hood* are so well known, that I have no intention of delving too deeply into them here. However, there are one or two things which might help to refresh one's memory. The Admiralty decided to detach *Hood* and *Prince of Wales* with instructions to intercept *Bismarck* who had been reported as heading towards the Denmark Straits. In doing so, they had no other choice, since these were practically the only heavy ships available with the necessary speed to catch *Bismarck*.

A further complication was the fact that *Prince of Wales* was a new ship, which had only just joined the fleet, with a crew not yet used to her. As a point of interest, the ship still had dockyardmen working onboard when she sailed. Add to this the fact that the new 14" guns were giving trouble, which had not as yet, been remedied, and you have a pretty tricky situation.

In sending *Hood* to intercept the *Bismarck* Sir John Tovey, the Commander-in-Chief, Home Fleet, must have been a very worried man. He, of all men, knew that *Hood's* big weakness lay in her absence of deck armour. She belonged to an obsolete design known as the battlecruiser and, of course, she was 25 years old.

In this class of ship, speed and gun power were the main features, consequently, in engaging an enemy of *Bismarck's* calibre, *Hood* had to close the range as quickly as possible to ensure that any hits received would strike the side which was armoured, rather than the deck which was not.

This range had to be below approximately 13,000 yards, when the trajectory of the enemy projectiles would be fairly flat. To fight an action above this range would be to invite plunging salvoes, which would penetrate her weak decks, thereby risking magazine explosion!

In the effort to close the range quickly, *Hood* put herself in an unfavourable attacking position, since only her forward guns could bear. At the same time she offered her full length of 860 feet as a target for *Bismarck's* guns, all of which were able to bear. Before *Hood* could turn to port to bring her after guns into action, she was struck in the vicinity of the mainmast and a fire broke out amongst the ready use A/A ammunition lockers. At 6 a.m. as the ship was turning to port, she was straddled by a salvo from either *Bismarck* or *Prinz Eugen*, the range was then approx between 13000 and 14000 yards. She was struck by this salvo, and immediately blew up in a colossal explosion. Only three survived out of a crew of some 1,400 men.

As an ex-member of *Hood's* crew I can recall numerous discussions we had in our mess about a possible meeting with either *Bismarck* or her sister *Tirpitz*. We were not at all happy about such a prospect. We knew our weakness and the risks of not having an armoured deck. We had the speed, yes, and we had the gun power, but we did not have our armour in the right place!

Another significant failure in our older capital ship design, was the siting of the magazines above the shell rooms, instead of the other way round; a fact which further increased the risk of magazine explosion from plunging shells.

All these factor we discussed among ourselves. We thought that with 23 years between the two wars, our older ships should have either been scrapped altogether, or at least modified to meet modern gunfire methods, even if it did hurt the taxpayers' pockets.

Even when *Nelson* and *Rodney* were built, the design fell short on the speed requirement. These two vessels were admirable for gun power and armour protection, but with only 23 knots as a maximum speed, what use were they against the fast ships then coming into use with other navies? Could not our people project their minds ahead a little? Could not they appreciate that even with armour and guns, one still had to catch the enemy?

The sublime complacence of pre-war governments in failing to provide sufficient funds to replace outdated warships, or the time to have them properly converted, was in my opinion, a national scandal. I am fully aware of the various naval treaties that existed, which prevented Britain renewing her navy, but if we were only to be allowed to retain certain units, then it was up to the nation to see that those units were the most modern available. As it was, we entered the war with 3 battlecruisers at least 21 years old and ten battleships built around about 1914-15. All of them potential risks to their crews in the light of modern high velocity naval gunnery. One or two had been modernized, but only so far as their speed and guns were concerned. Their decks and magazine siting remained the same.

I recall the unenviable position of Admiral Sir James Somerville, who, as C-in-C, Eastern Fleet, was fatuously expected to sally forth and do battle with the modern, fast Japanese Fleet, with a small force of old *Royal Sovereign* class battleships, built circa 1914–16, only capable of 21 knots if pushed and long overdue for the scrap heap.

It would have been funny, if it hadn't been so damned serious, and the men of the fleet who had to man these relics did not like being considered expendable! It is to the credit of Sir James that he evidently thought along very similar lines.

People may say that these old ships could be useful if used under this particular set of circumstances, or that particular tactical situation etc., but experience shows that these peculiar situations seldom, if ever, occur. These ideas are simply figments of the imagination, dreamed up by out-dated armchair tacticians, who, by voicing them, indicate that they belong to another and much older generation of thinking.

Modern wars demand modern machines, modern tactics, and most important of all, a fair fighting chance for the men who have to use them. It simply is not good enough to neglect the navy in times of peace, then send it into a modern war with out-dated weapons and badly designed warships, and expect their crews to work miracles. But in spite of all, miracles were worked, but at what cost in valuable lives.

Hood rests in position 63 degrees 20 minutes North Latitude, 31 degrees 50 minutes West Longitude, and inside her torn and battered hull lie most of my friends. Perhaps I can be excused being a little bitter about the neglect referred to.

It was a very long time before I got over the shock of *Hood*'s loss. As a ship's company, we had been together a very long time. We had shared the joys and excitement of peace. In war we had welded ourselves into a true comradeship that had weathered the Arctic gales and outshone the Mediterranean sun. As long as sea history is written, *Hood* and her gallant band of men will be remembered, and theirs will be a golden page in the book of time.

Married my 'Girl of the Storm'.

Chapter Ten

H.M.S. *VERNON* and ROEDEAN SCHOOL

<u>1941</u>

Arriving at Portsmouth on the lst of March, we were accommodated in the Royal Naval Barracks. I was amazed at the air raid damage that could be seen everywhere. The last time I had seen the city had been in May of the previous year, before the blitz had commenced. Whole areas had been reduced to rubble, and one had great difficulty in recognizing what had once been familiar ground. Poor old Pompey had certainly taken a beating.

Coming home from the sea, this scene of stark desolation shocked me into realizing what our people at home had been putting up with. We had our moments out there in the blue, but nothing like this! When a ship was sunk, that was the end of the matter. The cold clean sea took care of everything, nothing was left visible to offend the eye. Only the tragedy lived on, fixed in our minds. Here, ashore, it was different. The shattered wrecks of buildings remained as a poignant reminder, grotesque, almost obscene and I hated it. Already I was longing to get back to the fresh, wide, sunlit spaces of the open sea.

I was due to go to *Vernon* for my course on Friday, 13th March, but on Tuesday, 10th, Portsmouth sustained one of the worst air raids of the war. On this night when the tide was at its lowest level of the year, the Luftwaffe struck in an all night fire and bomb raid, which inflicted great loss of life and severe damage to the city.

Among the buildings hit and destroyed, was the torpedo workshops in *Vernon*. Also razed to the ground was the Custom House just outside the walls. It was not until some days later that I discovered that my father had been on duty in the Customs House and had been dug out by rescue workers. I wondered why he had returned home covered with dust the next morning.

I had been staying the night at my mother's house on this particular night, and had spent the whole of the night in the air raid shelter. On returning to barracks in the morning, a sorry sight met my eyes. One of the large Mess buildings had its top floor completely gutted.

There were fire hoses running in all directions across the roads, and in the asphalt of the parade ground was a small hole caused by one of our own AA shells. It had passed through the parade ground into the shelter below, where it had exploded, killing 8 of our men. They were bringing out their mutilated bodies as I passed by. The seamen carrying out this grim task had been given a stiff tot of rum beforehand. They needed it!

Due to *Vernon* being hit in this raid, my torpedo course was put off for a week, when it was decided to draft me to *Actaeon*, the Torpedo School at Chatham. In the meantime, however, I began my first duties in barracks as a Petty Officer. Two days after the raid, I was put in charge of a party of seamen, and told to report to the Royal Naval Hospital at Haslar.

Normally, these trips to the hospital were for the specific purpose of coaling all their galleys, and of course, this was in everybody's mind when we arrived. However, it turned out to be for a much grimmer purpose that we were required.

I had no suspicion as to the real nature of the job in hand, and it was not until I entered the long, low shed that the truth struck me like a douch of iced water in the face. There in the center of the room lay a row of empty pine coffins, each resting on its own trestles. Ranged around the white-washed walls and resting on the tables, were about 30 naked bodies; the naval dead of the air raid of two nights ago.

They lay there, peaceful and silent, as if carved in wax. The body nearest the door I recognized as a classmate of my pre-war *Vernon* days. In death they looked so young and beautiful. I was very close to tears, for the suddenness of coming upon this scene had shocked me deeply.

The Sick Berth Chief came over and very quietly gave me instructions as to what he wanted my party to do, and for the rest of the morning we were engaged in loading the coffins, now with their precious burdens, into a lorry and transporting them, to the Naval Cemetery, where we reverently lowered them, side by side, into a mass grave. It was a tragic morning's work, and it did not help when we returned from the cemetery, to see bloodstained stretchers propped up against the wall of the shed, some of which still had fragments of flesh adhering to them.

I raged inwardly at the senselessness of war, and at all the bloody stupid politicians who had allowed this state of affairs to come about. It was a long time before I got over this morning's work, and could enjoy a meal again.

On the following Friday, I was drafted to Chatham Barracks for course at *Actaeon* and on the Monday morning I began the course for Leading Torpedoman.

There were about a dozen of us in the class and we were billeted in the main barracks. After poor old blitzed Pompey, Chatham was peace indeed. In fact the pre-war "Bull" of Guard and Band was still being practised with all its red tape, a fact which peeved us, since we were not allowed to walk on the pavement in the vicinity of the Commodore's Office. Such bullshit had long been blasted out of Portsmouth Barracks by German bombs!

Having recently buried our dead in Haslar Cemetery, we did not take kindly to this tomfoolery. We thought that there were more urgent problems to be tackled; and that when men came in from sea, after facing all sorts of risks, they did not expect to be told to keep off the Commodore's pavement and to walk in the road. After all we were fighting this war to end such stupidity!

This was our only gripe about Chatham Barracks. In all other respects they did us proud. Their organization was terrific, spoiled only by this little piece of very irritating red tape.

The course lasted about 8 weeks, during which, in addition to torpedoes, we learned all about rendering mines safe, a job which would be our particular baby should the occasion arise. We also learned the latest demolition techniques, using TNT, Gelignite, and plastic explosive, besides depth charges and their release mechanisms. It was a most interesting period, which I enjoyed immensely.

Having completed the torpedo part of the course, I applied for, and was granted the other half of the course, which was purely electrical. It was necessary to do this in order to become fully qualified, and it had to be taken in *Vernon*, but due to bomb damage, the school had been transferred to Roedean Girl's School at Brighton, which the navy had taken over for the duration of the war. Before leaving Chatham, I was given a week's leave. A well earned rest.

Early June found me drafted to *Vernon* (R), the code name for Roedean School, which was situated on the coast road about 2 miles east of Brighton Pier. This fine old school added lustre to our course, and some of its old girls included names from some of the most aristocratic families in the country. To our amusement, notices to the effect that "Anyone requiring a mistress during the night please ring the bell", were still posted up in the bedrooms and dormitories. It has always been a source of pride to me that I received part of my education at this famous school.

Whilst on course here, I was able to have my wife down for about six weeks and we lodged in furnished rooms about a mile from the school. We were not bothered by air raids here, since the main targets were London and the large provincial cities and towns; although, now and again we had visits from tip and run raiders, who flying close to the water to dodge our radar defence, were able to zoom up over the cliff tops and plant their bombs indiscriminately.

The course lasted until August, and then we had ten days leave. After the leave period I was transferred up the road to the St. Dunstan's building which was also part of our electrical school. Since I had completed my course, I found myself in charge of the guard as a day time job, until such time as a draft came along. For weapons, we had one Boer war vintage rifle between every three men, the others were issued with a length of gas pipe with a bayonet soldered onto one end. Such was our plight in those days when invasion was more than a possibility.

August stretched into December and then, just before proceeding on Christmas leave I received a draft to H.M.S. *Ledbury* which I was to join in early January 1942. Nobody had ever heard of the ship, but judging by the fact that the vessel was new construction, now being completed at Thorneycroft's yard at Woolston, I had a idea that she was probably a destroyer of some sort, since that particular shipbuilder specialized in this type of craft.

There were two of us going to *Ledbury*, and we arrived one dark winter's evening in the black-out, and with a foot of snow on the ground. We had by this time discovered that the ship was indeed a destroyer of the newly designed "Hunt" class and since she was not yet finished, we had to find lodgings ashore.

Southampton, like Portsmouth had received a heavy blitzing from the Luftwaffe, and as we cast around for somewhere to stay, we could see the burned out shells of houses, with their skeleton like rafters, bare of slates, pointing at grotesque angles, faintly silhouetted against the night sky and contrasting obscenely against the white of the snow.

Arriving at the Civic Centre we found a Police Station and a friendly sergeant told us where to go for our lodgings, which turned out to be a boarding house opposite the Police Station and run by a retired actress. We were thankful to be able to have a hot meal and get to bed.

I lay awake for some time pondering over my new ship, which we would be joining the next day. Destroyers were not my cup of tea, and something seemed to tell me that I would not be very happy onboard this one. With a great deal of doubt and apprehension, I finally got to sleep.

My companion, who was a young Able Seaman Torpedoman, was not very keen on destroyers either, but I think that this was due to his inexperience more than the ships themselves. After discussing our prospects over an indifferent breakfast, we left our digs and caught the ferry across to Woolston and reported to the Shipyard Office where our advance party had their quarters. We had officially joined H.M.S. *Ledbury* and so began the most detested part of my Naval career.

At Brighton with my wife during a course at Roedean.

Promotion to Petty Officer

Chapter Eleven

H.M.S. *LEDBURY*

<u>1942</u>

After reporting to the dock office and making myself known, I went down to the fitting out basin. There were three destroyers still in the process of having their superstructures fitted, then, further along and quite apart from the others, lay *Ledbury*.

About 1,000 tons, with three twin 4" gun mountings; a single well raked mast and funnel, and a host of depth charge equipment, and, somewhere in the middle of it all, the soul of a new ship.

To begin with, I hated destroyer service. Not because of the ships themselves, but on account of my inability to master their violent movement in rough weather. These small vessels have a peculiar motion all of their own, which left me in a state whereby it was sheer misery to work at all, and this worried me because I had charge of a vital department, and it was essential that I was fit, since, in a small ship every man counted. To add to my worries, of the only other senior rates in my department, one was on permanent light duty on medical advice, and the other was a brand new Electrical Artificer straight from the school, and *Ledbury* was his first ship ever.

I envied those with cast iron stomachs, because destroyers were very chummy ships to serve in. Everyone knew each other, and there was a closer and more intimate relationship between the crew than one would find in a larger vessel. However, this was wartime, and I had to make the best of it, but I was conscious of the fact that, although I did my job, had I been in a bigger ship, it would have been done a lot better.

The *Ledbury* class of vessel was designed just before the war, as an escort vessel, primarily for use with convoys. They had sufficient speed, (28 knots) to catch any contemporary submarine, and sufficient dual purpose guns to give a good account of themselves in an air attack.

Some of these ships were designed to operate with the fleet. In such cases, they were fitted with a twin torpedo tube mounting at the expense of one twin gun mounting. *Ledbury* of course, was a convoy escort, and this was to be our main job.

Going onboard, I was met with air lines everywhere, wood shavings, wet red lead paint, and workmen everywhere. There was not much one could do at this stage except to have a look around and familiarize myself with the type of equipment I would be responsible for. With this in mind I began a minute tour of the ship.

Compared with *Hood*, this ship was a cockleshell and her various compartments were in proportion, there not being room to swing a cat around. I toured the electrical system and switchboards, also the depth charge throwers, traps, and release system, since all of these items were to be my responsibility. Then I ran into the Gunner, one of the most objectionable characters I have ever met.

For obvious reasons I shall call him "Fred". He was not a Torpedo Gunner, since we did not have tubes, but because our main armament consisted of guns, he found himself appointed to *Ledbury*. He was not a fully qualified Gunner, but, since he was within 3 years of his pension, he was offered, and accepted, the acting rank of Gunner (Warrant Officer).

To give Fred his due, he knew all about guns, as one would expect, but, although he knew little or nothing about depth charges or electrics, he was, by virtue of his rank, my immediate superior.

Had he left my side of the job to me, since I was well trained and qualified to do it, we would have got on well together; but in his parade ground manner, he interfered and caused me such unnecessary trouble, that I was obliged to take action to confine him to his own domain and to leave me and my staff in peace. We had quite enough work and responsibility without him putting a spanner in the works.

This caused Fred and I to be at daggers drawn, and this atmosphere did not help matters. Things came to a head between us, when, on one occasion I was fitting detonators to depth charge pistols. To do this, because of their great sensitivity to shock of any sort, one had to sit on the deck with a bunch of cotton waste between one's legs, so that if one dropped a detonator, it would fall on a soft bed, thereby eliminating the risk of explosion.

Fred, either not appreciating the reason for sitting, or out of sheer cussedness, started to rant, about my sitting to do this job. That, as far as I was concerned, was the last straw. I informed the Captain of this incident and requested that he take the necessary action to keep Fred out of my way. The skipper, appreciating the reason behind my request and knowing full well who was the qualified man, gave instructions that I and my department were to be left alone to get on with our jobs; from then on things began to run smoothly.

We were due to go on acceptance trials three weeks hence and the ship's company, having moved onboard, were busy painting, storing and ammunitioning ship. My staff and I had our hands full, fitting all the depth charges with pistols and primers and testing all the equipment. Then, one bright day in late January, we sailed for trials and after a couple of days during which we had speed, gun and depth charge trials, *Ledbury* was officially accepted into the Navy by the appending of the Captain's signature to the Dockyard receipt.

We sailed almost immediately for Scapa Flow, carrying out a depth charge attack on what we thought was a "U" boat on the way. I am glad to record that all of my charges exploded successfully, much to Fred's disgust.

On arrival at Scapa Flow we immediately began our working up programme. We carried out 4" surface and "AA firing and Asdic exercises with a Norwegian submarine, which was acting as our target.

During these exercises it was my job to fire small TNT charges, towed astern on wires. These were used to signal the submarine that she had been located. They were fired electrically, using the sea as an earth return circuit. One had to use great caution with these circuits since it was easy to fire one of the charges ready on the deck, instead of the one being towed astern.

I had an amusing experience whilst operating with the target submarine. To begin with, our skipper, Roger Hill, made it quite clear to all of us that his main ambition was to capture a "U" boat and to bring her into port. In order to be able to do this, he had to have a boarding party, suitably trained, to take over the "U" boat after it had surfaced. This party would capture the crew and remove all booby traps likely to result in the loss of the submarine. As the ship's electrical expert, I was chosen as the Chief Booby Trap Remover, and was therefore a member of the boarding boat's crew.

It so happened that one day, after we had been exercising with our Norwegian submarine, the "Old Man" decided to try out his submarine boarding theory. Unbeknown to us he had made arrangements with the submarine's Captain to surface his boat and to use what initiative he liked to prevent us taking over his vessel. This little arrangement caused a great deal of embarrassment to our boarding party, and much amusement to everyone else, except perhaps, our skipper, who almost tore us apart when we finally got back onboard.

The whole sorry episode went something like this. The boarding boat's crew were assembled, the whaler lowered, and we, armed with potatoes to simulate hand grenades, revolvers and a length of chain cable to dangle down the submarine's conning tower hatch to prevent them closing it, tumbled into the whaler and pulled cross the intervening stretch of water, watched by all our interested shipmates.

The submarine's skipper, being a wily bird, had concealed half a dozen of his crew under the upper deck casing. This, of course, we knew nothing of, and bringing our boat smartly alongside the submarine's saddle tanks, we left a boatkeeper in the whaler and jumped aboard.

We made a dash for the conning tower and, dropping a few "grenades" down the hatch, we quickly scrambled down into the control room. Holding up the crew with our guns, we began to take over the boat, then, suddenly from nowhere, there appeared six hulking great Norwegians, who surprising us, quickly took us prisoners. These were the men from the casing hideout. The conning tower hatch was quickly closed and amid the noise of a klaxon horn and the hissing of escaping air from the tanks as the valves allowed the sea in, the submarine slid below the surface, leaving our whaler, with its solitary occupant, drifting around the Flow.

For the rest of the afternoon we were submerged, and cruised up and down until, at about 4 p.m., just before dusk, the submarine returned to her parent vessel, and we, the deflated heroes, were returned to our own ship. I will not repeat our skipper's remarks when we finally got back on board, but after a while he began to see the funny side and reminded us that at least, we had learned a valuable lesson as to what could happen on one of these jaunts.

We completed our working up programme and became fully operational. Whilst at Scapa we had to take our turn as Emergency Destroyer which meant that we had to leave our existing anchorage and move over to a position on the far side of the Flow where we were completely isolated. It was as if we had been naughty schoolboys and had been sent over to a corner.

We hated this chore, particularly as, more often than not, it meant a sudden trip to sea to hunt some submarine, which usually turned out to be the figment of someone's imagination. This was one of the bad things about destroyer life. One did not get much rest. Coming in from sea, instead of a much wanted rest in one's hammock, it was often our lot to find ourselves detailed as emergency destroyer, when, before the night was over, one would probably be at sea again.

I always thought this system most unfair, as it seemed to me that it was only the destroyers with the junior captains who collected this duty. This may be a suitable arrangement in times of peace, but in war, rest was important to all, not just senior officers. I may be completely wrong in my supposition, for we had few destroyers to cover the many roles we had to play, but I cannot recall any occasion when our flotilla leader took a turn as emergency destroyer.

Our first duty was to form part of an escort for a small convoy to Iceland. In the dirty winter weather prevailing, and at the low speed of 10 knots, it was a bind. As we steamed slowly northwards, it gradually became colder, until soon it became necessary to chip ice away from our guns and depth charge release mechanism, and to introduce glycerine into the hydraulic system. We ran into occasional snow flurries, blotting out the convoy and reducing our visibility to nil. It was a horrible trip, and we were heartily glad to reach our destination, which was Sadiesfjiord.

On arrival, we berthed alongside an oiler and topped up our fuel tanks. The weather was bitterly cold, it penetrated one's thick clothing and gnawed at one's bones. The scenery was uninviting, the snow covered mountainous slopes funnelling the biting wind down to the scattered vessels in the anchorage.

We were alongside the oiler for about 4 hours, then, expecting a night of peace in a warm hammock, found ourselves browned off as emergency destroyer. Sure enough, within an hour or so, we were at sea again to hunt for an unidentified submarine reported by a Coastal Command aircraft. We "pinged" around all night and the best part of the following day without success. Tired, cold and not very happy, we returned to Sadiesfjiord, and topped up with oil. However, we stayed only long enough to fuel and without rest, off to sea again to escort a convoy back to Scapa Flow.

Destroyers, more than any other craft, were run off their feet. We had so few of them. Due to losses and our many commitments, they were more than overworked. When you realize that, when at sea, the crew were on a permanent watchkeeping basis of four hours on watch and four hours off, and add to this the fact that frequently they were at action stations when every man in the ship was on alert, one can appreciate the strain that was imposed on them.

One of the regular hazards we faced was the re-loading of the depth charge throwers, when the weather was rough. These throwers resembled a large calibre mortar into which is fitted a metal stalk. The free end of the stalk is fitted with a shallow tray into which is placed the 300 lb. depth charge. When fired, the complete stalk and charge is blown into the air and throws the charge some 50 odd yards from the ship. With the vessel rolling and pitching violently, one can imagine the dangerous job it is to hoist a fresh charge and stalk and to re-load the thrower, with heavy seas breaking onboard to complicate matters.

One also had to practise care when fitting a detonator into the depth charge pistol. In one particular destroyer, practically the whole of the depth charge thrower's crew were killed, and a goodly portion of the ship's stern blown off, because of the faulty fitting of a detonator into a pistol. A copper disc had been omitted. Had the charge been dropped from the stern traps, all would have been well. As it was, this particular charge was loaded onto a thrower, where the inertia of the discharge forced the detonator back on to the striker, thereby prematurely firing the charge as it left the thrower. Had the disc been fitted, the detonator could not have slid backwards. Each depth charge pistol box was supposed to contain one of these discs, but I have had to root around on more than one occasion to find another to replace the one missing in the box. When handling explosives of any kind, I always remembered the words of our Gunnery Instructor at *Ganges*, who used to regularly preach to us "Ammunition is safe, until you forget that it is dangerous". How right he was.

In addition to the normal discomforture, I also had to put up with Fred. Although he kept out of my way as much as possible, he didn't lose any opportunity at having a dig at me in any way he could. For instance, after I had turned in at night, he would sometimes send for me personally to report a small insignificant fault like a dud lamp, or a blown fuse. He knew perfectly well that a duty torpedoman existed to deal with these minor snags, but he preferred to dig me out of my hammock so that I could tell the duty man to do the job.

I tolerated this pettiness for a long while, until one night he sent for me, and I simply ignored him and stayed in my hammock. A stand had to be made against this fool, and I knew that if he reported my action to the Captain, it would have started an enquiry in which he would have had to do a lot of explaining. I heard nothing further from Fred, who, it seemed, appreciated the fact that he had taken his little jest far enough.

February passed into March, and our main job seemed to be convoy work either between Scapa and Iceland or between Iceland and a point half way to Russia, then, before we knew it we were back in Scapa and it was April.

The weather was getting warmer and we were grateful for that. Occasionally, when working about the depth charges I would see a seal pop his head above water and commence barking. At first I wondered where on earth the noise was coming from, for we did not have a dog in *Ledbury*. Then I saw "George" – for that was the name I gave him – his big round eyes looking right at me, and twitching his whiskers. I saw him often, after our first surprise meeting. He would watch me curiously as I went about my work.

One fine morning, during this spell at Scapa, I was bending over a depth charge on the stern, fiddling with the primer, when I heard seagulls whirling around above me. Suddenly I was "dive bombed" by one of them and he caught me fair and square on the back of my neck. I looked up at the wheeling birds who were screaming at me derisively. I shook my fist at the unknown culprit, and went below to the mess to clean up. I was greeted with laughter, the Coxswain remarking that it was considered to be very lucky to be crapped upon from a great height. I replied to the effect that if it brought me a draft out of this ruddy ship then it would be luck indeed! I had cause to remember this incident about a week later.

Ledbury had been running about for about four months, and was due for boiler cleaning, consequently we were ordered to Rosyth dockyard for minor repairs and to carry out the boiler clean. As soon as we arrived, I seized the chance to return our depth charge pistols for testing. Forty eight hours leave was given to each watch, but since I was living at Wembley, this was of no use to me, so I contented myself with a walk ashore to get out of the ship for a brief spell.

Since I had been promoted to Petty Officer I had not made any particular friends. The reason for this was probably because, in a Petty Officer's Mess one found older men, who, by virtue of their responsibilities, seemed to take life a little too seriously for my liking. I preferred youth around me. Although a Petty Officer myself, I did not let my rank rest too heavily upon me; it was not necessary. Also, it was not considered the thing among the "old boys" for a Petty Officer to go ashore with juniors in rank, although in fairness to the official view, there was no rule against doing so.

I always found the young company of my torpedomen, with their exuberant spirits and stimulating ideas on life preferable to the rather stuffy outlook of my equals. After all, it was the world of the young that we were fighting for, and I was only just turned 30 myself. Consequently, whilst in *Ledbury*, I usually went ashore alone, which, due to our circumstances, was extremely rare. Later on, however, I adopted an attitude of mind that made me choose my companions regardless of their rank, and I was all the happier for it.

After a week of boiler cleaning and repairs, I received the depth charge pistols back from the testing shop and re-fitted them to their charges, and on the following day, we received orders to sail for Scapa Flow at 5 p.m. Then a miracle happened! A draft arrived in the ship for me to proceed to *Vernon* for a Torpedo Gunner's Mates Course.

I was overjoyed at the prospect of leaving *Ledbury* for I had not been happy in her, and added to Fred and his antics, was the fact that destroyers did not agree with me physically. It was an oddity really, because sea sickness did not affect me in such tiny craft as Picket Boats, where I had enjoyed a rough buffeting. However, destroyers have a way of their own of upsetting one's equilibrium.

My relief joined the ship at noon and the skipper told me to give him a good look over the ship, and providing he was satisfied, I could get the night train to London.

All that afternoon I gave him a good insight into the workings of my department. Fortunately, he was a destroyer man, and was familiar with most of our equipment, and by 3 p.m. was quite happy to let me go. Fred, however, game to the last, tried to prevent my leaving the ship until we arrived at Scapa; but the skipper himself, by this time, had had enough of Fred and told him that I was to be off the ship before she sailed at 5 p.m.

As I stepped over the gangway at 3.30 the ship's company were singling up the wires ready for departure. At about 5.15 p.m. as my train was passing over the Forth Bridge I saw *Ledbury* steaming off into the distance. For once, and only once, in my whole naval career, I was glad to see the back of a ship.

Later on she was to distinguish herself in the Mediterranean by helping to escort the severely damaged tanker *Ohio* into Malta, and Roger Hill, her skipper, got his D.S.O. and, I believe, Fred received a D.S.C.

I have always had a soft spot for seagulls ever since, and I have a china replica of one of these graceful birds hanging on my lounge wall at this moment.

Chapter Twelve

"VERNON" (R) "ASSEGAI" ENGLISH POINT CAMP MOMBASA and "TEVIOTBANK"

1942 – 1943

Arriving back in the depot at Portsmouth I was sent on ten days leave, which was the custom during the war years when coming into barracks from a sea going ship. It was the middle of April, and since my wife was expecting our baby at any moment, the leave was doubly appreciated.

The blitz had eased off considerably, due, no doubt, to the German bombers being drawn off to the Russian Front, so my leave was much more peaceful than had been the case on previous occasions.

As my leave drew to a close, our baby had still not arrived and my wife had to go to hospital as her doctor forecast a difficult birth. On the last day of my leave I was obliged to ask for an extension, and was fortunate in getting a further 72 hours extension, during which time a son was born to us.

I was able to return to Portsmouth, where a draft to *Vernon* (R) was awaiting me to qualify Torpedo Gunner's Mate. This particular rating was much sought after. It was the top brick of the Torpedo Branch, and carried the rank of Instructor with it. I considered myself extremely lucky to have the chance of having a go at it. It was a long difficult course, involving mathematics, High and Low Power electrics, advanced Torpedo work, explosives, mines and depth charges. This course in peace time usually took a year to complete; now however, it had to be crammed into 8 months, and to make matters worse, we had all the newer devices and equipment to master as well. However, after *Ledbury* I was prepared to tackle anything.

For the next few months our class of 12 Petty Officers, sweated and strained through the various sections of the course. I had no illusions as to my own capabilities. To get through it at all successfully, I really had to swot. Many is the night when I have burned the midnight oil, and this in addition to voluntary attendance at night school. Looking back over the years I have often wondered how on earth I managed it. Manage it I did, however, and with a fairly reasonable pass mark.

During the course, we all managed a weekend or two at home, but it meant we had to lose a weekend of swotting, but there was a war on and those brief spells at home were precious.

By the end of November our course came to an end, and after the examinations we were given 10 days leave, which served to give our brains a rest.

At the end of our leave, most of us received drafts to various ships. Some went to submarines, some to destroyers, and five of us were allocated to H.M.S. *Assegai* which was a drafting depot, situated in Pietermaritzburg, South Africa, and was used as a personnel supply pool for the Eastern Fleet.

Whilst awaiting passage, I took one or two classes of Sub-Lieutenants through their Torpedo Course, and discovered that I liked instructional work. It was interesting work, explaining and lecturing on torpedoes and presented a challenge to me, particularly when one was asked an awkward question.

The war, at last, began to slowly turn in our favour. During the previous month, at El Alemein, the 8th Army, in a terrific offensive, and preceded by what was probably the greatest gun barrage in history, began to roll back the German Forces in North Africa.

At sea, in the central and eastern Mediterranean, our naval forces, particularly the submarines, were sinking everything that flew an enemy flag. In Russia, the Germans were engaged in titanic battles which drained their life blood. Not only did they have to contend with the implacable Russian forces and people, but also the bitter, vicious winter weather. In Western Europe they had to tie down valuable divisions and equipment, to counter a possible Allied invasion.

Germany's star was definitely beginning to sink, the writing was now appearing on the wall, and the Huns were now receiving in good measure the sort of treatment they had meted out to others, and they did not seem to like it.

The Mediterranean was still closed to traffic wishing to pass through the Suez Canal, with the result that all troop convoys to the far east had to go via the Cape of Good Hope. It was a great inconvenience, since to avoid the "U" Boats as much as possible, the ships had to steam well to the westward before altering course to make the southerly run to Cape Town, which brings me to the tale of my passage down to Durban.

About two weeks before Christmas, 1942, our draft for Pietermaritzburg left Roedean School for Portsmouth Barracks, where, after spending a night sleeping on the floor of a Nissen hut, we boarded a special train drawn up in the barrack siding. There were about 250 of us including 80 Wrens, all bound for Avonmouth, where our troopship was berthed.

It was dawn when our train drew out of Portsmouth and, after a most uncomfortable and cold journey, we arrived at Avonmouth docks at about 3 p.m. Our draft was joined by a like number from Chatham and Devonport, making the total naval draft up to approximately 680 including the Wrens. Also on the dockside being checked onboard the ship, were some 1,600 soldiers of the King's Own Regiment, bound, I believe, for the Burma area. It looked to me as if the ship was going to burst at the seams with all this lot going onboard!

The ship herself was the Shaw, Saville and Albion line's S.S. *Mataroa* In times of peace a meat carrier between U.K and New Zealand. Now her refrigerated holds had been converted into living quarters for the troops. Painted overall a drab dark grey, she looked a bedraggled old lady, the emphasis being on old.

Her crew were Merchant Navy men, and in my estimation, gleaned from experience, an unprincipled lot of fiddling scoundrels who put a price on every little favour asked of them, and who tried to create the need of the favour asked, for personal gain. It is one thing to expect tips from passengers in peace time, who, in the main, are usually able to afford it; but to expect, nay, even demand the same from lowly paid servicemen, who by force of circumstance, were obliged to travel in their wretched ship, is quite another and unforgivable matter.

To quote but two examples of what I mean. The ship's bakers, in order to make illicit booze to sell to the troops at inflated prices, deliberately starved the bread of its hop brew content, thereby supplying us with flat, soggy and practically uneatable bread. Then, as we could only use salt water to bath with, which left one's body sticky and uncomfortable, the stewards charged us a shilling for a bowl of fresh water to rinse off the stickiness. We Royal Navy men had a poor opinion of such men who called themselves seamen, particularly as they were already in receipt of danger pay, over and above their normal pay.

When we first arrived onboard, the messes were of a mixed nature. Some congenital idiot thought it a good idea to have soldiers and sailors in the same mess. It did not occur to him that it would cause problems of command between Corporals and Leading Seamen, and Sergeants and Petty Officers. Also the soldiers had all their equipment, rifles, Bren guns, tin hats, in fact, everything but the kitchen sink with them, which alone took up most of the available space, to the discomfort of the navy men.

The accommodation trouble we were able to put right by re-organising all the soldiers on one side of the ship and the R.N. personnel on the other, after which peace reigned once more.

Our next problem was the food they gave us. In all my service experience, I have never seen such atrocious food. The bread I have already mentioned, but such items as wet and soggy luncheon meat, rotten unwashed potatoes boiled in their skins and uneatable pastry were only a few of our complaints, and it takes a lot to make a hungry sailor complain. We had seen better food served as pigswill in our own Barracks.

We appreciated the fact that it was war time and, in the main, we accepted these conditions as cheerfully as possible, but it did not help to know that things could have been a whole lot better had some of these merchant navy crews played the game.

The first week of our six weeks journey, *Mataroa*, in convoy with about sixteen other vessels, steamed westward in the teeth of a typical Atlantic gale, which caused the ship to pitch and roll violently. Although not feeling too happy myself, I felt really sorry for the Army men, who, unused to such conditions, were fearfully and wonderfully seasick. The stuffy atmosphere between decks, plus the foul smell of vomit and overcrowded humanity, made life most unpleasant. Our only consolation was the fact that no "U" boat could successfully operate in such conditions. Things brightened up a bit after we altered course southwards and began zig-zagging towards Freetown, our first port of call.

Among our escort vessels was the armed merchant cruiser *Carnarvon Castle* which looked a magnificent sight as she steamed through the center of the convoy at 20 knots. It was typical balmy South Atlantic weather. The soldiers were fascinated at the antics of the porpoises leaping around our bows, while shoals of flying fish scudded over the surface of the now calm sea. We saw one or two sharks fins, as if to remind us that there were other enemies about beside "U" boats.

Most of we Navy men slept on deck, using our lifebelts as pillows, for apart from the hot weather, *Mataroa* was so overcrowded, we did not fancy sleeping below, particularly if an emergency arose. It was wonderful to lie on deck under a South Atlantic heaven, watching the thousands of scintillating stars, including the Southern Cross, which indicated that we were well under way with our journey.

We were free of duties of any kind during the trip, consequently I spent a lot of time reading, or just talking. On one occasion the Army asked me to give some of their men a talk on torpedoes, which of course I did, but apart from this, the long haul south was a rest cure, spoiled only by the food.

In due course the convoy arrived at Freetown, Sierra Leone, where we spent Christmas Day. The ships re-fuelled, watered, and took on fresh fruit and vegetables, before resuming our journey southwards 24 hours later. Soon we began to experience the long rolling swell peculiar to the approaches of Cape Town. We rounded the Cape and steamed on up the coast to Durban, where we eventually arrived one beautiful sunny morning, six weeks after leaving Avonmouth.

One of my outstanding memories of this beautiful city was the famous "Lady in White". She was a noted South African singer who greeted every convoy from Britain, by singing from the dockside as the ships came in to berth. As we slid slowly alongside the dock wall, we heard the lovely strains of "Land of Hope and Glory" floating across the still water. She entertained us right up until the *Mataroa* docked. It was something we will always remember, for it brought a little bit of England to us after our long and uncomfortable trip.

Our Naval draft left *Mataroa* at about 3 p.m., and as far as most of us were concerned, it was a jolly good riddance. We loaded our baggage into a special train at the dockside and took our seats. It was an electric train, fitted with overhead pantograph gear. The coaches had a center gangway, with the seats ranged either side facing the locomotive. At about 4 p.m. we left Durban for Pietermaritzburg, a trip which took us through the Valley of a thousand Hills.

At about 7 p.m. we stopped at a wayside halt which was about 2 miles from the camp, which, although shared by the South African Army, was know as H.M.S. *Assegai*.

While we had been travelling up, the storm clouds had been gathering over the veldt, and, as we began to detrain with our baggage, vivid flashes of lightning lit up the sky and the roll of distant thunder reached our ears. By the time we began our trek across the veldt towards our camp, it became obvious that we were in for a soaking. We got it! It began to rain, first in slow, large drops, then finally, in a heavy downpour This is all we wanted to complete the sorry story of our journey.

After six weeks of sea travel, under intolerable conditions, we arrived in camp like drowned rats......what the "U" boats couldn't do, the weather had. We were well and truly soaked. The one thing that cheered us was the bright lights of the camp, for here, in the inland towns and villages of South Africa, there was no black out.

Apart from wooden administration bungalows and dining halls, the rest of the camp accommodation was under canvas, and after being victualled in, we were provide with a hot meal and allocated temporary sleeping accommodation for the night. I found myself billeted in a tent with three others.

My first night in *Assegai* I shall never forget. To begin with there is an art in living in a tent; particularly in a hot climate. First of all there are the fleas. Hundreds of them, which we ignorant sailors, fresh out from home, had not even thought about. Then there were the termites, or white ants, which got into the seams of one's kit bag and ate away the stitching around the bottom with disastrous results.

The old stagers in the camp knew the answers to all these problems. We, of course, found out the hard way. For the first night, we all laid our bedding out on the earth floor of the tent. This was a fatal mistake to start with, since the ground was teeming with fleas; with the result that before long, we were nothing but flea bait. I stood this for as long as possible, then packing up my bedding, I slid quietly away in the dark and finished the rest of the night on the mess table in the dining hall. At least the fleas could not jump that high!

Next morning, I rolled up my bed and had a wash and shave in cold water. After a typical English Breakfast of eggs and bacon, I reported to the Torpedo Office, who, on finding I was an Instructor, welcomed me with open arms. They gave me a class of young New Zealanders, fresh, bronzed looking youngsters, to take through a maintenance course in Torpedoes. They also put me in a staff tent, which I shared with three other Instructors. Here they put me wise to the flea problem and the termites. First of all they helped me to build a wooden base about two feet high on which to rest my bed. Then my kit bag was hoisted up to the ceiling of the tent, this took care of the termites. Apart from an odd flea or two (which we got rid of by hanging our blankets out in the sun each morning) I was now fixed up.

Our torpedo school was a converted garage in the center of Pietermaritzburg. We had several 21" Mark IX★ torpedoes which had been salvaged from the wreck of H.M.S. *Hecla*, herself torpedoed and sunk in the Mediterranean.

Classes were transported to and from the garage by bus, leaving camp each morning at 8.30 a.m. and returning at noon for lunch. The afternoon session left at 1 p.m. returning to camp at 4.30 p.m., the rest of the day being our own.

It was while strolling up to the canteen one evening to buy cigarettes, that I ran into an old shipmate of pre-war days. Ted Jones and

I had been messmates in H.M.S. *Hood* He was the Leading Seaman in charge of my mess and had been a very popular figure. He was still a Leading Seaman, but had retired on pension, being recalled for further service on the outbreak of war. During the last six months of his pre-war service, he had acted as chauffeur to an Admiral serving in the Portsmouth Command. Because of this, the Captain of *Assegai* had taken him on in a similar capacity.

Meeting Joney was like old times, for he and I, with a few of *Hood's* torpedo party frequently went on swimming picnics in the warm and happy days of peace. We adjourned to his tent where he produced a bottle of "Commando" brandy, and we spent a pleasant nostalgic evening. From this time on, until I finally left *Assegai* we had several excursions ashore together, using the Captain's car as a ferry.

Our bathing facilities, whilst primitive in design, were exhilarating in use. We did not have baths in which to sit and dream. Neither did we have a roof. Ours was a thirty foot square of concrete, surrounded by a six foot high wooden stockade. Across the top was laid rows of copper shower roses. We did not have a door either, only a concealed entrance; but after a hot day's work in the garage, it was a wonderful sensation to stand naked in the brilliant sunshine, and let the ice cold water sting one's body into refreshing life, and to dry off in the hot sunshine with the vivid blue sky adding a splash of colour to the drab straw tints of the surrounding hills.

We had our minor perils such as one morning I awoke to find a green mamba snake a few feet from our tent. Someone had recently killed it, but it was not a nice thought to know that such creatures were with us, particularly such deadly ones.

After the summer heat of the day, we had frequent thunder storms at night, accompanied by vivid lightning which lit up the hills and momentarily turned the surrounding countryside into a floodlit arena. These tropical storms had to be seen to be believed and were a spectacle to watch.

I remained at Pietermaritzburg until about the end of March 1943, when *Assegai* closed down and was moved to Wentworth, a district some six miles out of Durban. At the expense of the British Government, the South Africans had built a complete Gunnery and Torpedo School, costing I believe about Eight million pounds and we were now going to commission it.

It was a modern establishment with separate cabins for Petty Officers, and brick built bungalow style lecture and work rooms. I could not hope to stay here long, since I was only on a supernumary basis, whilst awaiting draft to the Eastern Fleet. However, I did manage to take the first torpedo class through the new school before finally receiving a draft at the end of May. With a party of others, I was being sent to a jungle camp at English Point, Mombasa. Within a day or two, we embarked in H.M.S. *Resolution* at Durban for the voyage up the coast to Mombasa.

Resolution, due to condenser trouble, was on a fresh water rationing scheme for the ship's company's use. Imagine our surprise therefore, to find ourselves issued with a bucket when we joined the ship. We were all issued with a gallon of water which had to do for drinking and washing purposes. Under these illuminating conditions we began our trip.

A few days later found us entering Mombasa harbour, and a couple of hours later our small draft was taken out to English Point camp by lorry. To get to the camp we had to cross a bridge connecting it to the mainland. As we approached the structure, our lorry pulled up and a beaming ebony face glanced into the back of the truck, and before we knew what was happening, we were all treated to a generous helping of anti-malaria spray, from the gun operated by the smiling native boy. Apparently it was the custom to spray everything and everybody with the wretched stuff, before allowing them to cross the bridge.

After about ten minutes of bumping along a dusty road, leading through Palm trees, we arrived at the camp and began to unload our baggage. The camp itself consisted of administration bungalows which were made of plaited palm leaves and were known as Bandas. The accommodation for the men consisted of tents pitched among the palms. We had our own beach from which we could swim most of the day, since we were free of work, the camp chores being performed by natives.

There was always a breeze blowing over the camp. Producing a perpetual creaking and swaying from the tall coconut palms. Occasionally a coconut would fall to the ground with a heavy thump, and immediately there would be a mad scramble of humanity from the nearby tents to secure the trophy. Sometimes a nut would fall on a tent and, if any of the occupants happened to be standing up when it landed, there was the risk of being knocked out, since the tents did not have much headroom. We did have a couple of such cases.

After being victualled in, and allocated a billet in a tent, we had to attend a lecture by the camp doctor, to all newcomers. We all settled down and in a few moments, in came a young Surgeon Lieutenant. He began by welcoming us to English Point and started to explain the reasons for giving the lecture.

Anti-malarial precautions, dysentry, and general camp hygiene were covered, as was a warning to take a stick and a torch with us when visiting the lavatories at night, since scorpions frequently rested on the seats and they objected to being sat on!

During the course of the lecture, the doctor repeatedly made use of the phrase "when going to smoke your hams" – it was some little time before we caught the doc's meaning. It appeared that one of the methods used to combat the spread of dysentry was to light a fire of palm leaves underneath the dry lavatories, and to keep it well stoked with leaves, which produced a thick pungent smoke, keeping the flies away from the excreta, thereby minimising the spread of the infection.

It was the particular job of one of the natives to keep this fire going day and night. The lavatory therefore, was no place to hang about, or sit and browse in. When sitting to evacuate one's bowels, a continuous column of thick smoke would spiral up between one's legs, causing copious tears to stream down one's cheeks. This was not the end of the operation, for on rising, one usually had a black sooty ring around one's bottom. To leave the lavatory therefore, was a relief in more ways than one.

Apart from the lavatory, we had another hazard in the form of mamba snakes, but although we saw one or two, we never had any casualties from snake bite. Our days at the camp were idyllic, inasmuchas we had nothing to do except eat, read, swim and sleep. In the case of swimming we had to exercise care because the area was shark infested, but we kept fairly close to the beach. From our small stretch of golden sand, we could look across to the Arab trading section of Mombasa, where several dhows could be seen. These small vessels plied between Mombasa and the Arabian coast, and were always running in and out of Mombasa.

I enjoyed this life for a little while, then, getting bored, I went into the Drafting Office at Kilindini Barracks, and fixed myself a draft to H.M.S. *Adamant* the submarine depot ship in the harbour. The idea being that if I had to wait for a ship of my own at English Point camp, doing nothing, I may as well wait onboard *Adamant* where my qualifications would be made use of.

Arriving on board, I was given the job of testing the depth charge pistols belonging to the local flotilla of motor launches. This kept me occupied until such times as I received my own draft some six weeks later.

One Sunday morning I was requested to attend the Drafting Office ashore. Arriving at about 10 a.m. I was ushered into the presence of the Drafting Commander himself. He offered me a chair and a cigarette. This sort of treatment was most unusual, never had I received such courteous attention from the drafting department. It must be the climate, I thought. When we were both comfortable, he asked me if I would like a draft to a minelayer, a converted merchantship named *Teviotbank*. He would not say where she was to be found, but added that I would have to take passage out of Mombasa to join her. This did not require any thought on my part, for I had never served in a minelayer before, so I accepted the offer with alacrity.

It had been a pleasant interview, and a most unusual one, inasmuch that it was the first and only time that I had been asked if I would like to go to a ship. As I returned to *Adamant* I felt on top of the world; at last, my own ship. When I mentioned the draft in the mess at tot time, everyone looked mystified, and nobody had ever heard of the ship, and I was mortified to hear one unsympathetic messmate remark that 'it was probably some old crap barge rusting on its milk tins'.

In due course the draft note arrived in *Adamant* directing me to join H.M.S. *Teviotbank* and to take passage in a troopship then anchored in Mombasa harbour. I once more packed my kit, and was ferried across to a two funnelled P&O liner, whose name I cannot recall. There were about 250 of us taking passage across to Colombo, and after we had got nicely settled on board, a defect was discovered in the ship's main engines, which was going to be a long job to repair. This resulted in all of us being re-drafted back to English point Camp to await another passage.

After a day or two of mooning about the camp, I ran into no less a person than Admiral Sir James Somerville, who was the Commander in Chief, Eastern Fleet. He was strolling through the camp, entirely alone, and like the great man he was, lost no opportunity of a chat with his men. We talked for a few minutes about the camp, and our days in Force "H" when we served in *Hood*. He then asked me what I was doing in camp and hearing of my draft, he obligingly remarked, "Oh yes, she is my one and only minelayer, at present in Bombay." At last I knew where I was going and was told by no less a person than the C–in–C himself! A week later I joined SS *Khedive Ismail* for passage to Colombo via the Seychelles Islands.

I remembered this particular vessel from my pre–war Malta days. She used to run a service between Port Said, Alexandria, Malta and Marseilles, and many is the time I have seen her lying anchored off the Custom House in Valletta harbour.

We had a small naval draft onboard, bound, as I was, for H.M.S. *Lanka* which was the name given to St. Joseph's College in Colombo, which, at this time, was being used as a transit camp. Here we were to await further passage to our various units of the Eastern Fleet, most of whom were at Trincomalee on the N.E. corner of Ceylon.

Our first call was at the Seychelles Islands which lay to the eastward of Mombasa, here we dropped some civilian passengers and took on fresh water. From the ship, the islands looked beautiful and clean, with vivid green foliage, which, with the golden sand, and the bright blue sky, presented a pleasant contrast in colour I would have loved a trip ashore in this cool green haven, but as we were on passage, it was out of the question.

At this period of the war, naval personnel taking passage in troop ships were allowed to draw their daily rum ration, although later on, the practice was stopped. Our first issue in *Khedive Ismail* caused us a lot of amusement, inasmuch that the ship did not possess the regulation hand pump for getting the spirit out of the barrel. This caused great consternation among the matelots, and, of course, delay in issuing the rum. However, one bright spark suggested using the rubber tube belonging to the surgeon's stomach pump, and by siphoning the rum out of the barrel, we were able to enjoy our tot. There was, however, great competition among the officers as to who should be the Duty Officer at the rum issue, since it was his job to start the siphon going by sucking up on the tube.

During our trip across the Indian ocean the sea was like a mill pond. The furnace heat from the brassy sun reflected off the mirror like ocean and hurt our eyes. There was not a breath of wind to be had anywhere, and conditions below decks were decidedly uncomfortable, since the scuttles were small and the forced ventilation extremely poor.

Four days later we arrived at Colombo, and we naval types left the ship and entered *Lanka* barracks. The school had all the appearance of a Roman Catholic Convent. Pleasant gardens, spacious rooms and the usual square tower and bells one associates with these places. I reigned just long enough to get a haircut and a couple of nights board and lodging; then someone in authority woke up to the fact that, as I was going to Bombay, it would have been better had I remained in the *Khedive Ismail* since she too, was calling there. Once more, with my bag and hammock I boarded "*K.I.*" and, after a couple of days or so, we arrived in Bombay on a Sunday morning.

As we entered Bombay, over to port, I saw three famous structures, which, from time to time, I had seen mentioned in novels and books. They were the Taj Mahal hotel, Greens Club, and the Gateway of India. Everywere the kites were diving down and picking up scraps from the harbour. These birds, speckled brown in colour, with a hawk like beak, are scavengers, who keep the harbour waters clear of refuse. Unlike our seagulls who pick up their food with their beaks, the kite picks his up with his claws. It is entertaining to watch them trying to eat their catch whilst in flight, pecking away at the tasty morsel held in their claws.

At about ll a.m. I left the *Khedive Ismail* and reported to the Navy Office in the dockyard, who managed to find a boat to take me out to the *Teviotbank* which was anchored off the Gateway to India.

The first person I met when stepping onboard the ship was Harry Troke. We had served together as boys in the light cruiser *Centaur*. In those days, both Harry and I were the stroke oars in the Boy's racing whaler's crew. Now he was the Coxswain of *Teviotbank*. After welcoming me onboard he immediately shanghaied me into the Petty Officer's racing boat's crew, of which he himself was a member, and before my name was dry on the ship's books, I was away in a boat, pulling for dear life. This went on before breakfast each morning, and after tea each evening, until our regatta date, and I thoroughly enjoyed it.

This was one of the good things about shipboard life as opposed to barracks. In a ship you are immediately accepted as one of the ship's company. Your shipmates slowly disect you, find out what makes you tick, and then pass judgement. You are either a stinker and no bloody good, or else you are O.K. and accepted as "one of us". If you are of the former you are tolerated with the usual good humour of the sailor. If of the latter, then you are embraced into the fold and made to feel welcome in many ways. As for barracks, you are just a ship that passes in the night, few friendships are made, or sought, and you belong to nobody.

After the Coxswain, the first member of the crew to accept me unreservedly was the ship's mascot, "Chico", a small African monkey. We first met on the upper deck when I was talking to the Coxswain. Chico came over to me, took hold of my hand and smelled it. Deciding I was O.K. he climbed up on to my shoulder, and began going through my hair. From then on we were firm friends. This amazed the Coxswain, because apparently Chico was very hard to make friends with, and he had never been known to accept a newcomer so soon. As I remarked at the time, he probably recognised a brother.

I soon settled down in my new surroundings and took stock of my new domain, the mining deck. My staff consisted of about 20, with a Canadian RNVR Lieutenant in overall charge. We carried 280 mines, each holding a 500 lb. TNT charge, so we had quite a deadly cargo onboard. Once a week we carried out mine-laying drill the rest of the time being spent on care and maintenance routines on the mines, their sinkers, and the ship's electrical system.

Because of the very hot weather, we only worked forenoons, and life was very pleasant. Our Captain was a retired naval officer, getting on in years. He had been "axed" from the navy between the wars and had been called back for service. He was unusually gifted, because during his spell in "Civvy Street", he had studied medicine and had qualified as a doctor and surgeon. In addition to this, he held the electrical degree AMIEE, and was also a Master Mariner. He was a most interesting person to talk to, and when keeping a watch on the bridge at sea, would entertain the bridge staff to some of his experiences.

We had leave each day, when free of duty, and occasionally I would visit the "Metro" cinema, finishing up in a Chinese restaurant where one could obtain lobster salad, with pancakes to follow. Usually I went ashore with one or the other of my staff, and we mostly stuck to this cinema cum restaurant routine, with a bit of shopping thrown in now and again.

When first ashore in Bombay, I was appalled at the number of cripples, and disfigured people we saw around. In addition to this, hundreds of others had no homes at all and nightly, slept on the pavements of the city, using an old blanket to lie on and a rolled coat for a pillow.

This disturbed me greatly. If this was an example of our British rule in India, I did not think much of it. Heaven only knows what these poverty stricken Indians thought of us, looking well fed and smart in our clean white tropical uniforms.

At night, we slept on deck under the forward awning. Before going to sleep, we listened to All India Radio giving us the latest war news and the current swing and jazz music. Under this jewelled Indian night sky, the war seemed far away, and one felt a little guilty about this. Chico always slept beside me, and whenever I did my washing, he would sit on the edge of the bucket eating great fistfuls of soap suds. One day, one of the crew passing by, pushed him in and Chico, taking a dim view of this, chased the culprit around the ship. Although he never caught him, Chico never forgave him and the pair were at daggers drawn for a long time afterwards.

I was roped in to serve on the ship's Tombola committee, and on three evenings a week I was employed working out the percentage of winnings to be paid out during the games. Since we got a small rake off, plus tips left on the table by the lucky winners, this turned out to be a profitable business.

Once a month we Petty Officers gave a dinner in the mess to which we invited about 30 of the ship's company. The mess members contributed a few rupees a head which we turned over to the Ward Room Steward. He laid on lobster salad, trifles, fancy cakes etc. and by the time he had finished, we had a spread fit for a king. Drink, although not officially allowed, was provided by the mess members donating one third of their rum ration each day until we had enough to make a rum punch. These were highly successful evenings, the whole event being known as the "Golden Grommet Club" dinners.

Our ship's regatta loomed up over the horizon, and twice a day we took the boats away for practice. Twelve crews were entered, and it was exhilarating to get away in the boat and have a good pull. There is a fairly fast current in the Bombay roadstead, and whilst the outward leg of the practice run was fast and furious, the return trip was back breaking work. Our Petty Officer's crew of six, were all men with a fair time in the service, and our total ages amounted to over 200 years. Apart from the Officers and ourselves, the rest of our ship's company were youngsters of from 18 to 25 years of age. It is interesting to note that when regatta day came along, out of the twelve crews taking part, our Petty Officer's boat came second. A feat we were really proud of, even though most of us had sore bottoms and blistered hands.

While we were enjoying the golden sun of Bombay, decisions were being made at home regarding the second front in Europe. One of these was to cease minelaying operations in our theatre of war. This meant that *Teviotbank* would now be sent home and put to a more useful purpose. Meanwhile, around about Christmas, we learned of the action at North Cape, when *Duke of York* and *Jamaica* with destroyer escorts, intercepted and sank the German battle-cruiser *Scharnhorst*. This action made history for it was the first engagement fought by means of radar.

In January 1944, we received orders to proceed to Colombo and discharge our complement of mines, after which the ship was to proceed to U.K. Since I had only been on the station a year, I knew that a further draft would be coming my way to keep me out East. We weighed anchor and steamed southwards towards Ceylon.

Nights at sea in these waters were like something out of the Arabian Nights. A sea as smooth as glass, with stars like large diamonds, and the scent of spice, wafted off shore by the light night winds. There was something magical about it all. We were reminded of the war, however, when we heard that *Khedive Ismail* had been sunk by a Japanese submarine in the Indian Ocean, with considerable loss of life, including I believe, some WRNS girls taking passage. The submarine was destroyed by the escort destroyers. This was the trip following the one in which I had travelled in her. Fate had more than once taken a hand in my affairs.

Teviotbank arrived in Colombo late one afternoon and we began to prepare the derricks and winches for getting rid of our mines. Almost as soon as we arrived, a draft note arrived for me stating that, on completion of the off loading of mines, I was to proceed to Trincomalee and join H.M.S. *Resource* as the ship's Torpedo Gunner's Mate vice the present incumbent, who was going home to qualify as Torpedo Gunner.

We were given five complete days to get the mines out. It was a long-winded job, because we had to remove the top plate from each of the 280 mines, remove the primer, detonators, and the 500 lb. charge of TNT. Then the empty mine case and its sinker was hoisted out and lowered into a lighter at one side of the ship, whilst the TNT charges were placed in another lighter on the opposite side.

Since there are some 20 odd nuts to each top plate, you can see that we had our work cut out. To make matters worse, the weather in Colombo was extremely hot, and we were working, stripped to the waist, with the sweat running off of us in streams, in a between deck space which was like an oven.

On the fourth day, at about 5 p.m. we completed the job and replaced our hatch covers. We cleared up the mine deck and put away our tools. Alongside us was a lighter containing about 140,000 lbs. of TNT, then at about 11 p.m. that night, we had an air raid alert.

We were in the middle of a farewell party which my staff were giving for me. The mining officer provided the booze, and we had a sing song and a high old time, broken up only by the air-raid siren. With our little lot of trouble moored alongside the ship, to say that we were a little worried, would have been putting it mildly. Fortunately the air raid did not materialize, and, to our relief, the "All Clear" siren sounded and thankfully we went to bed.

Next morning, which I believe was Friday, I was put ashore with my kit and taken to the railway station for my journey North to Trincomalee.

It was a long, slow, and very uncomfortable journey. The carriage seats were of extremely hard wood, and unpadded. The locomotive was burning a vile type of coal which produced thick evil smelling smoke, of which we long suffering passengers got a generous share. The discomfort, however, was amply compensated for by the gorgeous scenery.

We passed through tropical jungle, chugged and panted up hills, where one could look across lush deep green valleys. We passed between high cliffs, with waterfalls tippling over their edges. It was a fantastic journey, and, although I arrived at Trincomalee aching in every bone, I would not have missed that trip for all the tea in China. It was simply magnificent. I was met at the station and taken down to the harbour by lorry, where *Resource's* launch was waiting to take me on board.

Trincomalee harbour is one of the finest natural harbours in the world. Flanked by rich vegetation, of all shades of green, it has a large stretch of deep water, which can take a fair sized fleet. At this particular time the Eastern Fleet had its base here and several units were at anchor in the harbour.

Resource was moored alongside a burned out wreck, bombed and sunk a year earlier by the Japanese. The wreck was a sizeable vessel, with a deck cargo of tanks and aeroplanes, all of which were burned out skeletons. She was resting on the bottom, with most of her upperworks showing, so that *Resource* was able to use her as a mooring jetty. Spirals of blue smoke still ascended from latent fires still smouldering in her holds. This then, was the scene that greeted me when the launch brought me alongside the ship, and in a few more minutes, I was being received by the man I was to relieve.

Chapter Thirteen

H.M.S. *RESOURCE*

<u>1944 – 1945</u>

Although I had not previously served in her, *Resource* was a familiar picture to me. I could remember the days before the war when she lay between her buoys alongside the Floating dock in Valletta harbour. One could see her great bulk towering above all else. She was the Fleet Repair Ship and her giant workshops were capable of carrying out some pretty hefty repair jobs. She was about 13,500 tons, had two funnels and carried four 4" A/A guns. Here at Trincomalee, she was attached to the Eastern Fleet and formed part of the newly constituted Fleet Train, which was designed to follow the fleet and serve as a mobile dockyard and supply base.

As soon as I stepped onboard, I recognized some old faces, and this is always a comfort when joining a new ship. Even George Adshead, whom I was relieving, had served in *Hood* with me in pre-war days. He introduced me to the Torpedo Party of whom I was to be in charge and I noted one or two youngsters I had trained whilst at *Assegai*. They were a friendly lot, with the accent on youth and I knew immediately that we were going to get along together.

In *Resource*, my cubby hole was a converted battery room on the top deck, which I used as an office and here it was that I kept my kit and also slept. My job onboard was purely supervisory, being responsible for the ship's electrical maintenance. Once every four days I took a turn of duty as Regulating Petty Officer when the responsibility of the ship's discipline rested on one's shoulders.

Unlike the rest of the fleet, we did not cease work at noon. There was so much repair work to be done for the fleet, that, hot weather or not, we kept on working. In the cool of the evening, however, we had our compensations. Our Chief Engine Room Artificer, myself, and some of my imps, would bring up deck chairs and form a semicircle near the guard rails and talk over events, spinning our yarns until the strident notes of the Boatswain's pipe informed us that it was time to go to bed. Even after "Pipe Down", one or two of us would still be smoking and, in contented silence, watch the stars until we nearly dropped asleep.

We had a good Chief and Petty Officer's mess, although, apart from meals, I spent very little time in it. My next door neighbour on the upper deck was a young Physical Training Instructor whom I first met onboard *Mataroa* on our way out from U.K. He had a P.T. store opposite mine. Our cubby holes sort of backed onto each other. We were firm friends, particularly when I was able to install a telephone for him.

We had beautiful weather in Trincomalee, with brilliant sunshine all day long, and about ten minutes of heavy rain each day to cool things off a bit. The light breeze from seaward kept us fairly comfortable above decks, but below it was a different story, one lived in a perpetual lather, in spite of the forced ventilation.

One of my special jobs was to operate the Main Derrick purchase motor when hoisting or lowering our boats. This required a good eye and judgement, since a mistake could quite easily smash in the bottom of the boat being lifted or lowered. I liked doing this job since it needed a bit of concentration.

As regards Trincomalee itself, I saw but little of it. Drink did not bother me, and apart from jungle and the small native market place, there was not a great deal to see, besides which, most of my pleasures were onboard. I had made friends of two young stores assistants and two artificers about 23 years of age, these with some of my own torpedomen, a comfortable deck chair and the radio programmes from our S.R.E. made my social life onboard. We enjoyed those evenings on the top deck, discussing this and that, and between the lot of them I was kept very much alive. I learned from experience that our youngsters were the salt of the earth and I liked to be in their exuberant company.

After about six months in the ship, I was given the opportunity to have ten days leave at the fleet rest camp at Diyatalawa, some 200 miles up in the hills of Ceylon, and, of course, I decided to go. It was the practice in this hot climate, that for health reasons alone, each man should be given the chance to have a break from ship routine and go up in the hills for a complete rest. It so happened that my two artificer friends and the stores assistants, who were the plague of my existence, were also coming along, so I was assured of some entertaining company.

We packed a few changes of clothes and, taking a packed lunch with us, we five, (with several other members of the ship's company,) were taken ashore and, scrambling aboard the lorry which was going to take us to the camp, we set off, a happy carefree lot, with a native driver at the wheel.

Apart from being the most hair raising trip I have ever had, with our lorry roaring around cliff edge, hairpin bends for mile after mile, with sheer drops to one side of us; it was also one of the most breathtaking for scenic views. We passed tea plantations, and saw the Tamil girls picking the tea. Of course, they got the wolf whistle, to which they replied with friendly waves. They were obviously used to this form of greeting.

As we climbed higher in the hills, the weather got noticeably colder, although the blue skies and brilliant sunshine persisted. At about noon we reached Kandy, where we stopped for about an hour. Some of us, we five included, went into an hotel, opposite the famous Buddhist Temple of the Tooth and had lunch, despite the fact that we had brought our own. We sat on the verandah sipping iced drinks and watching the colourful scene of the passing populace in their brightly coloured dresses, and the Buddhist monks in their gorgeous saffron robes.

After lunch, we resumed our journey. Due to the numerous bends in the road, and the insane speed at which we were being driven, one or two of our party were car sick. We sped on, ever climbing, towards Diyatalawa, until around about 4 p.m. we passed through the village of Bandaralawa, and there, a few miles up the road was the rest camp. We were relieved that, after our hair-raising, seasick journey, we had, at last arrived in one piece.

The camp consisted of several low bungalows containing beds and dining tables. At the end of each bungalow were the showers, which, although ice cold, we made great use of. We were told by the

Camp Commandant that while we were his guests, we could come and go as we pleased, and that we could lie abed in the mornings if we so desired. We were to enjoy the rest since there would not be any work to do. The weather up here in the hills was a sharp contrast to the sticky, close atmosphere of Trincomalee. The air was cool and fresh and the sun warm. We all went about in shorts and shirts, some never even bothered with the shirt when inside the camp boundary.

Every morning we were awakened by a Ceylonese boy and given a cup of tea, after which the rest of the day was our own. There was a small canteen in the camp at which one could buy the usual items such as cigarettes and sweets, but we were rationed to one bottle of beer a day and one tot of spirit.

Most days we five would go hiking over the hills. The surrounding views were magnificent. Close by was a tea plantation, and descending from the hills was a stream, cascading over the rocks in a series of waterfalls. At the base of these falls were fair sized, deep catchments of water, with overhanging projections of rock above them.

We found these ideal for swimming and, as we did not have trunks with us, we solved the problem by simply bathing in the nude. The combination of the ice cold mountain water and the hot sun gave one an exhilarating feeling.

Whenever we hiked over the hills, we always finished up with a cool swim in one or other of these catchments, drying ourselves in the sun afterwards. On one such occasion we were skylarking about in the water, quite naked, when we heard girlish giggling coming from some nearby bushes. It was then that we saw a couple of the Tamil tea pickers from the nearby plantation peeping through the foliage at us. We immediately sank down into the water and shooed them away. We could still hear them laughing in the distance as they went on their way.

Our only other menace was the fact that snakes abounded in Ceylon, particularly the notorious Tik-Palonga, or Russell's Viper, which was extremely deadly. One had to watch for these when bathing, for some varieties of snake loitered close to water courses. However, we were fortunate, they seemed to give us a wide berth.

After ten carefree, luxurious days, we returned to the ship, this time by train. We had completely rested our bodies and minds. We had lived in pure mountain air and splashed around in and under waterfalls. We had walked with the gods of nature amid their glorious greenery. We had, in fact, been in a different world, and now thoroughly rested, we were back to reality and our old routine. Those few days at Diyatalawa will live in my memory. They were a feast at the table of nature.

The hot steaming days passed us practically un-noticed. Our routine varied but little, just work and more work. The rest of the fleet came and went on their periodical patrols and forays against the Japanese. It was just beginning to get a little boring, when suddenly we sustained three accidents in the harbour, in as many weeks.

First of all, a brand new floating dock had been delivered to Trincomalee a few weeks earlier. It had been towed in three sections and was assembled as each section arrived. Two ships had already been lifted in it without trouble. The first, a 10,000 ton cruiser of the "London" class, and the other, a large oil tanker of similar tonnage. Then came the turn of the battleship *Valiant*, of about 30,000 tons.

She entered the floating dock at about 10 a.m. one bright morning, and by 4 p.m. the dock had risen and *Valiant* was high and dry. Everything appeared to be in order, and work was begun on scraping and painting her bottom, and the refitting of her underwater fittings.

As usual, my urchins and I were in our deck chairs either reading or talking. It was a beautiful night, warm, with a large yellow moon illuminating the harbour. At about 10 p.m. I announced that I was going to turn in, and packing up my chair, went into my office. Shortly after 10 p.m. I had just got into my hammock, when I heard a sharp, loud, cracking noise which appeared to come from across the water. At first I ignored it, then hearing a lot of shouting going on, I got up and pulling on a pair of shorts, went to see what all the fuss was about. Several searchlights had been switched on and were playing on the floating dock, and what a sight they revealed!

The whole dock was listed over to starboard, the forward section had fractured and was drooping downwards like a broken ankle.

Valiant was leaning over with the dock, but by some miracle or other, was keeping herself in her correct position relative to the dock itself. How the ship did not capsize we shall never know. It appeared to us that it was only the stout wooden shores which were keeping her upright. In theory, they should have snapped like matchsticks.

There was much activity in the fleet, with lifeboats arriving on the scene from all directions. The dockmaster was hurriedly brought on the scene and preparations made to gradually sink the dock and refloat *Valiant*. After a worrying night of feverish activity, the dock was finally sunk to everyone's relief. The ship was towed out into the harbour and anchored. An underwater examination of her hull revealed a bent propeller shaft and a hole in her bottom, caused when the floor of the dock reared up on fracturing. Luckily, there had been no casualties, but it was a miracle, nevertheless.

The second accident was caused by a submarine, which, when carrying out torpedo firing drill alongside her depot ship, accidentally fired a live torpedo, which careered up the harbour. Fortunately no damage or loss of life resulted.

When carrying out drill firings in a submarine, one of the torpedo tubes is unloaded and the tube is used for firing what is known as "water shots". In other words, the tube is flooded, the bow cap opened, and a charge of high pressure air blows the water out, thereby simulating the firing of a torpedo. This gives the tube's crew practice in the operation of their tube and at the same time tests the firing mechanism. It can only be assumed that, in this case, a live tube was fired by mistake.

A week later, two Beaufighters collided in mid-air immediately above the wreck of the dock, killing both pilots; and so ended our three week run of bad luck. The dock incident finished *Valiant*'s career. She was eventually towed home and broken up. Built around about 1914/15, she had been present at the Battle of Jutland, and had served almost continuously ever since. A fine record indeed and a worthy member of the fleet.

As Christmas approached, the war in Europe was nearing its close, and in our part of the world the Japanese were beginning to realize that, for them too, the writing was on the wall. With the situation at home going more and more in our favour, we were receiving reinforcements of newer ships from home. Our Eastern Fleet now became the British Pacific Fleet and was composed of such modern ships as *Anson* and *Victorious*, and the fleet moved into the Pacific and began to operate with the United States 7th Fleet.

As a result of this, the Fleet Train of repair ships, oilers, store ships etc. moved across to Sydney as the first of our moves. We, in *Resource* remained at Sydney for about a week, re-storing and victualling, then we moved up to Manus in the Admiralty Islands (New Guinea Territory), where we acted as repair ship for a while. The Americans had driven out the Japs, and had built a dockyard and township almost in record time.

We had to admire their methods. Once they made up their minds to build a runway, town, or what have you, an avalanche of labour, mechanical tools and skilled know-how descended on the proposed site, and in no time at all, the job was completed! This included all the services provided such as Coco Cola machines, Juke boxes, clubs, radio station and bars.

We envied their system and their thoroughness. Most of all we envied their personnel, for they were treated like very important people for whom nothing was too good. While they sat in their comfortable air conditioned buildings drinking iced beer and soft drinks, we under our very antiquated system, had to go ashore in our launch, queue up on the beach, and be dished out with one bottle of warm beer per man by a very indifferent N.A.A.F.I. assistant!

Here, we were really under the Southern Cross. After dark we would be in our deck chairs listening to the local American Forces Radio Network, announced as the "Voice of the Admiralties". After a hot day's work, mainly below decks, it was sheer luxury to relax, and talk over the day's events, and the war news, among one's friends. Long after "Pipe Down" we lay in our hammocks, under the stars, talking or just listening to Glen Miller's orchestra over the radio. Suggate, or Suggy as we called him, a recent addition to my Torpedo party, would talk on all sorts of subjects, until we both dozed off, to awaken with the early morning Pacific sun in our eyes.

Further to the north the 7th Fleet were bombarding Japanese installations, and at the same time being attacked by "Kamikaze" or suicide planes. It was now only a question of time before Japan would be forced to capitulate and they were using desperate tactics. It was now the end of March 1945, and within three months the war in Europe ended, and all our efforts were now directed towards the final obliteration of Japan.

Resource moved further north to Leyte in the Philippine Islands, where we continued to service the fleet. I had now been away from England almost two and a half years, and this was about the time that one obtained a relief. Accordingly, I informed the Captain's Office, and an application for my relief was made to the Pacific Fleet Drafting Office in H.M.S. *Golden Hind*, a shore base at Sydney.

Towards the end of June, my relief arrived in an Escort Carrier, H.M.S. *Striker*. I turned everything over to him and bade farewell to my torpedo party, who did not seem very happy at my leaving them. We had all been good friends and had been a happy Division. My five particular friends, who had made my stay in *Resource* so pleasant and entertaining, wished me well. We didn't say much, for it was one of those occasions when the least said was the most understood, but I knew that in leaving their vivacious company I would possess a gap that would be difficult, if not impossible, to fill.

I boarded the launch with my kit, and, as we left the side of the ship and were waving our farewells, I thought of those hikes over the hills in Ceylon, and the bathing in the mountain streams, and I felt a little sad at our parting. We had been happy together, and *Resource* had been a good ship. However, I was going home now, and the happy prospect of seeing my wife and son far outweighed my present sadness.

Striker sailed within ten minutes of my boarding her. In fact they were about to hoist the accommodation ladder when our launch bumped alongside. So I only just made it! A week later, we entered Sydney harbour, and passing Garden Island, we secured alongside the Circular Quay. I disembarked, and was taken by lorry to *Golden Hind*, the naval camp at Sydney Race Track.

After about four days in this camp, living under canvas, I enquired about a passage home, but was told that it would probably be some time before this could be arranged. It so happened that when *Striker* entered Sydey harbour, I had seen the Dutch liner *Nieu Amsterdam* lying alongside the jetty, and a member of *Striker's* crew had told me that the Dutchman was sailing for U.K. within a week. I lost no time in informing the Drafting Office of this, and was politely told that this information was top secret, and that I was not supposed to know it. However, the Chief Writer said that he would see what could be done. He certainly did, for the next day, I, and a few others who were in the know, found ourselves onboard *Nieu Amsterdam* and before the day was over, we were steaming through Sydney Heads. Then, turning south, we began the first leg of our journey home.

This beautiful Dutch vessel of 35,000 tons was used as an R.AF. troopship. She still had her pre-war crew onboard, and they kept the vessel like a new pin. The food was something out of this world; the Chef and his staff even made fancy cream cakes for the boys' teas! What a startling comparison to the *Mataroa* of our outward bound trip.

Altogether we had about 800 service personnel onboard, of which the greater number were Air Force, and we lived like fighting cocks. The war in Europe had ended, so we were all in a happy, carefree mood as we ploughed westward towards Freemantle, our first stop. We only stopped a few hours to pick up mails and fresh water, then we headed out across the southern portion of the Indian Ocean towards Durban.

Nieu Amsterdam was returning to U.K. via the Cape of Good Hope, since we had to pick up homebound drafts at Durban, Cape Town and Freetown. During this trip across the Indian Ocean I had a dose of dysentry which lasted about three days. However, the ship's doctor soon put that right. We entertained ourselves as best we could, either by reading, listening to radio programmes, or, as some did, playing cards. This latter pastime always seemed a mug's game to me, and considerable sums of money were won or lost at it.

Arriving at Durban we picked up a further R.A.F. draft and their families, and after re-fuelling and watering, continued on our way to Cape Town. We stayed at Cape Town about four days, and I was able to get ashore and buy a few things to take home.

It was here that we first saw an exhibition of the Belsen Concentration Camp photographs. Even we hardened old sea dogs were shocked at what we saw and the remarks of some of the South Africa people who were looking at them are unprintable.

Soon, we were on our way again, and rounding the Cape, steamed northwards up the Atlantic towards Freetown. It was balmy weather, with golden sunshine, light winds, and lots of flying fish. With the European war over, we now steamed with all our lights on, and our scuttles open. This was luxury indeed, because it was over five years since we were able to do this and we began to realize how the folks at home felt when the street lights went on again!

Arriving at Freetown, we took on water and a small naval draft and once more proceeded on our way. The draft we took onboard had yellow tinted skins which was caused by the daily dose of a quinine substitute drug, which they were obliged to take to combat malaria. As real quinine was unobtainable due to the Japanese occupation of the producing area, this substitute was issued, which produced a saffron tint on one's body.

Nieu Amsterdam was a fast ship, and exactly five weeks after leaving Sydney, we were nosing our way up the Mersey. It gave me a thrill to see those familiar birds on top of the Liver Building as we nudged alongside the jetty at Liverpool. England looked good after my long stay abroad. A few hours later, the naval draft had passed through the Customs, and boarding a special train we were soon on our way to Portsmouth.

Within the next 24 hours, we were all on a month's well-earned foreign service leave, a little thinner perhaps, but glad to be home. It was during this leave that America dropped the first atomic bomb on Hiroshima, followed a day or two later by another on Nagasaki. The Japanese finally got the message and capitulated. The atomic age had arrived, with all its problems, re-adjustments and fears.

H.M.S. *Resource*

Chapter Fourteen

H.M.S. *DOLPHIN* and H.M.S. *COLLINGWOOD*

<u>1945 – 1948</u>

The war, at last, was over. Looking back to the days of Dunkirk, and the collapse of France, a miracle had been wrought. There had been times when most of us were unable to see a chink of light anywhere in the gloom. Spurred on by our own determination, and the indomitable fighting spirit of Winston Churchill, we had come out into the brilliant sunshine of victory. All were thankful that it was over; particularly we servicemen, who sometimes wondered if we would come through it.

As in most other wars, it was the young who had won the victory. Fresh youngsters who had blazed a trail across the skies and ploughed their furrows through sea and land. It was they who sowed the seeds of victory and carefully tended the green shoots of a better world and civilization in the hope that one day, when it was all over, they could live peacefully on the fruits of their blood, sweat, yes, and their tears.

It did not happen like this. The harvest so carefully nurtured was, as ever, being ruined by the politicians, the old ones. The seeds of fresh conflagrations were already being sown in the shape of Iron Curtains, Lines of Demarcation, Air Corridors etc., only next time it will end civilization as we know it. Atom bombs know no compromise, nor can they discriminate. Lawrence of Arabia once wrote, "Youth could win, but had not learned to keep". This was history repeating itself. Even now we are jeering at modern youth and its Ban the Bomb organization, but who is right? It is their world, their future, their lives at stake! Have the old the right to ignore them? There are obviously two sides to this question, but when dealing with Atom and Hydrogen bombs, I for one take the side of youth, for this time it will be a question of survival.

In the first post war election, the country returned a Labour Government, which was, I suppose, a poor way of thanking Mr. Churchill for his war efforts. However, most people had had enough of war and wanted to build a brave new world, and they could not see this being one under a Conservative majority. Rightly or wrongly, the issue was as simple as that.

Amid the excitement and hustle of the election, I received a draft to H.M.S. *Dolphin* the submarine base at Gosport, as a staff Torpedo Gunner's Mate. For the first time in my Naval career I was glad to be posted to a shore base. Here at *Dolphin* I would be employed on overhauling the submarine's torpedoes, which was not only a very interesting job, but meant also that I could get ashore every night, also weekends.

My wife came down to Portsmouth for a fortnight and we cast around and bought a house, then we moved our effects down from Wembley and set up our first permanent home. After our long separation during the war years, we were happily engaged in putting our new house to rights. Each evening I came ashore found me with a paintbrush in my hands, and between us we soon had things looking ship-shape.

At *Dolphin* we were kept busy unloading torpedoes from submarines returning from Japanese waters. Since the "fish" still had their warheads and pistols fitted, we first of all had to take out the pistol and primer and remove the detonators. Then the warhead was taken off the torpedo, boxed up and returned to the depot.

Unfitting the pistol was always a job requiring extreme care on account of the detonators, and I frequently had to spend long periods doing this tricky work. After the heads and pistols had been attended to, the torpedoes themselves were given an annual overhaul which involved stripping the weapons down to the bare shell, renewing washers, worn parts etc., re-assembling and thoroughly testing the completed torpedo. Then one signed its History Sheet and if anything went wrong with the torpedo after this, then having signed the sheet, one awaited the enquiry which was bound to follow. This particular type of overhaul took four weeks to complete.

I did this work, day in and day out for three years, apart from a short break, when I was selected to become President of the Petty Officer's Mess. Until my appointment by the Captain, this job had always been performed by a submarine man. However, due to mismanagement, the Mess was almost on the verge of insolvency, and the skipper decided to appoint a General Service Petty Officer.

It went against the grain for me to have to take on this job. I was of the opinion that a submarine Petty Officer's Mess should be run by their own kind. I was a General Service Petty Officer, and was therefore only an interloper, but the powers that be were firm about this and reluctantly I took on the job.

There had been quite a bit of peculiar housekeeping going on as I soon discovered when going through the mess accounts. I called a Mess Meeting and introduced a levy to clear off existing debt. Then we sold an old carpet for fifty pounds and, after six months, the mess was again back on its feet and a going concern. All this time I had been away from the Torpedo shop and I longed to get back there. One got to love these tempermental weapons and I felt that I had been away from them long enough, particularly as the staff were one man short, due to my absence.

With this in mind I paid a visit to the Commander and requested that I be relieved of the duty of Mess President. After hearing my story, he agreed that it should be a submarine man in charge and at last I returned to the old familiar workshop with its perpetual smell of shale oil.

I was very happy here, fiddling and messing around with the tin fish, and of course, I had my spell of home life. At about this time, the Admiralty decided to introduce a separate Electrical Branch into the service and this posed a problem for me, since it involved a big change in my professional status.

Hitherto, all electrical maintenance work in the navy had been carried out by the Torpedo Branch, the fitting and turning work being carried out by Artificers. However, with the complicated systems being fitted in the modern vessels, it was now considered necessary to have a separate branch to enable full time attention to be given to the installations. This meant that a new rating had to be introduced, since one could no longer afford the time to be a seaman, a torpedoman and an electrician.

In order to start off the new branch, certain existing torpedo ratings were to be given the chance to change over to electrician ratings. It meant that, on transfer, they would lose their identity as seamen. Also they would no longer be responsible for torpedo maintenance, depth charges, explosives or mines, since a further branch was being instituted to combine submarine detection duties with the torpedo work.

I was therefore faced with the choice of either being an Electrician or a Torpedo/Anti Submarine rating. Electrical work I had always liked, since it produced some interesting problems which one could get one's teeth into. However, I also liked messing about with torpedoes, but to choose the anti submarine branch would mean that I would have to learn an entirely new subject, and also I would be condemning myself to service in small ships, which was something I did not want. It was therefore to my advantage, in many ways, to transfer to Electrician, and I duly made application to undergo the necessary conversion course at H.M.S. *Collingwood*, the newly created Electrical school at Fareham.

It was not until early in 1948 that I managed to get this course in *Collingwood* and finally gave up the coveted rating of Torpedo Gunner's Mate; and so died a particular rank, which had been much sought after and which I had achieved only after years of effort and much study.

At *Collingwood* we ex-Torpedo Gunner's Mates were transferred to the equivalent rank in the new branch, which was Electrician. It was with sadness that we removed our T.G.M's badges, which consisted of crossed torpedoes with a crown above and a star below, the whole being done in gold wire. In return we were issued with an insignificant badge in red silk, consisting of crossed flashes of lightning with the letter "L" in the centre. We felt bald, but the badge was later modified to include a crown above it for the Petty Officer rating.

We all had to go back to school again, and for the next six months we swotted at our books, delving deeply into electronics, auto-switchgear, complicated High Power and Low Power systems, Fire Control instruments and tables etc. until our brains were saturated. At the end of the course we passed the examinations and were given a week's course at the Damage Control School H.M.S. *Phoenix* at Portsmouth. Here we learned to fight oil and electrical fires, combat flooding, and repair action damage under difficulties. We learned how to save a damaged ship by means of counter flooding. Yes, the war had taught us a lot, and at last we were profiting by our experience.

Our most exciting day was spent in the "mock up" section of a ship, where we had to effect electrical and other repairs under action conditions. This was an actual ship section with its compartments containing sections of an electrical ring main and switch gear; also fuse boxes, machinery, lighting, etc.

The bulkheads were pierced here and there with actual shell holes, complete with jagged edges. These holes were connected from outside to water pipes controlled by valves on the top deck.

The idea of the training was to put the repair crew into the lower compartment and close all doors. At the start of the exercise, all lights were switched on, as one would normally expect. Suddenly a "Thunder Flash" would be thrown into the compartment, to explode with an ear splitting noise. All lights would immediately go out and streams of water under pressure commenced to pour out of the shell holes and slowly flood the compartment.

After the initial shock and surprise, the repair team would then go into action. Some would arrest the flooding using battery floodlights to see by, and fitting temporary patches or boxes over the holes. Others rigged up emergency electrical circuits to restore power and lighting and get the pumps working to get rid of the flood water, which, by this time, had risen half way up one's legs.

Standing in water, trying to effect electrical repairs, often resulted in one or the other of us receiving an electrical shock, but we all seemed to survive. It was great fun, particularly when a smoke bomb was added to the chaos; and when it was realized that the longer one took to restore power and get the pumps working, the higher the water was going to get.

We learned a lot during this week. It was proved to us with the aid of scale model ships in a large tank of water, that more than one ship could have been saved during the war had their crews received this type of training.

All of us returned to *Collingwood* much wiser men and considered the Damage Control Course to have been well worth while; we had all enjoyed it. We were given 14 days Summer leave and, on our return, we were employed on routine camp duties whilst awaiting ships of our own.

One day, coming into the Mess for dinner, I found a draft note awaiting me, and was overjoyed to find that it was for H.M.S. *Glasgow*, a 10,000 ton cruiser, which was going to the West Indies Station to take over as flagship of the Station for two years. This news made my day, for this station was the plum of the navy and I could not think of a better class of ship to serve in.

At about this time, the Admiralty had introduced a scheme whereby one could take one's wife and family overseas at Government expense, and although rather despondent when she first heard my news, she soon perked up when I mentioned the possibility of her coming too!

I had inoculations and was vaccinated, and proceeded on 10 days draft leave, a lot of which was spent in making plans to set up home in Bermuda. Fortunately, my wife's parents were living with us, therefore we could leave our own house in safe hands for the two years that we would be away. It only remained for me to get out to Bermuda and find somewhere for us to live.

Towards the end of September I joined *Glasgow*, which was lying in a basin in Portsmouth Dockyard. As our lorry drew up abreast the ship, I had time to cast a quick eye over her. She was a handsome looking ship, even the daubs of red lead paint, and the accumulated dockyard dirt could not spoil her classical lines and rakish looking funnels.

The moment I stepped onboard this beauty I knew that it was going to be a happy partnership. I just had that feeling about *Glasgow* and, since, due to my length of service she was likely to be my last ship in the Royal Navy, I was determined to make the most of our association.

Group – H.M.S. Collingwood

Chapter Fifteen

H.M.S. "GLASGOW"

1948 – 1950

One of the first persons I met in *Glasgow's* Petty Officer's Mess was Alf Staden. He was the President of the Mess and an old ship-mate of mine from my *Marlborough* days. The last time we had seen each other was in 1928 when we had been boys together. We had quite a conversation, going over the years between.

Our mess was at forecastle deck level, right under the bridge on the port side of the ship. It was a large, airy compartment, with several large scuttles to give us plenty of fresh air. We also had a skylight, which, in fine weather we were able to open.

We were about 60 strong and one of the finest collection of messmates I've sailed with. One of our number, Paul by name, was a brilliant pianist, and of all things, he brought his piano on board and installed it in the mess. He was to give us many hours of pleasure when we were at sea.

Our Captain, Charles Firth, was also an old shipmate. We had both served in the old light cruiser *Centaur* in 1929, he as a young Flag Lieutenant and I as a boy and Ordinary Seaman. Charles Firth D.S.O. and bar was one of nature's gentlemen, and was probably the finest Captain I have ever served with. He was a signals specialist and a destroyer expert, and had spent most of his nine years as Captain in command of these vessels as a Flotilla Leader. We thought the world of him. Our other officers were also an excellent sample of what naval officers should be. Our commission had all the makings of being an extremely happy one.

My first job onboard was as Electrician in charge of the 6" gun fire control system, and since the dockyard had been refitting all of our gun turrets, my staff and I had a full time job on our hands.

The first thing we had to do was to re-new all the 50 volt/50 cycle magslip transmitters and receivers throughout the whole system. Also, the turret batteries were still ashore in the dockyard battery shed. These had to be drawn, fitted into three turrets and charged up. All of this work kept us busy, almost up to the time of our departure.

We were due to sail for Bermuda in October, and the ship's company were busy storing, provisioning, and painting ship. After receiving her coat of light grey paint, *Glasgow* looked a really smart and beautiful ship. Since we were going to take over as Flagship on our arrival in Bermuda, extra care was taken with the painting and cleaning up, and about the middle of October, we sailed first to Portland for a few days, then on to Bermuda.

The Atlantic this October, behaved itself beautifully. It was a wonderful crossing with nothing but light airs and a gentle swell all the way. As for me, I was glad to feel the lift of a deck under my feet after my 3 years of stagnating ashore. It was great to feel the salt wind on one's face and to see the white horses capping the deep blue of the Atlantic. *Glasgow* rolled but little and from my later experience of her, she was a marvellous ship to be in during bad weather.

Not once in the two years I was in her did I suffer the slightest pang of seasickness. After about eight days, we sighted the tall radio masts of H.M.S. *Malabar*, the Bermuda base radio station; and we began to approach the deep water channel which would take us through the reefs and into the dockyard at Ireland Island.

After our Atlantic crossing, here was a feast of colour! The vivid green foliage, golden sands, blue skies and deeper blue sea, gradually changing to pale green, before bursting on the beaches in a chaotic riot of white.

We passed the little town of St. George to port, and I was fascinated at the gay bungalows with their pink, blue or yellow walls and white stepped roofs, peeping through the scattered cedar trees. Occasionally one could smell the faint odour of cedarwood as it wafted off shore on the light breeze. With the sunlight dancing on the sparkling sea, Bermuda looked a paradise. This was my first visit to these lovely islands. I was already captivated by them. My wife and son were going to love this place.

Glasgow rounded the marker buoy and headed for the entrance of the dockyard breakwater. It was now that we witnessed a sample of Captain Firth's superb ship handling. There is not a great deal of room in the harbour to manoeuvre a ship of *Glasgow's* length and tonnage, particularly as other ships, including *Sheffield* (another 10,000 ton cruiser) were berthed alongside the jetty, further limiting the space available. As we entered the breakwater opening, the ship slowly turned to port, then, when the Captain had lined up the ship's stern with the point he had in mind, he reversed engines and we began to rapidly slide astern. *Sheffield's* crew watched us goggle-eyed as we slid past them stern first, to bring up neatly alongside the wall ahead of her. We had our berthing wires and gangways out in no time at all. It was a first class bit of seamanship which earned us a congratulatory signal from the Admiral in *Sheffield*. We, a 10,000 ton cruiser had entered a restricted harbour and berthed as if we had been a mere destroyer.

It was Saturday, and after lunch I went ashore with the idea of looking for accommodation for my wife and son. We had made arrangements with another Petty Officer and his wife to share a house in Bermuda, and George and I set out to try and find one. Bermuda consists of a series of small islands linked by bridges and ferries, the whole being almost in the shape of a horseshoe. Ireland Island was the particular one containing the dockyard, and it was here that we commenced our house hunting.

The dockyard itself was simply a few buildings, built of sandstone, which housed the power station, naval stores and victualling departments, and on the headland was *Malabar* radio station. To seaward and enclosing the small harbour, was the breakwater; and right up in one corner was moored a floating dock capable of lifting our class of cruiser.

Leaving the dockyard area, George and I walked over a bridge into the greenery and houses of Ireland Island. Of the Bermuda islands, I would say that this was the most straggly and unimpressive, and we decided that we would have to look further afield for what we wanted.

Next day, Sunday, we went onboard *Sheffield* to find out if any of her crew were giving up their houses, since they were leaving the station. We were advised to try the Spanish Point and Hamilton areas across the water. As I was on duty that day, George had to go ashore alone. He returned with news of a house, or rather rooms in a house at Spanish Point. However, he emphasized the fact that it was only suitable for one family, more or less hinting that he was going to take them himself. He added that there was a brand new outhouse in the garden which could easily be fitted up as a bedroom and used until I could find something better. The main thing was to obtain an address so that a passage could be booked for my wife and son.

To cut a long story short, I went ashore and inspected the outhouse and found it ideally suited as a temporary address and on returning onboard immediately applied for a passage at Admiralty expense.

In the meantime, we did a little working up routine. Admiral Sir William Tennant had transferred his flag to *Glasgow*, and *Sheffield*, having said her farewells, sailed for the United Kingdom. As a point of interest, Admiral Tennant had been the wartime captain of H.M.S. *Repulse* when she had been sunk off the coast of Malaya with *Prince of Wales* in 1941. Captain Tennant had been so well thought of by his crew, that they personally made sure of his safety, otherwise he would have been lost with his ship.

Before we knew it, Christmas was upon us, and we were getting ready for our first Spring cruise, which was to take us to, among other places, Trinidad, Jamaica, Punta-del-Este, Montevideo, Buenos Aires, Rio-de-Janeiro, Port Stanley in the Falkland Islands and Grytviken in South Georgia Island.

We began to refit our floodlighting gear, since it would be needed at each port we called at. It was customary to give an official reception and cocktail party at each of the places we visited, and on these occasions we floodlit the ship, and the Royal Marines Guard and Band, resplendent in their full dress uniforms with medals, would Beat the Retreat. The ceremony finished up with the sunset hymn "The day thou gavest, Lord, is ended". The whole performance was illuminated by our searchlights, which caused the medals, and polished brass of the band instruments to literally blaze. It was most effective and was greatly appreciated by the local populations, who would sometimes come miles to see it. *Glasgow*'s visits to the various countries did more to spread goodwill than all the diplomatic humbug and some of the local newspapers said as much.

Early in January, 1949, *Glasgow* sailed. My wife and son's passage had been booked in M.V. *Reina del Pacifico* due to sail from Liverpool in January, which meant that they would be arriving whilst we were away on our cruise. However, the Commander-in-Chief's wife, Lady Tennant and her navy wives committee, always received new arrivals from home, so I had no worries on that score. It was nice to know that they would be waiting when I arrived back from the cruise. I was glad for their sakes, because back home they were still rationed with some foodstuffs and clothing, whereas here in Bermuda, rationing had come to an end and one could obtain anything.

Our first port of call was Jamaica, and as we entered Kingston harbour, we passed the old site of Port Royal, noted as the Caribbean headquarters of Henry Morgan and his pirates. This particular part of the world has many historical, romantic and piratical associations, and the place positively reeks of history.

We stayed here about a week, berthing alongside the jetty at Kingston. I managed a trip ashore, also a duty trip as Petty Officer in charge of the Naval Patrol. One of the things that struck me about Kingston was the amount of poverty abounding.

Hundreds of native families were living in settlements, the huts of which were made from flattened petrol tins. One was continually pestered by young and middle aged women, offering themselves as prostitutes. As we left Jamaica and moved south to Trinidad, I went over our stay at Kingston. Here the wealthy soaked themselves in sunshine on the island's golden beaches. On the other side of the canvas, people lived in tin shanties, under insanitary conditions, breeding communism, of which we had received demonstrations from some of the dock workers. I left the place with very mixed feelings. I felt that Britain, after all these years, might have done a lot more for Jamaica; that is for the real people of the island, not the layabouts!

Arriving at Trinidad, we berthed alongside the British Regent Petroleum Jetty at Port of Spain. That evening we had a visit from a local Steel Band who gave us an interesting night's entertainment. It was the first time we had seen and heard a steel band. I was amazed at the range of notes one could obtain from an empty oil drum!

Trinidad contains the great Asphalt Lakes, also the oil wells of British Regent, which run out under the sea. I went ashore and had a look around, but the islands are very similar, and having seen one or two of them, one has seen the lot. After a week, we left Trinidad and began the long journey down to Rio-de-Janeiro in Brazil.

It was beautiful weather during our run down the South American coast. Most of us sunbathed in our off duty moments, including myself. We saw several sharks and on the evening prior to our arrival at Rio, we stopped the ship and put hands over the side on stages to wash it in order to smarten us up a bit.

While stopped, we saw between 15 to 20 fair sized sharks circling around close to the ship. Our torpedo party fitted up some one and a quarter pound TNT charges and threw them in amongst the vicious brutes. The explosions drove them off for a while, but they soon came back, so we stationed one or two men on the forecastle armed with rifles and sub-machine guns to keep them off.

Next morning at 9 a.m. we entered the famous harbour of Rio-de-Janeiro. Passing the Sugar Loaf mountain and the Corcavado, we berthed alongside a jetty which ran parallel to one of the city's main thoroughfares. Rio harbour is probably the most beautiful in the world, indeed, the most beautiful I have ever seen. Flanked by the Sugar Loaf, Corcovado, and the fabulous Copocabana beach, stretching in a curve of golden sand with its Ritzy skyscraper hotels behind it, presented a picture of paradise; particularly with the lush green foliage and hills as a backdrop to the city.

One of the things that struck me about Rio was the apparent happiness of its population. Dressed in highly coloured suits and dresses, everyone seemed to be smiling. At night, the city put on its jewellery in some of the most brilliant lighting I have seen in many a year. For miles around, Rio harbour reflected the city lights in its dark waters, like diamonds sparkling in the night, whilst high up on the summit of the Corcavado, the huge illuminated figure of Christ could be seen dominating the star studded sky. There was a feeling of carnival in the air and Rio was certainly keeping up its reputation for being a gay, carefree city.

We experienced several tropical downpours during our stay. It would rain solidly for about fifteen minutes, when the streets would be flooded to a depth of about a foot. Then, as suddenly as it had started, the rain would cease and the hot, bright sun would re-appear and dry up the streets amid clouds of steam.

On the evening of our official cocktail party, we rigged *Glasgow* for the reception. We had spent all day rigging and connecting up the floodlight circuits, which consisted of rows of wooden booms sticking out from the ship's side. At the outboard end of each boom was a 1,000 watt tungsten lamp shaded in such a way as to throw the light against the ship's structure. All around the decks and superstructure, other lamps were placed in strategic positions to illuminate the masts, bridge and funnels.

During the evening, after darkness had descended and the party was in full swing, down came a tropical storm. The cold deluge, suddenly striking the hot floodlights, caused total havoc, since most of them blew to pieces, reducing the ship down to her normal lighting. The floodlighting was completely ruined for that night. However, this was the only occasion it happened to us. The following day I received news that my wife and son had arrived in Bermuda, per *Reina del Pacifico* and were happily settling in, so I began to look forward to our return.

Our next call was to Buenos Aires further down the coast. Our relations with the Argentine at this particular period were not all they could have been. To begin with, they laid claim to the Falkland Islands, and even went as far as to issue stamps showing the Islands as their property. Furthermore, a line of demarcation was agreed to between our two Governments which forbade our naval vessels to enter waters below the 60 deg. Parallel of latitude. This was to prove very awkward for *Glasgow* later on in the cruise, when rescue operations involving one of our frigates were called for.

We duly arrived at Buenos Aires and were given a berth close to the city centre. It was also noticed that armed Argentine police were posted close to the ship. Our visit to this apparently hostile country proved to be a great success. Admiral Tennant and his Officers entertained President and Madam Peron onboard, and relations seemed to improve after this.

During the visit, *Glasgow* was open to visitors each day, and two of us took an English couple around the ship. The man turned out to be the Agent of a London Tea Company, and as a mark of his appreciation, he and his wife invited us out the following day, on a tour of Buenos Aires, with a tea to round it off. After dinner a large car arrived at the ship and our friend of the day before got out and rounded we two up. Getting aboard the car we were taken on a tour of the city, our hosts pointing out the various places of interest. After a lovely tea, we went to the city railway station and saw our friends off on their journey up country, where they had their home. The railway station surprised us, since it was an exact replica of our own Waterloo Station in London.

One day the ship received an invitation from Anglo Refrigeration, a local corned beef plant, to send a party for lunch and to tour their factory. As I had always been curious about the canning of beef, I put my name on the list. It turned out to be one of the most interesting and informative tours I had ever undertaken.

We were taken to the plant by special buses, about a hundred of us all told, and we were shown the whole process from A to Z. It was a huge factory, which had its own ocean terminal to enable the refrigerated ships to receive their cargoes direct from the plant.

We saw the cattle coming in from the Pampas beyond, midst clouds of dust kicked up by hundreds of hooves. We saw them passing through the disinfectant baths and then on up to the veterinary surgeons, who thoroughly examined each animal. Occasionally they would reject one and it would be isolated and funnelled off to another part of the factory, to emerge as fertilizer, already in sacks. Nothing was wasted, for every part of the animal's anatomy had its uses, right up to its horns.

All animals passing the vet were directed on to an escalator which conveyed them up to the top floor of the plant. We followed each stage of the process; the killing, skinning, boning, cutting, boiling, canning, labelling and finally, the standing period of ten days. If the cans did not blow after this time had elapsed, then they were packed, so many tins to a box and loaded onboard the waiting ship.

I was particularly interested to see how the actual cans were filled with meat. Before filling, the cans are already fitted with their lids, which have a hole in them about the size of a shilling. A pipe from the boiling plant fits into this hole and fills the can under pressure. The hole is then sealed with a disc, which also has a tiny hole in its centre. From this stage it passes to a vacuum machine which removes all air out of the tin via the hole in the disc, and at the same time seals the hole with solder.

In addition to corned beef, this particular plant produced hams, tongues, luncheon sausage, liver pate, and a host of other meat products. The firm gave us a wonderful lunch, which consisted of all their products, with crusty rolls and butter and iced beer to swill it down with. I returned to the ship well satisfied as to how corned beef is produced.

The weather here was very hot and being berthed close to the city thoroughfare, there was very little breeze to cool us down, so we were not sorry when our visit came to an end. We had enjoyed ourselves and I think that our stay had helped, in a small way, to mend the rift that had grown between our two countries over the ownership of the Falklands. The general opinion seemed to be that it was Madam Peron who had all the say in Argentina. It could have been right, at that!

We left Buenos Aires – the city of statues – and steamed south towards Port Stanley in the Falklands. As we moved down the coast, the weather became decidedly colder, and before long, we were beginning to shiver in our shoes. Putting away our white uniforms, we once again appeared in our blue serge.

The America and West Indies Station is the largest of our Naval Commitments. It covers the whole of the North and South

American coastlines on both sides, also the Antarctic. It was possible, as in our case, to be sweltering in the heat of the tropics one day and a few days later to be amid the icebergs down South Georgia way.

We duly arrived at Port Stanley, in weather very similar to our Orkney Islands in winter. We could see the snow on the hills, and it looked and felt, exceedingly bleak. *Glasgow* anchored off the harbour entrance, a few cables away from *John Biscoe*, the Falklands Dependencies vessel. Here we met our first penguins, and cute birds they are. Completely unafraid of humans, they possess a very inquisitive nature, coming right up close to us and giving us the once over.

Most of the islanders make their living from sheep rearing and while here, the ship re-stocked her refrigerators with mutton. For the local population it was a hard sort of existence, taking into consideration the weather conditions and the barren countryside; and this much could be seen from the inhabitants in the poor way they dressed, collars and ties being conspicuous by their absence.

After about three days at Port Stanley, we received an S.O.S. from one of our squadron frigates, H.M.S. *Sparrow*. She was caught in the ice further south and, if unable to break free by the end of the month, the ice would have trapped her for the winter. The first thing we thought of was the Anglo Argentine agreement which would now prevent our going to her assistance since she was trapped below the 60th parallel of latitude. *Sparrow's* own position was perfectly legal under the agreement, since she had been paying a routine visit to our whaling station in that area.

After a lot of diplomatic exchanges between Whitehall and our C-in-C, it was decided to send *John Biscoe* down, since she was not a warship, and to try and break *Sparrow* free of the ice. In the meantime, we, in *Glasgow* left Port Stanley and made our way down to Gritvyken, the whaling station in South Georgia, in order to be closer to the scene, and also to pay a visit to the whaling fleet.

The drop in temperature as we steamed further south was very marked, and we placed extra lookouts to assist in spotting icebergs. These were in addition to the use of our radar. We passed one or two spouting whales, also some fairly large icebergs. As we passed the bergs, one could feel a sudden drop in temperature until we actually passed them, when the temperature would go up again.

One morning, at about 9 a.m. we saw Gritvyken ahead of us. The sea was as smooth as glass, and although a brilliant sun was shining, it was bitterly cold. As we approached our anchorage, we were passed by several whalers, with inflated whales lashed to their sides, making their way over to the depot slipway, which we could see over on our starboard bow. Behind the small township of scattered huts, the black mountains capped with snow, reared towards the sky. Overall hung the stench of gutted whale, altogether it was a dismal looking place.

Under a cairn of stones, Sir Ernest Shackleton lies buried here in Gritvyken. Here also, hardy seamen spend six months of every year catching and processing whales. We were told that, during this period, it is possible for a man to earn as much as one thousand pounds. We considered that they more than earned it!

During our stay a reindeer hunt was organized for the Ward Room and, at the end of the day, our launch returned to the ship loaded with reindeer carcasses, with the result that we had venison for dinner for weeks afterwards. I personally, did not like the stuff – it tasted like very strong mutton – besides which, I felt sorry for the reindeer. The senseless slaughter of these graceful beasts annoyed me.

Eventually, we received news from *Sparrow* that, with the help of *John Biscoe*, she was free of the ice, and was on her way back to Bermuda. It was just as well, because we would certainly have gone to her assistance had it become necessary, treaty or no treaty.

After a week's stay, *Glasgow* left Gritvyken and headed north for Montevideo, where we were to spend a week at the invitation of the Government of Uraguay. We were glad to leave South Georgia, it was far too cold for our liking, besides which, we could not get ashore for a look around.

As we steamed towards the River Plate, the weather once more began to warm up, until soon, we packed away our blue uniforms and began to appear in shorts and shirts once more. Eventually we arrived off the River Plate, scene of that famous action in December

1939 between *Ajax, Exeter and Achilles* and the German Pocket Battleship *Graf Spee*. It was a glorious morning as we steamed up the Plate towards Montevideo. We passed the wreck of *Graf Spee*, although all her upperworks had been removed, all that was left being the hull, and that was gradually being broken up for salvage.

Our reception at Montevideo was much better than it had been at Buenos Aires. The population here was very pro-British, and we were made to feel at home. There were no armed police patrolling near our berth, and our ship's company had the freedom of the city, more or less.

We entertained the President of Uraguay onboard and of course, we gave our customary cocktail party and reception, with the floodlighting and "Beating the Retreat" as our pièce de résistance. The quarterdeck on these occasions was all spit and polish. We had a red and white candy striped awning which we stretched under the existing one. Coloured electric lamps lined the edges and a centre backbone of multi-coloured lamps stretched from the roof of the gun turret to the ensign staff at the stern. Flags were used as side curtains and an illuminated fountain played in the center of the deck. The whole arrangement was most tastefully laid out, with potted ferns and plants, obtained from shore, scattered around the deck.

I did not personally go ashore at Montevideo, but the ship's company thoroughly enjoyed themselves and we sailed away with regret. Even the ship did not want to leave, because she got caught in an abnormal current, which carried us over a shallow patch in the harbour and bunged up our condenser inlets with mud, which delayed our departure for Punta del Este, until a diver went down and cleared them.

Late that afternoon we were once again steaming seawards down the Plate. Our departure from Montevideo had been a bit of a fiasco, because we had taken the President of Uraguay onboard with the intention of taking him with us to Punta del Este, but because of our condenser trouble, he had to be put ashore again, which caused a lot of red faces in high places. However, accidents will happen, and it was not our fault that the current had proved to be other than was stated in the Tidal Atlas for that area.

We arrived at Punta del Este that evening, but we stayed only a few hours, then we began the long haul northward, back to the Caribbean where we were due to take part in some tactical exercises with the U.S. Fleet. About a week later, we met up with the Americans and were with them for a few days, carrying out manoeuvres and other drills, then, bidding them farewell, we set course for Bermuda and, for me, a welcome re-union with my wife and son.

It had been a most interesting cruise. We had steamed thousands of miles, both in tropical and Antarctic waters; from highly coloured tropical birds to penguins in evening dress. We had seen the breathless beauty of Rio's fabulous harbour and the grim barren wastes of South Georgia. It had been an education in itself and we had all enjoyed the wonderful experience.

On the way back to Bermuda, I happened to be in the bathroom one evening, when our Yeoman of Signals informed me that a draft had been received for me to be transferred to the frigate *Bigbury Bay* on *Glasgow*'s arrival at Bermuda. This was bad enough news, but he went on to say that *Bigbury Bay* was being sent to the China station to reinforce their squadron. I was stunned at this news, because my wife and son were now in Bermuda, and would have been left there until a passage could be arranged for them to return to U.K. Fate was most unkind, because there were nine electricians carried in *Glasgow* and I was the only one whose wife had come out to be with me. On top of this, I hated small ships.

After supper, the ship's Electrical Officer sent for me and broke the news, but he added that, on going through my service papers he had come across an entry made by the Captain of *Ledbury* back in 1942, which had also been entered on my Medical History Sheet. It was to the effect that both he and the Doctor considered me as medically unfit for service in small ships due to sea sickness.

This was my straw in the wind. The Electrical Officer knew of my wife's arrival in Bermuda and he immediately sent a signal to the Drafting Officer in Portsmouth, pointing out the entry on my Medical sheet and requesting my draft be cancelled. I went to bed that night a very worried man.

At about 10 a.m. next morning, I was again sent for and informed that the draft had been cancelled. A load had been lifted from my mind. I was happy again and went about my work in great heart. Two days later we entered the deep water channel, past the ancient town of St. George and into the approach to the dockyard. It was a beautiful morning, and a boisterous chop on the water caused the waves to sparkle in the brilliant sunshine. It was a wonderful homecoming for me.

Before entering the dockyard, we lowered the Admiral's barge – a high speed launch in green and white enamel, a really beautiful boat – this was sent across to Admiralty House at Spanish Point to bring over Lady Tennant to meet her husband.

As we were securing the ship alongside the jetty, I saw the barge, bouncing her way across the sparkling sea towards us. As we ran out the two gangways, the barge came alongside the after accommodation ladder. Lady Tennant came up the steps and to my surprise and delight, my wife and son followed her up, and so we were reunited onboard ship. This made my day, it was so like Lady Tennant to think of little things like giving lifts in her husband's barge to sailors' wives, so that they too could enjoy a reunion as soon as the ship arrived. This is why she was held in such high regard. Her husband, the Admiral, was no less considerate. Small wonder that *Repulse's* crew made sure of his safety back in 1941!

After our meeting, I went ashore for the rest of the day, and from then on, until *Glasgow* sailed for the summer cruise, we enjoyed an idyllic family life with me coming home from the ship each day at 4 p.m. Before tea, we would go for a swim in the natural bay at the end of our garden. We taught our son to swim and we had a wonderful time. I was also able to get 10 days station leave from time to time which made life very pleasant.

Towards the middle of May, we began to prepare for our Summer cruise, which was to take us to Canada, Newfoundland and the U.S.A. The ship was repainted, and we stored and provisioned. I had changed my job from Low Power Fire Control to High Power, which brought me into contact with the ship's domestic power system, such as bakery ovens, lighting, ventilating fans, winches, cranes, etc. I was now the senior Electrician and as our Chief Electrician was close to his pension, I was next in line for his job, particularly as my own promotion to Chief could not be far off. This change of job every six months helped me to get thoroughly used to *Glasgow's* installation, ready for the time when I took overall charge in an administration capacity.

At the end of May I said my farewells to my family, and *Glasgow* left Bermuda for Halifax, Nova Scotia. It was only a couple of days run and soon we were securing alongside the Naval dockyard jetty. It was a sort of semi official visit both to Halifax, which was celebrating its 200th anniversary and to the Royal Canadian Navy, whose Atlantic coast base it was.

The weather here was rather dull during most of our stay, something like our own back home. I was not very impressed with Halifax. It seemed a drab looking town, although the population were warm hearted enough. We stayed here about ten days, after which we headed north to St. John's Newfoundland. This proved to be a similar place to Halifax; rather bleak and drab, and must have been a grim place to live in during the winter months. I had a trip ashore, but did not stay long. I thought it most uninteresting.

Our next port of call was Cornerbrook, also in Newfoundland. Here was a huge paper making plant belonging to the Bowater Corporation, who supply newsprint for the world's newspapers.

We berthed alongside their jetty, which, as we found a day or two later, was a silly thing to do, because the air around the plant was full of acid fumes which turned our nice new paint a dirty shade of brown. We hastily moved out into the harbour, and had to wash and repaint the whole ship, much to our disgust. However, the Bowater Corporation were very apologetic and supplied the paint for us to do the job.

During our stay, we saw the giant rafts of logs being towed into the paper mills, and on a tour of the plant, saw the whole process of making newsprint. A few of we electrical types were invited to the Deer Lake Hydro-electric power station, which was about sixty five miles up in the hills. I went on this excursion, and we passed over some of the roughest roads it has been my misfortune to travel on.

How the car's springs stood up to it I do not know, but the scenery on the way was magnificent, all pine forests and lakes. The generating station itself was quite a modern one, and to us members of the electrical branch, it was most interesting. We spent most of the day in this place, returning to the ship just before dark.

The ship was also presented with sufficient fresh salmon to provide the crew with three days of fish dinners. It was a rare treat to be able to enjoy fresh salmon cutlets. They would have cost the earth back home.

Our visit came to an end. It had only been, more or less, a fishing holiday for the Admiral and his officers. There was not much in it for the ship's company, since there were no bright lights or cabarets. Cornerbrook was, in reality, only a settlement of people who worked for the Bowater Organisation.

We sailed for Quebec, and I was particularly looking forward to the long trip up the St. Lawrence river. It turned out to be a journey of great beauty. The weather was brilliant, and the river wide, with a surface like a mirror. On both sides we had a mass of green foliage and trees, with here and there, a small slender spired church appearing amid the greenery, indicating signs of habitation. We were in French Canadian country and the French influence was very evident everywhere. After almost two days steaming we arrived at Quebec and berthed alongside the famous Heights of Abraham and immediately opposite the Chateau Fontenac.

Quebec, the city of dreaming churches, its streets teeming with gaily dressed French Canadians, who seemed to use their forefathers' tongue more than their own. The large numbers of Roman Catholic clergy and nuns gave away the very religious atmosphere of the city. It was like living in a typical French town rather than a Canadian one.

There is a fairly fast current running at Quebec, and one wonders how on earth a British sailing fleet ever got as far as this in the days of General Wolfe.

We did our usual cocktail party and the ship looked a picture when floodlit and viewed from the opposite bank of the river. The ship's company enjoyed themselves during our stay, making quite a number of friends among the men of the local army garrison.

After a stay of ten days, we left Quebec and continued on our way up the St. Lawrence to Montreal, where we arrived one bright morning and secured alongside a large wharf, behind which stood a row of gigantic granaries and, beyond them, the tall buildings and skyscrapers of Montreal.

If Quebec reminded one of France, then without doubt, this gay city of Montreal could well have been its Paris. Its highly coloured neon signs at night, in both French and English, its music, in fact the very air of the place, conveyed to all of us a real life picture of France.

I had a couple of trips ashore and bought a pair of Indian moccasins, and with a party from our Electrical division, I visited the Bell Telephone Exchange, also a local brewery, where we were regaled with samples of the firm's products.

We received a visit from the Blackfleet tribe of Indians, dressed in full feathers. Their Chief, a magnificent figure of a man in his eagle feathered headdress, had come onboard to make our Captain an Honorary Chief of his Tribe, and to entertain our ship's company to an exhibition of Indian dancing. It was amusing to see some of these redskins wearing modern spectacles and dancing the tribal war dance with all the wild abandonment of savages.

After the dance, a chair was brought up onto the forecastle and the skipper was made to sit down. The Chief then adorned the "Old Man" with a glorious feathered bonnet, and presented him with the pipe of peace. They both took turns at puffing it with their right arms raised. How the skipper was taking all this mumbo jumbo was anybody's guess, because the best part of our ship's company were either perched up on the two forward gun turrets, or standing around watching the ceremony. Afterwards, the tribe were entertained to tea onboard before leaving.

We all enjoyed this wonderful "Paris of the West" and were sorry when our visit came to an end. Soon we were slipping our berthing wires and, heading seaward commenced our long trip down the beautiful St. Lawrence river, and on our way to New York.

Quebec Province had been an eye opener to me. I had expected to see a piece of country which was typically Canadian, but I found instead, what might have been France itself. Certainly the people retained their French way of life, and a lot of the buildings had a typically French style about them, and of course, the people were all bi-lingual.

After three days we were clear of the St. Lawrence, and steaming down the eastern coast of Canada, we entered the Hudson River and there ahead of us was the Statue of Liberty and the famous Manhattan skyline. I had always wanted to see New York; at last a cherished ambition was realized.

We secured alongside one of the Ocean liner berths and for the next couple of hours the Official calls were exchanged, in between pipe music played by the local branch of the Caledonian Society, complete with kilts and sporrans. It was very hot weather, and the breeze off the Hudson did little to alleviate the oven-like atmosphere caused by the high city buildings.

I went ashore with the ship's painter (or Putty as we called him) and the writer, to do a bit of shopping. We did most of it in or around Times Square and Broadway. "Scribes" bought a slide projector, and some coloured slides of nude girl models. We had great fun in the store, choosing these, particularly as it was a curvy dish who served us and helped to pick out the good ones. That evening we had a superb picture show in the mess, and one can imagine the remarks that were passed as each beauty appeared on the screen!

While we were in New York, our Government at home was having one of its periodical financial crises, and to our dismay devalued the Pound sterling. This had the effect of almost halving our spending power. The day prior to the devaluation, we were getting four and a half dollars to the pound when changing our money, but now the pound was only worth two point eight dollars. It was a bitter blow to us, but the navy found a way to get around this, and at no expense to themselves.

Some of the ship's company discovered that the New York hospitals were willing to pay five dollars for a pint of blood to volunteer donors, with the result that several local hospitals received literally gallons of good British naval blood, both to the medical satisfaction of themselves and the financial improvement of our sailors. Where there's a will, there's a way.

New York is a marvellous city in which to find one's way around. The numbering of the streets and the block system of layout, made it a simple matter to get around. However, the traffic flowed at a much faster rate than at home. Here, the limit was forty miles an hour in the city, and since their traffic lights do not have an amber light, it made road crossing a hazardous business.

I found the skyscrapers a bit frightening, one felt like an ant trapped between the compartments of a toaster. The stifling atmosphere caused by the height of the buildings and the narrowness of the streets in comparison, was overpowering. It was not a city in which I would have liked to live or work, and the amount of litter hanging about the back streets was appalling. I satisfied myself on one point however, most of New York's policemen really are Irish!

The time came for us to leave this forest of skyscrapers, and amidst the skirling pipes of the Caledonian Society's band, we slid astern from the dockside, and with a toot or two on our siren, we steamed slowly down the Hudson river, towards the open sea. Another highly successful visit behind us. We were now bound for Portsmouth, New Hampshire, a U.S. Naval Base. On arrival we were given a berth in the Inner harbour, and for most of the morning we were occupied in exchanging calls with this Admiral and that, which is usually the case when visiting a foreign naval base.

During our stay, our skipper decided that it would be an excellent thing to foster relations between the ship's company and the local population. In order to have them meet each other, he suggested a big church parade to the local church on Sunday morning, led by our Royal Marine band. In order to get volunteers for this, he bribed the boys by excusing them scrubbing decks that morning and allowing them an extra half hour lie in. He craftily pointed out that after the service was the time when the vicar would introduce the congregation to our lads. He painted such a rosy picture, that next day, which was Sunday, we had over half of the crew, all decked out in clean white uniforms and raring to go.

With the band playing, they marched off, skipper and all. They looked most impressive and, at the church, created such a good impression, that it found its way to our Ambassador's ears in Washington, and was favourably commented on by the Foreign Office and the Admiralty. Furthermore, the skipper's plan paid off, for as our lads left the church, the vicar, delighted at having a British congregation at his church, introduced everybody and for the rest of our stay at Portsmouth, these friendships formed on Sunday, flourished; and a good time was had by all.

Before returning to Bermuda, we visited one or two of the West Indian islands, including St. Kitts and St. Lucia, where we poodled around until mid September, then, heading northward, we made for Bermuda, where we were to remain until after Christmas. It had been a wonderful cruise, both for weather and for what we had seen and been able to do. Now we were going back to our base, and for me a happy spell with my wife and son.

Bermuda, whilst being ideal for those of us fortunate enough to have our families with us, was not a good place for the rest. The main reason being the high cost of living. Even I was paid an extra ten pounds a week subsistence allowance for my wife, otherwise we could not have made ends meet. Apart from the Naval Canteen in the dockyard, the main form of entertainment was fishing.

The one good sport that Bermuda could offer was its marvellous fishing. From the dockyard breakwater, we caught shark, bream and on occasion, a large turtle, which we released again, and watched him racing out to sea for dear life. After dark was the time when Johnny Shark came in close, although we did not catch many due to the barrier of reefs to seaward, which kept most of them out.

About a fortnight before Christmas, Bermuda dressed its harbour front trees with coloured fairy lights and large illuminated stars appeared on top of some of the buildings. Occasionally one heard the distant church bells playing carols, such as Silent Night and We Three Kings. It seemed a peaceful world, as we heard the sweet notes floating across the starlit, silent waters of the harbour.

Another attraction of the Island was the local Commercial

Radio Station, which, in between adverts, churned out all sorts of popular music throughout the day and night. I well remember the show sponsored by Libby, the tinned meat and fruit organization. Between 7.30 a.m. and 8 a.m. each morning we had selections from the musical "Oklahoma". It was most pleasant sitting in the mess having breakfast to the tune of "Oh what a beautiful morning", with the brilliant sunshine streaming through our open skylight and scuttles; it really made my day.

By this time, Kay, Clive and I had moved our place of residence twice and now we were living in a bungalow in Hamilton, the main town of Bermuda. The road had a name which savoured of the Wild West, Happy Valley Road, and many was the night when, returning from a cinema show, we could hear the flippety flop of the giant toads as they leapt out of our way.

When we first took up residence here we lay awake at nights listening to the cricket-like chirping of the miniature frogs, tiny creatures no bigger than a small fingernail. The chorus would go on all night and eventually one grew used to the noise and it went unnoticed. We also had red cardinal birds in our garden and small birds of a vivid shade of blue. Red Christmas flowers grew there too. It was a wonderful place to live in and we were very happy.

Returning to the ship one morning, with brilliant sunshine and a flat sea, I was scared out of my life, for without any sort of warning, a giant Mantau Ray leapt out of the sea ahead of our boat. It rose out of the water like a huge aeroplane, so high that I could see the paler colour of its belly, then, with a terrific clap, like thunder, it flopped back into the sea. Had it dropped on our boat, it would have flattened us. It must have weighed well over a thousand pounds.

Another feature of life in Bermuda was the water supply. There is no Public Water Supply as we know it in England. All fresh water is collected from the rainfall. In order that each house has its supply, a large tank is built under the house. The roofs of the houses are limewashed by law, and are stepped in design. They are guttered in such a way that the rain is guided via pipes, into the tank below. The water is then pumped up to a gravity tank on the roof and used as required via the normal house tap system. Should one run out of water, then one had to purchase a tanker load from the company that distilled water from the sea. As this was a most expensive business, one had to exercise great economy in the use of fresh water.

One of the hazards of life in the Bermudas was the hurricanes. We usually received plenty of warning of these in advance, the season being between September and November. Providing one barricaded one's windows and doors and left no opening whatsoever, one was fairly safe. Failure to adopt these elementary precautions often resulted in the roof of one's house being completely removed, since these hurricane force winds blew at anything between 90 to 160 miles per hour.

Another unpleasantry was the centipedes, found in certain parts of the islands. These insects were really harmless, but if one crawled upon any exposed part of the body, one had to be careful to ensure that one flicked it off in the direction it was moving. To brush it the opposite way resulted in the insect leaving its legs embedded in one's anatomy, and so requiring medical attention for their removal since they invariably turned septic.

After Christmas, about mid January 1950, we sailed on our first cruise of the year. This time it was to our own West Indies Islands. We cruised around most of the Windward and Leeward Group, which took us up to April, when once more, we returned to Bermuda, where we were dry docked in the floating dock for a bottom scrape and paint, and the overhaul of our underwater fittings.

During April I was promoted to Chief Electrician. Since the beginning of the year I had been carrying out Chief's duties, our own Chief having returned to U.K. I was now the Chief Electrician of H.M.S. *Glasgow*, and was human enough to feel very proud of the fact. From now on, life would be much easier for me, although, heaven only knows, I had no reason to complain before my promotion. I was very sorry to leave the Petty Officer's Mess; I had been very happy in it, for its members were a fine lot. However, I was made very welcome in the Chief's Mess and as I already knew them all, I did not take very long to settle in.

At the end of May we began our Summer cruise, visiting Halifax again, San Juan in Puerta Rica, Norfolk Virginia, Nassau in the Bahamas, Georgetown in British Guiana, Port of Spain (Trinidad), Kingston (Jamaica), Mexico, and the Dominican Republic.

During this cruise, we were originally due to go through the Panama Canal and visit San Francisco and the Western seaboard of the United States, but 24 hours before we arrived at the Atlantic end of the canal, we were diverted back to Kingston (Jamaica) and the rest of our cruise cut short. This was caused by the war in Korea. The British Ambassador in Washington did not think it very diplomatic to have a British cruiser paying courtesy calls in U.S. Ports at a time when U.S. naval vessels were taking part in military operations against North Korea. The fact that we, too, had ships doing precisely the same thing, seemed to have escaped His Excellency's notice!

Whilst *Glasgow* was at what is now named Santo Domingo (Dominican Republic), Kay and Clive returned to Britain in the Cunard White Star Liner *Georgic*. This was in September. As *Glasgow* was also returning to U.K. in October, I thought it advisable to get them settled back home before *Glasgow* left Bermuda, rather than afterwards, since passages were not all that frequent.

At the end of our cruise, *Glasgow* returned to Bermuda for a week or two, then, one bright morning we left Ireland Island dockyard for the last time, and, passing the old familiar landmarks, we headed north eastwards for Portsmouth. Across the heaving Atlantic ocean, passing successfully between two hurricanes en-route

Ten days later, we steamed up the Solent, past the Nab Tower, Warner Lightship, Fort Blockhouse and into Portsmouth Harbour, securing alongside Fountain Lake Jetty, our long Paying Off pennant trailing languidly behind us.

We were home again, after having covered thousands of miles. From the tip of Newfoundland down to the Antarctic. From the Tropics to the ice floes. We had seen the huge log rafts, manipulated by touch lumberjacks, into the giant Bowater plant at one end of the American continent. At the other end, we had seen the whales towed into the processing plant in South Georgia.

We had seen cattle coming off the Pampas in the Argentine, to emerge as tinned beef from the corned beef factory. We had experienced the hot winds of the Caribbean, and the bone chilling cold of the Antarctic. It had been a memorable commission for all of us, and an extremely happy one for me, since I had my wife and son with me.

Now it was over and I felt a sort of emptiness. No more would I awake to new horizons, new faces and strange lands, for this had been my last ship. In another year I would be leaving the service I loved so well.

A few days after our arrival at Portsmouth it was decided that *Glasgow* should have a refit at Chatham dockyard. With this end in view the bulk of the ship's company were drafted into barracks for their Foreign Service leave, and the ship, with a skeleton crew of key men onboard, steamed to Chatham, where on our arrival, we were given a berth in an inner basin and work began on the refit.

As the Chief Electrician, I had to remain with the ship during the refit, which lasted around to approximately the end of August 1951, when, on arrival of a new Chief Electrician, I was drafted to H.M.S. *Collingwood* as a Staff Instructor, attached to the Apprentices Training Section.

I was more than sorry to leave *Glasgow*. I had enjoyed every moment I had been in her. She had been the best ship, next to *Hood*, that I had served in, and we were a very happy crew. It was with mixed feelings that I turned and watched her familiar outline – now a bit patchy with dockyard grime – receding in the distance, as my lorry rattled over the cobblestones towards the dockyard gates. As she finally vanished, the words of an old song passed through my mind as aptly fitting the occasion – "Goodbye old ship of mine."

HM.S. *Glasgow with paying-off pennant
entering Portsmouth, October 1950*

Chapter Sixteen

H.M.S. *COLLINGWOOD*

1951 – 1953

I took up my duties with the Apprentices at the beginning of September, and was attached to a division as an Administration Instructor. My main job was to be a sort of father to these youngsters. To see that they kept their quarters clean, and to more or less help to organize their service life.

The Naval Apprentice starts his career at between 15 and 16 years of age, and after a rigorous eighteen months initial training at H.M.S. *Fisguard* at Torpoint, they then decide for themselves which particular field of engineering they wish to follow. They can specialize in either Marine Engines, Electrical Engineering, Aeronautical Engineering or Armament and Ordnance Engineering. At *Collingwood* we received all the Radio and Electrical optants, and, for a further four years, they were put through a course of electrical engineering, fitting and turning, far better than could ever be received in civilian life.

I thoroughly enjoyed my job with these boys. After long service as a Petty Officer and Chief, I was inclined to be a bit 'stuffy', but these lads, with their high bubbling spirits, soon unwound my spring, and it was as much as I could do to keep one jump ahead of them.

Every fourth day I had a night duty, acting as Duty Chief, which involved seeing that discipline was maintained during off duty hours, and that the boys got to bed and got out again next morning at the ordained times. Also I had to carry out a round of their dormitories during the night accompanied by the Duty Officer. They were a fresh, clean and intelligent lot, and we got along very well.

During my first months in *Collingwood* my period of service was extended by a further eighteen months, due to the war in Korea. I did not mind this, since it meant that I would be remaining with the Apprentices.

After six months, the Apprentices Divisional Officer was drafted to the China Station and we got another Lieutenant Commander in his place. This change over made a difference to my job, because the incoming officer was a Navy boxer and ran the local naval boxing circuit, which involved quite a lot of administration work over and above his divisional duties with the Apprentices. One day I was able to help him out by typing boxing correspondence and writing some letters for him. This resulted in my taking over the clerical side of the boxing circuit, and, from then on, I wrote and typed all letters and memos, and became his secretary to all intents and purposes.

In order to do this full time, I was relieved of my day time duties with the boys, although I still did my night duty with them every fourth day. This arrangement suited me very well, and my memory went back some 25 odd years, when as a boy at Shotley, I got myself a nice quiet office job through my ability to type and organize. I had come full circle.

It was the custom among the Apprentices classes that, at the end of their final year, and after the examinations were over, each class held a Passing Out dinner with a show to follow. In order to do this, they appointed a dinner secretary immediately they joined *Collingwood* and began paying a regular subscription each pay day, which went on for the full four years, by which time, a tidy sum would be in the kitty.

These dinners were hilarious affairs, and when the coach returned to base, usually in the early hours of the morning, it was the duty Chief's job to get all the boys to bed. Since most of the little beggars were overloaded with booze and food, this often became a hazardous and extremely unpopular job.

It did not always end with the boys being put to bed. On more than one occasion one would find a pair of lady's knickers flying from the masthead on the Parade ground. On other occasions I have seen a chamber pot at the yard arm and a Watney's beer barrel flag flying aloft. On these occasions the Duty Chief would have to nip out smartly in the morning, before anybody was about and remove the offending items.

It was also the custom for the passing out class to invite a Chief to their dinner and show, the Chief concerned being elected by the whole class on a unanimous vote. It was recognized as a mark of their appreciation of the particular Chief's qualities, and we Chiefs considered it an honour to receive such an invitation since one had to be held in pretty high esteem to get it. I was therefore very glad and honoured to be invited to one of these affairs, and spent a very happy evening at the Mapleton Hotel, Leicester Square, and at the Adelphi Theatre afterwards, where we saw the show "Talk of the Town".

My extended service soon came to an end, and on 13th April, 1953, I packed up a few things I wanted and returned my kit bag and bedding. I said 'Goodbye' to the boys with whom I had spent numerous happy hours, and to the staff. Getting astride my bicycle, I pedaled off towards the Main Gate.

Arriving at the Officer of the Day's Office, I dismounted, and for the last time saluted the Duty Officer and requested permission to proceed ashore. Permission being granted, I walked my bike through the gate and out onto the country road. About a hundred yards down the road, I halted and looked back at the old familiar buildings. At the snowy white ensign floating from the gaff of the mast. At the smart Wrens and sailors passing in and out of the gates about their various duties. My mind went back over twenty-six and a half momentous years. To the day when I, an unimportant, fearful rookie, waited on the pierhead at Harwich for the launch to take me across to Shotley and H.M.S. *Ganges*.

Since that day, I have travelled hundreds of thousands of miles. I have visited forty-nine countries; crossed the Equator ten times, and sailed in eighteen different seas and oceans. I have lived with and enjoyed the company of, thousands of seamen in all parts of the world and have seen many wonderful things. I can honestly say that I have enjoyed practically every hour of it.

The Royal Navy, in peace or in war, is in my opinion, a very fine institution to belong to. It has trained and shaped me to be a useful citizen and to appreciate fine things. I have had my ups and downs, my rough times and my smooth ones. Now it was ended. As I remounted my bike, and began to ride off down the road, I heard the bugle call summoning the boys to their rum ration. The call which for years has called generations of seamen to their rum ration. Without another backward glance, I pedaled off into Civvy Street and obscurity; glad that, for over a quarter of a century, I had belonged to the Royal Navy, the finest character building ground in the world.

H.M.S. *Glasgow*

At H.M.S. *Collingwood instructing apprentices*

END PIECE

Sometimes my wife will catch me gazing into space with a distant look in my eyes – the look of the sailor – and she will ask me where I am. It is a good question, because at that moment, Snowy and I will probably be in Malta, strolling down the narrow sunlit Strada Stretta, in our clean white uniforms, making our way to the Morning Star bar, or perhaps the Silver Horse, with the strident music of the Honky Tonk Orchestras floating through the swing doors of the various bars as we pass.

Or we may be swimming in the blue sunkissed waters of the Mediterranean, racing each other from the harbour breakwater to the nearest mooring buoy. Possibly, I may even be lying in my hammock, beneath a million brilliant Pacific stars, talking to Suggy, as the ship lies peacefully at anchor off the Admiralty Isles.

It may even be Bermuda, strolling along the coral by-ways with my wife and small son, the white roofs and coloured walls of the fairy like villas peeping through the scented cedar trees, as we walk with the music of the surf in our ears.

Wherever it is, you may be sure that it is one of many far distant places, each with its many happy memories. As I go back over the years, I feel sorry for those who are condemned to fight for a seat in a bus or train, each morning and evening, all the working days of their lives. Theirs is the everyday boredom of a humdrum job. Where is the adventure, excitement and colourful variety so common to the sailor? What sort of memories will they have in their old age?

In the writing of my story, I have re-lived my youth, and have enjoyed every moment of it, and my only regret, when I hear the youngsters of today moaning about having nothing to do, is that I cannot steal their youth, and once more go down to the sea in ships; for in that medium, one can really live, and have one's roses in December too!!

The End.

When I have fears as Keats had fears
Of the moment I'll cease to be,
I console myself with vanished years,
Remembered laughter, remembered tears,
The peace of the changing sea
And remembered friends who are dead and gone.
How happy they are I cannot know,
But happy am I who loved them so.

Noel Coward.

"If I take the wings of the morning
and dwell in the uttermost parts of the sea,
Even there shall thy hand lead me and thy
Right hand uphold me."

Psalm 39

The Lord watch between me and thee
When we are absent one from another

Gen. 31 : 49

Death is nothing at all.
I have only slipped away into the next room.
I am I, and you are you:
Whatever we were to each other, that we are still.
Wear no forced air of solemnity or sorrow.
Laugh as we always laughed
At the little jokes that we enjoyed together..
Play, smile, think of me, pray for me.
Let my name be ever the household word that it always was.
I am but waiting for you just round the corner.
All is well.

Canon Scott Holland.

"It's what you learn after you know it all that counts."

President Truman.

Words I shall never forget.
I said to a man who stood at the gate of the year
"Give me a light that I may tread safely into the unknown"
And he replied:
"Go out into the darkness and put your hand
   into the hand of God.
That shall be to you better than a light
   and safer than a known way."

Minnie Louis Haskins.
Quoted by King George VI
in his first wartime Christmas broadcast, 1939.

Reflections on borrowed time:

When I awake each morning,
I say to myself:- "Thank you God, for another day."

Len. October 16th, 1986.

To sail beyond the sunset,
   and the paths of all the Western stars until I die,
It may be that the gulfs will wash us down,
It may be we shall touch the Happy Isles,
   and see the great Achilles,
Whom we knew.
Tho' much is taken, much abides;
   and tho' we are not now that strength
Which in old days moved earth and heaven;
   that which we are, we are;
One equal temper of heroic hearts,
Made weak by time and fate, but strong in will
To strive, to seek, to find and not to yield.

From Lord Tennyson's "Ullysses"

When I pass on, beyond this hasty world,
Scatter my ashes across a windswept place,
A field, where midst the sweet smelling grass
I'll feel the pulsing silence of the stars.

L.C.W. 20.9.74

Under the wide and starry sky   )
Scatter my ashes and let me lie   ) My epitaph.
Here he lies where he longed to be   )
Home is the sailor home from sea   )

L.C.W. with apologies to R.L.Stevenson.

Remember me when I am gone away
Gone far away into the silent land,
When you can no more hold me by the hand,
Nor I half turn to go, yet turning stay.
Remember me when no more day by day,
You tell me of our future that you planned;
Only remember me; you understand
It will be late to counsel then or pray.
Yet if you should forget me for a while
And afterwards remember, do not grieve,
For if the darkness and corruption leave
A vestige of the thoughts that once I had,
Better by far you should forget and smile
Than that you should remember and be sad.

Christina Georgina Rossetti.

<u>Simon</u>
I know a boy called Simon,
He's the apple of my eye,
He quells my fears of advancing years
And lifts me to the sky.
I hope one day he'll meet a girl
As equally nice as he,
And that I'll be spared to watch them wed –
For he's my Grandson, don't you see
And I love him!

Grandpop – 17.4.75